A Weird Writer in Our Midst

THE HIPPOCAMPUS PRESS LIBRARY OF CRITICISM

S. T. Joshi, *Primal Sources: Essays on H. P. Lovecraft* (2003)
S. T. Joshi, *The Evolution of the Weird Tale* (2004)
Robert W. Waugh, *The Monster in the Mirror: Looking for H. P. Lovecraft* (2006)
Scott Connors, ed., *The Freedom of Fantastic Things: Selected Criticism on Clark Ashton Smith* (2006)
Ben Szumskyj, ed., *Two-Gun Bob: A Centennial Study of Robert E. Howard* (2006)
S. T. Joshi and Rosemary Pardoe, ed., *Warnings to the Curious: A Sheaf of Criticism on M. R. James*
Kenneth W. Faig, *The Unknown Lovecraft* (2009)
Lovecraft Annual (2007–)
Dead Reckonings (2007–)

A Weird Writer in Our Midst
Early Criticism of H. P. Lovecraft

Edited by S. T. Joshi

Hippocampus Press
New York

Copyright © 2010 by S. T. Joshi

Published by Hippocampus Press
P.O. Box 641, New York, NY 10156.
http://www.hippocampuspress.com

All rights reserved.
No part of this work may be reproduced in any form or by any means
without the written permission of the publisher.

Cover art by Jason C. Eckhardt.
Cover design by Barbara Briggs Silbert.
Hippocampus Press logo designed by Anastasia Damianakos.

First Edition
1 3 5 7 9 8 6 4 2

ISBN13: 978-0-9844802-1-0

Contents

Introduction by S. T. Joshi..9

I. Recollections of Lovecraft 19

    Howard P. Lovecraft [1890–1937]...21
    Walter J. Coates

    Amateur Affairs..22
    Hyman Bradofsky

    [Letter to the Editor] 25
    Robert Bloch

    Interlude with Lovecraft..28
    Stuart M. Boland

    Howard Phillips Lovecraft..32
    Muriel E. Eddy

    I Met Lovecraft 40
    Paul Livingston Keil

    The Man Who Came at Midnight..41
    Ruth M. Eddy

II. Criticism in Lovecraft's Lifetime 45

    A Note on Howard P. Lovecraft's Verse....................................47
    Rheinhart Kleiner

    Howard P. Lovecraft's Fiction..48
    W. Paul Cook

    The Vivisector 49
    Zoilus [Alfred Galpin]

    Preface to The Shunned House 50
    Frank Belknap Long, Jr.

    A Weird Writer Is in Our Midst 51
    Vrest Orton

    The Sideshow 54
    B. K. Hart

    What Makes a Story Click? 56
    J. Randle Luten

III. Comments from Readers 63

IV. Criticism from the Fan World 119

H. P. Lovecraft, Outsider 121
August Derleth

A Master of the Macabre 124
August Derleth

Disbelievers Ever 127
R. W. Sherman

The Last of H. P. Lovecraft 128
J. B. Michel

What of H. P. Lovecraft? or, A Commentary upon J. B. Michel 131
Autolycus

H. P. Lovecraft: Strange Weaver 135
J. Chapman Miske

Lovecraft and Benefit Street 140
Dorothy Walter

[Letters to the Editor] 145
Thomas Ollive Mabbott

A Plea for Lovecraft 148
W. Paul Cook

Let's All Jump on H.P.L. 150
P. Schuyler Miller

Howard Phillips Lovecraft 153
Michael Harrison

The Lovecraft Cult 157
Arthur F. Hillman

Lovecraft Is 86 161
Francis T. Laney

Rusty Chains 164
John Brunner

Some Notes on HPL 170
Sam Moskowitz, Fritz Leiber, Edward Wood, and John Brunner

V. Notices from the Literary Community 177

Mystery and Adventure 179
Will Cuppy

Horror Story Author Published by Fellow Writers 180

[Review of The Outsider and Others] 183
T. O. Mabbott

Such Pulp as Dreams Are Made On 184
Robert Allerton Parker

Macabre, Lyrical and Weird 193
Peter De Vries

Mystery and Adventure 194
Will Cuppy

Nightmare in Cthulu 195
William Poster

Books Alive 196
Vincent Starrett

Bookman's Holiday 198
Charles Collins

Mystery and Adventure 201
Will Cuppy

Poesque Doodles 203
By Marjorie Farber

Books Alive 204
Vincent Starrett

The Phoenix Nest 205
William Rose Benét

[Review of Supernatural Horror in Literature] 207
Fred Lewis Pattee

Pilgrims through Space and Time 209
J. O. Bailey

Imagination Runs Wild 213
Richard B. Gehman

Books Alive 220
Vincent Starrett

A Bookman's Notebook 221
Joseph Henry Jackson

Sabbat-Night Reading 222
E. O. D. Keown

Of Good and Evil 223
[Anthony Powell]

The Genius Who Lived Backwards 223
Vincent H. Gaddis

Appendix: Some Vignettes 231

Notes 233

Index 253

Introduction

The emergence of H. P. Lovecraft from a titan in the tiny fields of amateur journalism and pulp fiction to a writer of canonical status in American and world literature is little short of incredible—perhaps unparalleled by any other writer in Western literature. The present volume seeks to chart the earliest phases of that transformation, reprinting articles, reviews, and other matter during and just after Lovecraft's lifetime, up to about 1955.

The degree to which Lovecraft achieved a kind of "famous obscurity" in his own time is made clear in Section II of this book, which includes many of the most noteworthy discussions of Lovecraft's work in his lifetime. The paucity of this material—especially that coming from mainstream venues—is painfully evident. What criticism exists generally appeared in the amateur press. The first critical article on Lovecraft— Rheinhart Kleiner's "A Note on Howard P. Lovecraft's Verse" (1919)—is still of value, highlighting Lovecraft's satirical verse as the capstone of his poetic work. (The essay was written well before Lovecraft had generated any significant amount of weird verse—probably the only other body of his poetic output that is of any genuine or lasting value.) Not long thereafter, W. Paul Cook printed one of the first of Lovecraft's "mature" works of fiction—"Dagon" (1917), written after a nine-year hiatus in fiction-writing— and prefaced it with a remarkably perspicacious analysis of his work as a fiction writer.

There were, to be sure, any number of other discussions of Lovecraft in the amateur press, but many of these concerned the at times heated controversies—literary, political, cultural, and associational—in which Lovecraft quickly became embroiled after his entrance into amateur journalism in 1914. These latter articles have not been printed here, although many of them are both entertaining and insightful (such as James F. Morton's "'Conservatism' Gone Mad" [*In a Minor Key*, 1915], a pungent criticism of Lovecraft's racial and literary views as expressed in an early issue of his amateur paper, the *Conservative*). What I have included are articles dealing specifically with Lovecraft's literary work. Hence, Alfred Galpin keenly analyses "Facts concerning the Late Arthur Jermyn and His Family" (*Wolverine*, March and June 1921), noting that "it is unquestionably original and does not derive from Poe, Dunsany, or any other of Mr. Lovecraft's favorites and predecessors."

Just after Lovecraft ended the first phase of his work in amateur journalism (in 1926, when the United Amateur Press Association collapsed),

Frank Belknap Long—who began as an amateur associate but evolved into a close friend and colleague, sharing Lovecraft's devotion to weird fiction and achieving even more success than Lovecraft himself in the publication of pulp fiction—wrote a generous if somewhat flamboyant brief introduction to W. Paul Cook's stillborn edition of *The Shunned House* (1928). It was around this time—when he had become a leading figure in *Weird Tales* and had placed a few contributions in other pulps such as *Amazing Stories* and *Tales of Magic and Mystery*—that Lovecraft began to attract a bit of attention from newspapers. During a visit to Brattleboro, Vermont, in the summer of 1928, he was written up twice in the *Brattleboro Reformer*—first in a brief piece (not included here) about a "literary gathering" at the home of the poet Arthur Goodenough in nearby Guilford, and then in a much more significant article by Lovecraft's friend Vrest Orton. This article, which has supplied the title for this book, is remarkably prescient. Orton, while claiming that weird literature is not at all to his taste, nonetheless recognises Lovecraft as a master of the form, perhaps even exceeding his mentor, Poe. His final remark can only be quoted: ". . . as a scholar and research worker in the one subject of the weird from his point of view, and a writer on that subject exclusively, H. P. Lovecraft is the greatest this century has ever seen or maybe will ever see." More locally, B. K. Hart of the *Providence Journal* touted Lovecraft in several instalments of his "Sideshow" column in 1929-30, and he continued to discuss Lovecraft sporadically in other columns of the 1930s.

From Orton and Hart to the unwitting buffoonery of one J. Randle Luten is decidedly a transition from the sublime to the ridiculous. Luten, who has now descended into the maw of oblivion except for his one article ("What Makes a Story Click?" *American Author*, July 1932) in which Lovecraft is discussed in part, was attempting to determine what makes for "glamor" in short fiction writing. His article was published in a writer's magazine that has similarly been deservedly forgotten, if the quality of this article is representative of its contents. Lovecraft, who was aware of the piece, was probably not keen on having his named linked with that of the pulp hack Edmond Hamilton—just as he did not care to be mentioned in the same breath with Otis Adelbert Kline in William Bolitho's 1930 article on "Pulp Magazines" (see Appendix).

As it is, the bulk of "critical" work on Lovecraft, if it can be called that, is found in the readers' columns of the pulp magazines—in this case, *Weird Tales* and *Astounding Stories*. The numerous comments that Lovecraft's tales elicited in *Weird Tales*—not only from professionals like Robert E. Howard and E. Hoffmann Price, but from general readers, some of whom later came directly in touch with Lovecraft through correspondence—is a testament to his immense popularity in the magazine, a popularity that was only augmented when, in the 1930s, a number of factors—the rejection of some of his most dynamic and innovative work by timid editor Farnsworth Wright; the radical reduction in his fictional output; the increasing self-doubts that he had about the merits of his own work—caused his tales to appear less and less frequently in its pages. To be sure, Wright exercised a certain restraint in choosing letters for publication: for example, Lovecraft noted that Wright had told him that readers had "violently disliked" "The Silver Key" when it appeared in the January 1929 issue, but Wright tactfully printed no letters expressing disapprobation of the story. The only truly critical letter Wright printed about Lovecraft was the brash young Henry Kuttner's remark, in reference to the collaboration "Through the Gates of the Silver Key," that Lovecraft "is getting trite as hell." (This was a few years before Kuttner began corresponding with Lovecraft.)

And yet, I suspect that both Wright and Lovecraft gained a certain wry amusement when readers found merits in tales that Lovecraft had ghostwritten. The most priceless comment, from this perspective, is Bernard J. Kenton's remark on Hazel Heald's "The Horror in the Museum," which Lovecraft surely wrote from beginning to end: "Even Lovecraft—as powerful and artistic as he is with macabre suggestiveness—could hardly, I suspect, have surpassed the grotesque scene in which the other-dimensional scrambler leaps out upon the hero." Let it pass that this scene, as with the story as a whole, was probably meant as a parody; Kenton, the future creator of *Superman*, was not likely to appreciate such subtleties.

As for the readers' comments to *At the Mountains of Madness* and "The Shadow out of Time" as appearing in *Astounding Stories*, the one remark that can be made at once is that, overall, these readers seemed to be on a substantially lower literary level than those of *Weird Tales*. Their letters are more crudely written, more captious in their attempts at criticism, and in general betray a devotion to the "action" plots that constituted a substantial proportion of the pulp science fiction of the day. Carl Bennett's remark that "*At the Mountains of Madness* would be good if you leave about half the description out of it" is representative—a remark that the learned if critically naive Sam Moskowitz would repeat in the 1950s and maintain to the end of his life. I am still debating whether Harold Z. Taylor was attempting a bit of dry humour when he observed that Lovecraft's novel "was rather dry, although a pretty girl and the appearance of the Elders [whoever they might be] would have made it an excellent story for a weird magazine."

That last remark points to one of the significant motifs in those *Astounding* letters that strongly criticised the two Lovecraft tales: they were not science fiction as then understood. This contention is probably correct, and both *At the Mountains of Madness* and "The Shadow out of Time" gain their aesthetic significance by a fusion of horrific and science-fictional elements. But this fusion clearly did not sit well with some readers, notably Cleveland C. Soper, whose intemperate letter asserts remarkably that "there is no science in it [*At the Mountains of Madness*] at all" and resents the very appearance of the work in a science fiction magazine. Remarks of this sort bring to mind the short-lived "Boiling Point" controversy in the *Fantasy Fan* (1933–34), in which Forrest J Ackerman attacked Clark Ashton Smith's "The Dweller in the Gulf" (published in butchered form in *Wonder Stories* as "The Dweller in Martian Depths") both on the grounds that it was not true science fiction (probably correct) and on the grounds that it was a bad story (probably false).

And yet, the degree to which Lovecraft's tales were "panned" in the *Astounding* letter column has been considerably exaggerated by some critics. Looking at the letters *in toto* (and the present volume prints every single mention of Lovecraft in the letter columns of April–August 1936), the verdict on *At the Mountains of Madness* is perhaps a wash, while the overall opinion of "The Shadow out of Time" is probably somewhat more negative than positive, but only slightly so. For every comment such as Andy Aprea's sober judgment that *At the Mountains of Madness* was "drivel," we can find a remark like that of Cameron D. Lewis that "The Shadow out of Time" was "absolutely magnificent!" And, as we can now see in hindsight, W. B. Hoskins was entirely correct in remarking: "You have only three or four authors who could qualify as authors *only*, not merely as authors of science-fiction, and Lovecraft is one of them."

Lovecraft's early and, to many, unexpected death elicited an outpouring of grief and reminiscence in the amateur press, the letter columns of *Weird Tales*, and in the burgeoning world of fantasy fandom. For months after his death was announced in *Weird Tales* for June 1937 (the issue probably appeared at least a month or two before its cover date), letters from fans and from Lovecraft's colleagues poured in. It is remarkable to read the comment of Robert Leonard Russell, who never knew Lovecraft except from his published writings: "I feel, as will many other readers of *Weird Tales*, that I have lost a real friend." Is it any wonder that Lovecraft's actual correspondents, even though they may never have met him, felt an even more fervent loyalty to his memory? Such late correspondents as Robert Bloch, Robert A. W. Lowndes, Kenneth Sterling, and Henry Kuttner ("I've been feeling extremely depressed about Lovecraft's death") wrote poignant letters, testifying not only to Lovecraft's greatness as a writer but to his remarkable kindness and generosity as a man.

From writing letters it was a short step to writing full-fledged memoirs and reminiscences of a man who, posthumously, appeared to be ascending step by step to a pinnacle of hallowed reverence in both amateur journalism and weird fiction. The great majority of these memoirs have been included in Peter Cannon's nearly definitive compilation *Lovecraft Remembered* (1998), so that we need here reprint only a few items that Cannon could not be troubled to include. Hyman Bradofsky's "Amateur Affairs" (1937) is a poignant introduction to a special issue of his amateur journal, the *Californian*, devoted to Lovecraft; Paul Livingston Keil's slight "I Met Lovecraft" (1946) tells of how he took the celebrated photograph of Lovecraft, Long, and James F. Morton in front of the Poe cottage in Fordham; Stuart M. Boland's "Interlude with Lovecraft" (1945) is a (possibly unreliable) memoir by a late correspondent; Ruth Eddy's "The Man Who Came at Midnight" (1949) is a charming brief memoir by a woman who had met Lovecraft when she was a child.

Ruth Eddy's mother, Muriel E. Eddy, is a bit of a puzzle. Peter Cannon included her later memoir, *The Gentleman from Angell Street* (1961), in *Lovecraft Remembered*, but in my judgment this memoir is full of unverified and possibly false details. Specifically, Mrs. Eddy asserts that she and her husband, the pulp writer C. M. Eddy, Jr., had become acquainted with Lovecraft as early as 1918, because her mother and Lovecraft's mother were both involved in the woman suffrage movement. There is no evidence to support this contention, and all the evidence from Lovecraft's letters suggests that he came in touch with the Eddys, who lived in North Providence, only in 1923. Indeed, Muriel's first memoir, "Howard Phillips Lovecraft" (1945), reprinted here, begins with the sentence: "It was in the middle of August, 1923, that the late Howard Phillips Lovecraft, Esquire, made his first personal appearance in our lives." There may be a deliberate ambiguity in this remark—does it suggest that Lovecraft had become acquainted by correspondence earlier than 1923? Nothing in the rest of Muriel's memoir suggests such a thing. Muriel's grandson, Jim Dyer, claims that he has letters from Lovecraft dating to 1918, but he has not made them available for consultation. Barring additional evidence, it would seem that Muriel's first memoir is the most reliable of the several she wrote over her lifetime.

Mrs. Eddy's article appeared in the slim pamphlet *Rhode Island on Lovecraft* (1945), one of the first books about Lovecraft to appear. It emerged at a time when the world of fantasy fandom was taking over the discussion of Lovecraft the man and writer. In 1945 Robert Bloch noted: "During the past two years . . . I've read scores of items concerning Lovecraft's life, personality and works." Possibly Bloch was exaggerating somewhat, but the fan press of the 1940s certainly featured an abundance of widely varying articles on Lovecraft. Since much of this commentary was oriented toward science fiction, it is not surprising that it reflects some of the same criticisms that had been made of Lovecraft's work in the pages of *Astounding*. We need not take very seriously J. B. Michel's idiosyncratic comment—written at the end of a poignant account of a visit to Lovecraft's final residence in Providence and a meeting with his bereaved aunt, Annie E. Phillips Gamwell—that "Lovecraft . . . was the deadly enemy of all that to me is everything," a remark that suggests the emergence of a seriously flawed myth about Lovecraft as an archaic fossil hurling imprecations at the contemporary world from his ivory tower in Providence. To be sure, Lovecraft was in part responsible for the development of this fantasy-image, given his oft-expressed devotion to the eighteenth century; but I suspect that Michel would have had a very different view if he could have known of Lovecraft's fervent support of FDR's New Deal and his conversion from monarchism to moderate socialism in the latter stages of his life. Analogously, P. Schuyler Miller chastises Lovecraft for creating an "artificial mythology" (the exact phrase that Lovecraft himself used to designate his pseudomythology) in such a manner that "the uninitiated" could not enter into that fictive world. But the argument is self-refuting, for the mere existence of such a legion of fans as Miller himself acknowledges ("he automatically created a cult of readers . . .") means that it is eminently possible for any determined reader to enter the world of the Cthulhu Mythos.

As for Francis T. Laney's "Lovecraft Is 86" (1948)—the title is meant to suggest that Lovecraft is *passé*—it appears to be largely a product of his jaundiced disgust with the whole fantasy fandom movement, as expressed in his amusing autobiography, *Ah! Sweet Idiocy!* (1948). In seeking to find every possible means to attack Lovecraft, Laney wildly asserts that Lovecraft was a "failure" not only commercially (something no one is likely to deny) but also artistically. Specifically, Laney denies the quality of "realism" to Lovecraft's work because he "knew life only fourth or fifth hand." There are two problems with this view. Firstly, the realism Lovecraft spoke of in "Notes on Writing Weird Fiction" as essential to the creation of weird fiction was not only a realism of human character; in Lovecraft's work there is an intense (and surely successful) focus on realism of *setting*, whether it be the New England locale of "The Colour out of Space" or the Antarctica of *At the Mountains of Madness*. Secondly, Laney's comment is one more testament to the prevalence of the myth of Lovecraft as the unworldly recluse—a myth that his letters have now overwhelmingly refuted.

The general disfavour with which fans and writers of science fiction in the 1940s and 1950s regarded Lovecraft is no more evident than in John Brunner's celebrated article "Rusty Chains" (1956). Here the young Brunner brashly dismisses Lovecraft—after reading about half of *At the Mountains of Madness*—as "the first writer with a big reputation that I had yet run across who had *nothing whatever* to recommend him for it" (Brunner's emphasis). And yet, the reasons for Brunner's disapproval do not become particularly clear as his somewhat unfocused article proceeds. Although he makes a parade of his learning in literature and other fields, it does not seem as if Brunner is very sensitive to any prose aside from the brisk, businesslike writing that dominated science fiction at the time: when he notes that Lovecraft appears to have written prose using a Roget's thesaurus, he is testifying only to his own deficiencies in understanding the English language. But Brunner goes on to remark, astoundingly, that the entire genre of horror appears to be *passé* because, it appears, the development of psychology has resulted in a revolution in human thought and feeling: ". . . now the demons walk in sunlight." And Brunner repeats once again the complaint that Lovecraft's emphasis on "nameless" creatures was an aesthetic cop-out, not realising the detail with which Lovecraft did indeed describe those "nameless" creatures (the shoggoth in *At the Mountains of Madness*, Wilbur Whateley's twin in "The Dunwich Horror") so that they are brought clearly and terrifyingly before the reader's eyes. Brunner's final contention that "Lovecraft was a throwback, an atavism, deliberately cultivating the modes and manners of an earlier and vanished day" once again plays into the myth of Lovecraft as an anachronism and seeks to contrast that myth with the sprightly, up-to-date world of science fiction.

At the same time, it cannot be said that those who sought to come to Lovecraft's defence against such criticisms did so in the most competent manner. Fritz Leiber and Edward Wood keenly and perspicaciously rebutted many of Brunner's remarks, but Sam Moskowitz caved in when he admitted that he was unable to finish reading *At the Mountains of Madness*. Elsewhere, W. Paul Cook, in "A Plea for Lovecraft" (1945), although correctly seeking to keep Lovecraft's devotees to some level of sanity (he reports that someone had come up to him and said, "Lovecraft is almost a god to me"), went on to endorse a reviewer's ignorant comment that "The

Rats in the Walls" is "pure clap-trap"—and then compounded his error by admitting that the story is "superb clap-trap," whatever that may be. Cook, as is well known, disapproved of Lovecraft's later, scientifically based narratives, and his article displays disappointment with even such an early specimen as "The Outsider" (1921). What inspired Cook to make the remarkably myopic comment that the second Lovecraft omnibus from Arkham House, *Beyond the Wall of Sleep* (1943), "should never have been published" is beyond conjecture.

The guiding force behind the emergence of Lovecraft as a literary figure in the late 1930s and 1940s was, of course, August Derleth. His determination to found Arkham House after he was unable to persuade mainstream publishers to issue the enormous *Outsider and Others* (although, by his own testimony, those publishers might well have accepted a smaller volume of the best of Lovecraft's stories—exactly the sort of volume that Derleth compiled in the *Best Supernatural Stories of H. P. Lovecraft* [1945], which sold tens of thousands of copies) is now legendary. Derleth also contributed to the "Lovecraft legend" by writing any number of articles purportedly praising his mentor, but in the process fostering several serious misconceptions of Lovecraft the man and writer. Perhaps his most culpable act was in disseminating the spurious quotation "All my stories, unconnected as they may be, are based on the fundamental lore or legend that this world was inhabited at one time by another race who, in practising black magic, lost their foothold and were expelled, yet live on outside ever ready to take possession of this earth again"—a statement that was in fact fabricated by Lovecraft's correspondent Harold S. Farnese and passed on to Derleth as a quotation from a Lovecraft letter. The frequency with which this comment—first cited by Derleth in "H. P. Lovecraft, Outsider" (1937)—is quoted by other critics is sufficient testimonial to the authority Derleth exercised as Lovecraft's champion and publisher.

The early reviews of *The Outsider and Others* (1939) and other Arkham House volumes in the mainstream press are of great interest: the focus, in several of the reviews, is not the quality (or lack of it) of the work itself but the mere existence of the books as a testament to friendship. This is the burden of the anonymous *Publishers' Weekly* review-article of 24 February 1940, which occupied a full two pages of the magazine but said almost nothing about the substance of Lovecraft's writing. The early Arkham House volumes never received extensive notices, but the enthusiasm of mystery devotee Will Cuppy is evident in his several reviews for the *New York Herald Tribune*. T. O. Mabbott expressed pride in being the first academician to review Lovecraft, and his laconic comment in *American Litera-*

ture (March 1940)—"Time will tell if his place be very high in our literary history; that he has a place seems certain"—is as true today as it was seventy years ago.

To be sure, not all mainstream reviewers liked Lovecraft. Peter De Vries, an acclaimed comic novelist, admitted that Lovecraft "is not quite on my wavelength" and went on to dismiss his work as a "competently wrought anachronism"; but even he felt that "There are moments when he strikes fire, achieving exquisite eerie details." William Poster, otherwise unknown but in his day prestigious enough to be a reviewer for the *New York Times Book Review*, could not be troubled to spell "Cthulhu" correctly, but nonetheless made the pungent remark: "Lovecraft was one of those rare individuals who seem to have been perfectly fitted by nature to do one thing surpassingly well." As for Marjorie Farber, her amateur psychoanalysis ("Only as an *undiscovered* genius can a writer really protect himself from failure") is about as sound as the amateur sociological analysis of Robert Allerton Parker's "Such Pulp as Dreams Are Made On" (1943).

Apparently, the negative reviews that the Arkham House volumes (not merely the Lovecraft books but also books by other writers) received gradually impelled Derleth to cease sending out review copies to the mainstream press, with the result that Lovecraft largely disappeared from public view for much of the 1950s and 1960s. The most negative review of all, of course, is not included here: Edmund Wilson's "Tales of the Marvellous and the Ridiculous" (*New Yorker*, 24 November 1945) is credited with almost single-handedly destroying Lovecraft's reputation for a generation. And yet, the existence of several other reviews and notices in the 1940s and 1950s makes one doubt such a blanket assessment. Only a few months after Wilson's blast, Fred Lewis Pattee praised Lovecraft's "Supernatural Horror in Literature" as "a brilliant piece of criticism"; J. O. Bailey (who had briefly corresponded with Lovecraft as early as 1930), in the first academic treatise on science fiction, *Pilgrims through Space and Time* (1947), spoke warmly of Lovecraft's contributions to the genre; Richard B. Gehman, in a popular article on science fiction, "Imagination Runs Wild" (1949), although he misspells Lovecraft's middle name, finds much to praise in Lovecraft's work and influence. Joseph Henry Jackson, a well-known critic at the *San Francisco Chronicle*, cited the early Arkham House volumes as having "something quite special in the line of shudders." When the first British editions of Lovecraft appeared in 1951, Eric Keown and the noted British novelist Anthony Powell generally praised Lovecraft, although not without equivocation.

The greatest champion of Lovecraft in the mainstream press in the 1940s was his erstwhile correspondent of 1927-28, Vincent Starrett. And yet, in some senses Starrett's praise—expressed repeatedly in his "Books Alive" column in the *Chicago Tribune*—did more harm than condemnation would have done. It was Starrett who propounded the view that Lovecraft was "his own most fantastic creation"—but in outlining what that "creation" was, Starrett yielded to the developing myth of Lovecraft as a "cadaverous, mysterious figure of the night," a "self-conscious *poseur*, a macabre *precieuse*," and so on. Starrett reveals his prejudice in an unwittingly candid moment when he declares that, in his judgment, Lovecraft's tales are "only superior experiments in pastiche."

What a volume like this indicates is the degree to which misconceptions about Lovecraft's life and work emerged at a relatively early period following his death. A late article in a writer's magazine, Vincent J. Gaddis's "The Genius Who Lived Backwards" (1954), shows how such misconceptions had become inveterate, although overall this article is a relatively sound piece of work. We also learn the supreme importance of the publication of Lovecraft's letters in finally helping to overturn these misconceptions—and the central role of scholars of the 1970s, notably Dirk W. Mosig, Richard L. Tierney, and Donald R. Burleson, in fostering a newer and deeper understanding of Lovecraft the man and writer. If much of the criticism in this volume now appears quaint, superficial, and wrong-headed, it is only because these and other scholars have worked so tirelessly in dismantling the Lovecraft myth and replacing it with sound facts and interpretations. The emergence of this newer and truer Lovecraft—a Lovecraft who was not only the creator of Cthulhu but the propounder of a detailed philosophy of life; who was not only an enthusiast of Dryden and Pope but a reader of Bertrand Russell and Havelock Ellis; who not only liked cats and ate immoderate quantities of ice cream but argued searchingly about the nature and causes of the Great Depression—makes him an even more compelling literary and intellectual figure than ever, and augurs well for his endurance in the centuries to come.

—S. T. Joshi

I. Recollections of Lovecraft

Howard P. Lovecraft [1890–1937]

Walter J. Coates

> Walter John Coates (1880–1941) was a colleague of HPL's who lived in Vermont. He came in touch with HPL in 1926 through W. Paul Cook. In that year he established the monthly periodical *Driftwind*, focusing chiefly on Vermont affairs but including fiction and poetry; HPL served as an associate editor from 1935 to 1937 and also published several poems (sonnets from *Fungi from Yuggoth*) and other matter in the magazine. Coates issued HPL's rare pamphlet *The Materialist Today* (1926)—originally a letter to him—under the imprint of the Driftwind Press. The following is an obituary published in *Driftwind* 11, No. 9 (April 1937): 343–44.

With a keen sense of personal loss and a profound sorrow the editor of DRIFTWIND records the death of Howard P. Lovecraft. The end came, most unexpectedly to us and all his friends, on Sunday, March 14th,[1] and was made public in Monday's papers.

He died in Providence, where he had spent most of his life. He was born there August 20, 1890, and resided, for many years, with an only aunt. Educated at local schools and under private tutors, he was early attracted to literature, and to psychic literature—the weird, the eerie—especially. The philosophy of the occult, the unearthly, the mysterious, obsessed him. And his early writings, published mainly in amateur magazines, reflected this trend. Attracting the attention of *Weird Tales*, he soon became one of the most popular contributors to this "pulp journal," and other similar publications. He was easily among the first American master-writers of weird fiction—comparable to Bram Stoker or Elliott O'Donnell in England—a master genius amidst phenomena unusual and bizarre.

Lovecraft was one of the earliest and most valued friends of DRIFTWIND. He encouraged us at the start, and did not withdraw his support, as many do, at the last. He was no "fair weather friend," merely. It was always a pleasure to publish his work; a pleasure to get, every issue, his cordial and appreciative comments; a pleasure to receive innumerable post-cards from him—post-cards that were as unique and exceptional in character as were the thoughts in his own mind. He loved old colonial architecture, antique doorways, embellished with the witches' cross, antique church spires, curious gabled houses, haunted or ruined mansions, old wooden covered bridges, dank wharves and slimy-green canals—anything that could stimulate his exotic imagination. Even his poetry exhaled this essential aroma. His was an abnormal yet strangely gentle and lovable disposition.

In The National Amateur Press Association Lovecraft served as an official critic, and at one time as President.[2] He did a lot of revising and editing for other writers, mature and immature. His own works include such divergent titles as "Idealism and Materialism" and "The Materialist Today" (essays); "Supernatural Horror in Literature" (treatise); "Vermont: a First Impression" (sketch);[3] "Fungi from Yuggoth" (poem)—and innumerable short mystery stories in the "pulps." His works, including "The Shunned House"—a novelette—will appear in an omnibus volume in the near future, under the able editorial guidance of August Derleth of Sauk City, Wisconsin.[4]

As a materialist Lovecraft sleeps "dust to dust"; yet, despite his own often expressed convictions, one cannot help feeling that, even now after the dissolution of his earth life, the spirit we knew and loved may be something more tangible than the poetic image of

"a painted ship
Upon a painted ocean."[5]

Amateur Affairs

Hyman Bradofsky

> Hyman Bradofsky (1906–2002) established the amateur journal the *Californian* in the 1930s and published a number of essays and other work by HPL and his colleagues. When he was president of the National Amateur Press Association (1935–36), he became embroiled in various bitter controversies, and HPL came to his defence with the essay "Some Current Motives and Practices" (1936). The following, an editorial prefacing a Lovecraft memorial issue, appeared in the *Californian* 5, No. 1 (Summer 1937): 28–31.

The news that Howard Lovecraft was gone seemed incredible. It was like an unicorn dying, or an amoretto, or one of those sinewy and eternal children of Pan. It came like a shock, as if a calamity had happened. There was an eternal quality in him, and his passing disturbed our feeling of the essential durableness of things. And yet a short while after, we became adjusted to the change in our ideas concerning him.

Years come and go. Centuries pass, nations rise and decay. Peoples perish. Here and there on the pages of history a name appears, fadeless and enduring—names of men and women who, because of strength of character, of loyalty to cause, of unselfish devotion to friends have stamped their personality and deeds upon the life and time in which they lived. These are the men and women who are courageous, gentle, just, generous. Into the very warp and woof of eternity these names are traced. As the years slip by their memories, brightened and burnished, shine with ever increasing luster.

Great as was Howard Lovecraft in heart and mind, we of today are unable to evaluate him at his true worth. Time and the march of events will bring increased understanding of him and of his tangible legacies.

In this age of materialism and mad pursuit after wealth, there are but few who care for the higher things of life. And because the men whose gaze penetrates beyond the trivialities and superficialities of our modern civilization are so few, we value those who have given us the more. And we grieve all the more when they are taken away from us.

Howard Lovecraft would have been a glory to any age, even the Golden Age of Amateur Journalism, but his brightness shone with an unusual brilliancy in our times, because so many of us have deserted the things for which he stood from his earliest years until his leaving us a brief time ago.

And what were the things for which he stood? The identical things which were sponsored and advocated in the amateur press by such notables as Truman J. Spencer, Ernest A. Edkins, James F. Morton, Edward H. Cole, Maurice W. Moe and Rheinhart Kleiner. Lovecraft stood for something highly important. By his life he demonstrated that it was possible in amateur journalism to make a career of so illusive and unsubstantial a thing as beauty. This was no insignificant achievement. It was an extremely important accomplishment in the eyes of the above-named group who know the stirrings of an awakening urge to create, and interpret and live, beauty.

Lovecraft reviewed hundreds and hundreds of writings appearing in tiny publications. Himself a discerning critic, he was at home in the field of analysis and interpretation, and yet the kindest of mentors.

Perhaps the pithiest of all Lovecraft legend is forever buried in his personal letters. Here he was free to damn or bless; either of which he could do to the king's taste. To quote the present day apostles, he "let himself out." They were rich in wisdom and health. They were unrestrained and glorious! He would parody anything from the psalms to Eddie Guest[6]—and do it with keen relish. He reserved nothing, letting the ripe essence of a life richly lived scatter over the pages. His advice to the young writers he knew, and whom he trusted, was the most exquisite philosophical classicism ever put to paper. A tragedy this is lost to the unhallowed multitude. We have no idea how he managed to be so exact and meticulous in answering letters. Nor has anyone else.

Authors all too frequently write much and say little. Not so Howard Lovecraft. His pen pictures of the fantasy are interesting in the extreme as showing not only descriptive ability, but the genius mind. All of his poems were exactly polished and beautifully written. He was filled with all sorts of good story material which he flung right and left to those who could use it. He wrote admirable prose. Few literary men were more versatile than Lovecraft. His work was scholarly while at the same time it possessed a glow and enthusiasm that held the interest. He was a true student of the classics—the Maecenas of letters.[7]

The psychopathic fallacy of nature was not in Howard Lovecraft. He might write about the moon. But he didn't hold that the moon was young Mancata, sterile and subject to convulsions, and a worshiper before a red-and-vermillion shrine. Nonsense, the moon was an orb of poetic uses but also of deep astronomical interest. In fact, he could cover reams of paper with sines and cosines in the laudable effort to determine its correct trajectory. In other words, he was also scientist.

Howard Lovecraft made many friends. The amateur and professional press have spoken generously of his work and contribution. The tributes from friends and admirers indicate the vast company that would wish to add their word. Lovecraft was a man of the deepest human sympathies. Scores of writers and hundreds of would-be writers know how generous he was with his time in reading and criticising their efforts, and many are the friends who know how his great heart was the first to feel for them in misfortune and to help when it lay in his power. His greatest joy was in giving and in serving. He was extra-human in his sense of duty.

Lovecraft's passing is a distinct loss to this writer. When we visit Boston we will not see him. That hurts, when we force ourselves to realize it. But Lovecraft lives on in his work; lives, too, in the memory of those who knew him, and lives well.

[Letter to the Editor]

Robert Bloch

> Robert Bloch (1917–1994) was one of HPL's most accomplished late correspondents and disciples. The following letter—published in *Fantasy Commentator* 1, No. 7 (Summer 1945): 164–65—is one of his earliest published recollections of HPL, preceded only by his letter to *Weird Tales* (see pp. 84–85) and preceding such memoirs as "Out of the Ivory Tower" (1959).

I'd like to comment briefly on "The Lord of R'lyeh,"[8] which makes several points and makes them well—but before rambling on, I must take the precaution of stating that what I say is not to be construed as either criticism or objection.

But I am curiously impressed with the entire phenomenon of Lovecraft-appraisal. During the past two years, particularly, I've read scores of items concerning HPL's life, personality and works. And I see but a small fraction of the fan publications. Strange that he should be more alive in the minds of fandom eight years after his death than at any time during his actual existence . . . or is it?

It took the accolade of book-publication, general critical recognition and successful reprinting to awaken even Lovecraft-aficionados to the man's literary importance. I can well remember when the really dyed-in-the-wool Lovecraft fan of the late twenties and early thirties was actually looked down upon by the lofty readers of *Astounding* and *Wonder Stories*, to say nothing of the *Weird Tales* group which preferred "fast-action" authors. The Lovecraftophiles were then distinguished by their *intensity* rather than their numerical supremacy.

But now (needless to point out the obvious reasons) the picture has changed. Everybody who knew him seems to have come out with an "I knew him when" piece . . . and those who didn't at least manage an "analysis" of the Master's works.

Far be it from me to carp or cavil. I personally have enjoyed each and every bit—and it delights me to find such recognition (even belated and posthumous recognition) of his importance in the fantasy field.

Still, I confess to a certain uneasiness as I contemplate the aggregate content of these articles. They tend, I fear, to place emphasis on aspects of Lovecraft's life and writings which obscure the man himself.

There are many readers who never knew HPL through either personal correspondence or personal contact . . . many more who didn't even read his stories during his lifetime. They must therefore depend upon existing articles for a picture of the man and an interpretation of his literary efforts. And the picture is distorted.

Too often the sincere attempts at reminiscence on the part of his social intimates and correspondents resolve inevitably into the presentation of a series of trivial anecdotes unconsciously emphasizing the pride of the narrator in his friendship with Lovecraft. And frequently the analyses display an erudition of the author at the expense of an accurate appraisal of his subject.

For this reason I have never written a line about him for publication save for a brief, impulsive statement in *Weird Tales* immediately upon receiving news of his death. For I too feel myself liable to unconscious bias. I *did* correspond with him, *was* a great admirer, and *am* proud of his friendship. Indeed, I must admit that his dedication of "The Haunter of the Dark" to me, and his use of me as protagonist of that tale remains the high spot of my life to date—and I've had some pretty gaudy high spots. But in the face of the growing mass of Lovecraftiana extant, I'd like to mention one aspect of HPL's life and times that has never (to my knowledge) been properly presented to fandom.

When I think of Lovecraft the man, I think of a rather different picture than the one generally presented. (The tall, thin, ascetic eccentric; encyclopedic in his knowledge, picturesque in his philosophy, renowned as a recluse—you know the story; you've read it in almost everything written about him.)

When I think of H. P. Lovecraft I think mainly of his most outstanding attributes . . . his kindness and his courtesy.

Lovecraft was the kindest, most courteous man I have ever encountered.

(And dammit, I'm not given to gushing or to using such hackneyed words loosely or profanely.)

In order to elucidate I must descend for a moment to that "I knew him when" level . . . but I trust the spirit will not be misinterpreted. I wrote the first (and just about the last) "fan letter" of my life to Lovecraft in the early months of 1933, when I was fifteen. As I recall it, the letter contained a specific request for information as to where I could purchase magazines containing his older stories that I had not read.

So you get a letter from a fifteen-year-old kid wanting to know about magazines . . . you tell him to try the second-hand bookstores, and forget it.

Not Howard Phillips Lovecraft.

I got back a complete typed list of all his published stories, together with an invitation to send for them in any order I chose. He would mail me the tear-sheets, and if they were unavailable, he'd send me the original manuscripts or carbons. And of course I must feel free to write again.

I felt free. The second letter mentioned my general interest in fantasy and some of the reading I'd done.

Lovecraft didn't rattle off a list of supplementary book titles. Instead, he sent me a handwritten complete list of every fantasy book in his own library—again with an invitation to borrow at will.

His later kindnesses in introducing me to the "gang," his interest, encouragement, critical readings of and suggestions for my early stories—all were typical of the man. His delicacy, unfailing tact and finesse in the critical approach were unsurpassed. Of course his letters were magnificent—but it is the spirit behind the letters that overshadows all else for me; the erudition, the profundities, the prodigality of his correspondence.

As to the psychological and philosophical motives which led to the creation of his stories, I am not qualified to speak. But in all that I have read, I have never heard one important consideration mentioned as a factor in Lovecraft's work . . . and to me it was the most human aspect. I refer to his *enthusiasm* for writing the weird tale. He loved to turn out a story, and through all his misgivings and self-recriminations and self-criticism it is impossible to read through a sheaf of his letters referring to work in progress without consciousness of that enthusiasm shining through.

Lovecraft wrote weird fiction because he enjoyed it; because it gave expression to escape-fantasies. In other words, he wrote for the same reason that most of us in the fantasy field write our yarns. The fact that he wrote much better stuff does not mean that his motives in doing so were any loftier, or that he was consciously attempting to build up a cosmological philosophy or create a new school of writing.

I don't know whether I'm coherent or not—I rather doubt it. But one point is important to me: having been one of the "Lovecraft circle" of correspondents, I cannot think of the man as primarily a genius, an eccentric, or a literary prodigy. To me, first and foremost, Howard Phillips Lovecraft was a hell of a swell guy.

Interlude with Lovecraft

Stuart M. Boland

> Stuart Morton Boland (1909–1973) was a San Francisco librarian who appears to have established a correspondence with HPL in late 1936. The following memoir appeared in the *Acolyte* 3, No. 3 (Summer 1945): 15–18. The article contains some editorial notes by the editor of the *Acolyte*, Francis T. Laney.

In the Spring of 1935 I was making a library survey tour of the European continent. At the quaint little hill town of Orvieto, in Italy, I came upon an amazing mural high on the walls of the local Duomo or Cathedral. The painting represented mighty figures of ebon-hued men (not angels or demons) with great wings, flying through etheric space carrying beauteous pinionless mortals—men and women who were rapturously accompanying them on their voyage through eternity.

I photographed the scene and sent a print to Robert E. Howard, telling him it reminded me of one of his Conan stories. With the print I included a colored reproduction of a rare illuminated manuscript of the 10th Century which I had seen in the Royal Archives at Budapest. Howard, for some reason, sent this facsimile to Lovecraft, asking if he thought his *Necronomicon* would look anything like the reproduction of the parchment.[9]

* * *

Three months later, when I reached my home by the Presidio in San Francisco, I found awaiting me two letters from Howard and an extensive missive from Lovecraft. I was extremely pleased and surprised to hear from these masters of fantasy. Lovecraft inquired if I had another copy of the illuminated facsimile; then proceeded to give me his version of the history of the *Necronomicon*. The small and cryptic handwriting interested me considerably, but Lovecraft's statement to the effect that the *Necronomicon* was not in any way, shape, or form a thing of beauty stirred my imagination. Even the Egyptian *Book of the Dead* was a testimony to the bibliographical arts and accomplishments of the strange high-priests who produced it, no matter what immortal horror lay locked within its sheets.

Lovecraft said that the brightly colored and gilded manuscript was a far cry from what he had in mind; in fact, the *Necronomicon* was intended to be a tome of stark terror and diabolical utility. "The ultimate horror whose secrets would curdle and boil the seething organ of the brain in its bone-pot as its ghastly mysteries unfolded to the eyes of those who dared to read it." Incidentally, Howard claimed that the name *Necronomicon* was compounded from the words "Necro," meaning death; "nomi," meaning name, and "con," meaning with—literally, "With the Name of Death."[10] It should be noted, however, that Lovecraft gave me a long explanation about the *Necronomicon* without thus defining the origin of his word.

Lovecraft asked me if I thought that San Francisco's Ambrose Bierce and George Sterling wrote stories under nom de plumes for pulp magazines. He ventured the suspicion that they did, because in certain fanciful stories he had read, he thought he clearly detected the imprint and character of their respective styles. [So far as we know, Lovecraft was mistaken in this assumption.—FTL]

In my reply to HPL, I stated that I thought his opinion was well-founded, and furthermore that the references of both men to odd, ancient gods were ideas they must have borrowed from Mayan, Toltec, and Aztec mythology. Such references, I suggested, were disguised from their original source by cloaking the identity of the gods in different environments and baptizing them with new names.

Lovecraft wrote promptly back to me and asked if I had much knowledge of the history and lore of the ancient Mayan, Toltec, and Aztec civilizations. He also asked if I harbored the thought that he might have gotten some of his ideas about gods from these same sources.

In my reply I mentioned that I had studied first-hand the cultures of the American aborigines of yesteryear, and that there were similarities between his gods and those of the early Mexican Indians.

Lovecraft's next communication showed rare humor, and I got the impression that the Lovecraft Theology was a source of considerable amusement and secret mirth to him; also that anyone with any kind of imagination could invent any number of odd-gods and there would always be people willing and eager to believe in them. He seemed to be bubbling over with a deep Jovian inner laughter because supposedly intelligent readers of his tales took his gods for granted as real existing powers. I further sensed that his attitude was that Man *"created god in his own image and likeness"* to serve his own ends and purposes. I felt a sardonic impulse at play here, but one which with all its burden of tremendous knowledge faced the future with a courage and fortitude unmatched in my experience; Lovecraft, the *"man who created the gods who created men"*; was my instinctive thought as I gleaned his lines. Moreover, Lovecraft seemed to have pride in the fact he portrayed his gods so realistically that many of his credulous readers believed in them as implicitly and emphatically as a Fakir Fanatic. He said he had letters from people expressing overwhelming faith and fear with all the rabidity of frenzied zealots, who considered him the high-priest of an archaic cult rescued in these latter years from the oblivion of doubt. But it was his Gargantuan sense of humor which led him to "feed the poblacho fodder for their figments of the imagination."

Lovecraft put in a post-script asking me if I had any ideas or suggestions from my knowledge of the Mexican deities who would make suitable candidates for his pantheon. [Note. It might be mentioned as an aside that August Derleth, in "The Trail of Cthulhu," applies the Aztec name of *Huitzilopochtli* to Cthulhu, and that much of this story centers around a Peruvian manifestation of Cthulhu and his minions.—FTL]

I sent him several clay and jade figurines of Aztec and Mayan gods and godlings that I had gotten in Quintana Roo, Mexico; and some publications on the subject, including the splendid brochure put out by the American Museum of Natural History in New York. Then after a few moments contemplation, I sent him the following list of extremely Lovecraftish gods.

Chiminig-Agua. A violent deity and keeper of the Cosmic Light. Creator of the colossal Black Avians that distribute light about the Universe during the daytime and who gobbled it up every night.

Cen-Teatl. A gigantic, squat, frog-like female with a thousand udders, whose embrace was fatal to the Elder Gods and the Ghoul Gods of the Aztec Lethe (World of Oblivion).

Tonantzin. Supreme Being in the form of an ever-sneering serpent whose long sinewy body coils about the entire firmament. The eggs she lays are solar orbs and planets. Cannibal-like, she devours her own children and hence is oftimes called "The Star-Eater."

Camazotz. Mayan vampire bat-god who flies into the reeking pits and caverns of the Abysmal Cesspools of Creation to drag forth the vile monstrous maggot life dwelling therein. He drops these revolting entities on planets whose inhabitants refuse to worship him. The maggot life-forms smother the fated orbs with their slime and spittle before sucking out the steaming, living viscera of the earth-bodies.

Kinich-Kakimo. Fiery visaged Lord of the Overworlds, whose chief duty is to hew out meteors from the mighty solar orbs in the Celestial Mansions. He also chops the tributary planets into form from great suns with his flint axe.

Noh-Ek. (Star-Killer) Who sets the stars dancing down the corridors of space and time to their doom in the charnel cellars of creation. As each star reaches the Portals of Mitla (or Cosmic Slaughterhouse) it is felled with a soul-shattering blow by *Noh-Ek's* brother. The remains of the murdered stars are mixed with the ichor of fallen gods and served as fodder to the lost spirits of *Omacetl.*

Tamoancan. The god of the Waiting World or Abode of Descent where wait the souls of demons, outer world fiends, and hell-spawned effluvia. *Tamoancan* secretly slips the souls of these hideous devils into the bodies of infants about to be born on earth. Once in human form they must remain bound to that body until they are freed by performing some noteworthy cosmic crime whose "evil effect can blot out the stars."

Tlau-Izcal-Pante-Cutli. Beauteous, sadistic, lustful, lecherous female voluptuary who purchased the *Five Firmaments* in order to find a supreme lover who could satiate her overwhelming passions. So far, all lovers have perished gallantly in the attempt. In vengeance and frustration she destroys the solar circuits of the planet from whence the failures sprang. She has frequently disguised herself as the newlywed bride of some brawny swain, usurping the place of his wife who is spirited away into the Starless Void beyond the Eternal. The groom is usually found with his life completely drained away, succubus-like. This goddess has been known to kidnap the entire male population of a planet, leaving the stricken womenfolk with a desolate, manless world. (Lovecraft thought this deific character would make the basis of a splendid Robert E. Howard story.)

Yum-Cimil. The Supreme Horror who steals the possessions, life-forces, and finally the soul of every sentient creature in the Universe. His head is the skull of a dead planet; his beard the entrails of the savage quag-god; his eyes the living fires of hell; and his voice the agonizing cry of frightened thunder.

Lovecraft studied over the choice items carefully and said they were fertile with ideas he "might choose to use" but they were "crude and require a great deal of interpretation and modification." He said that he felt his own writings depicted man as the hapless victim of vast cosmic conspiracies, and that the suggested Mexican gods fitted in with this principle. He went on to venture the thought that Clark Ashton Smith would likewise be interested "because he wrote of man as the pre-destined tool of death," and assuredly the garish gods of the Aztecs bore out such a premise. He went on to declare that Catherine Moore wrote as "an incurable optimist rescuing man from an ill-omened fate by the means of a 'Star-destined fortune-favored' element; and that she would take over these old Mexican gods and dispose of them one by one through the valor, courage, and will power of her characters." He said she believed that the animal "man" had the undeniable ability to recover from the most hell-shattering catastrophe. The immortal potentialities of mankind, as she saw them, were too enormous a factor to be submerged or intimidated by mere "terror-gods." Such would make excellent straw-men for her heroes to vanquish.

Lovecraft finished his comparisons by asserting that "Robert Howard created men like gods and gods like men, with the men invincible conquerors over all the woe and misery the Powers of the Absolute could throw at them." He averred that Howard would find the Maya-Toltec-Aztec gods easy meat for his blood-lusting warriors, except that the divinities should have more sex-appeal to be worth his heroes' trouble in dispatching them! In the light of this basic philosophy of Howard's it was a titanic life-quake when the full shock of his passing struck his friends. Such a reversal of fundamental nature seemed unbelievable. So vital and dynamic a personality seemed eternal and immutable. He and Lovecraft were good friends and perhaps together they are exploring the infinite with the same zest and joyous spirit they possessed on the mundane sphere. They make a perfect pair of Immortals, each with stupendous understanding of life, creation and the universe; each the complement of the other, in realms and dimensions and planes undreamed.

I cannot but wonder if the Great God Lovecraft is now enthroned with the God of Gods, telling him chilling, enthralling tales of mankind and the demoniacal deeds of that dire, dread, planet-spawned, earthbound biped; telling him and his fellow gods the horrific, spine-freezing truth about the erratic mammal whose feet tread the earth but who betimes sends his soul a-voyaging through the starry vastness; tales of the two-legged mystery incarnate who caresses with one hand and kills with the other! Undoubtedly the gods find Lovecraft's sagas equally as exciting and intriguing as do his fellow men.

Howard Phillips Lovecraft

Muriel E. Eddy

Muriel E. Eddy (1896–1978) was the wife of Clifford Martin Eddy, Jr. (1896–1967), who collaborated with HPL on four stories. The following is her first memoir of HPL, published in *Rhode Island on Lovecraft*, ed. Donald M. Grant and Thomas P. Hadley (Providence, RI: Grant-Hadley, 1945), pp. 14–22. In later memoirs—e.g., *The Gentleman from Angell Street* (1961) Eddy adds numerous details to her account, such as the assertion that she and her husband came in touch with HPL as early as 1918 because Clifford's mother and HPL's mother knew each other and shared an interest in woman suffrage. Many of these details seem suspect and are not confirmed by other evidence, especially the testimony of

HPL's letters, in which he indicates (see, e.g., *SL* 1.254) he came in touch with the Eddys only in 1923.

It was in the middle of August, 1923, that the late Howard Phillips Lovecraft, Esquire, first made his personal appearance in our lives. The first thing we noticed about Lovecraft was his eyes, which, behind their spectacles, beamed upon us in friendliness,—they were gentle, benign, smiling, such a deep brown that they seemed almost black. He wore a straw sailor hat, an immaculate light gray Palm Beach suit, a white shirt and a black four-in-hand tie. When he removed his hat we saw that his hair was carefully groomed and a glossy jet black. At that time he was inclined to plumpness, and despite an unmistakable "lantern jaw" his face seemed cherubic in its contour. Extending lean white fingers in what we came to regard as a typical Lovecraftian gesture, we noticed that, although the day was extremely hot and sultry, his hands were cold.

Under his arm he carried a leather brief-case, bursting with "National Amateur" publications and manuscripts from his own pen. At that time he contributed freely to amateur writers' periodicals, not having thought seriously of commercializing his work.

From our first meeting, we knew that here was a man who would be a loyal friend. Over a period of months we had discussed writing and its fine points, and Lovecraft had put us in touch with a few amateur publications in which our poems had subsequently appeared. At that time Lovecraft himself was no mean poet, and we had learned a lot regarding poetic construction by correspondence with him. Our telephone conversations had been few, as Lovecraft had a deep-seated aversion to anything that smacked of present-day mechanical inventions, preferring to imagine himself a gentleman of the past, long before the days of the telephone and similar timesavers.

At that time we lived but three miles, "as the crow flies," from each other—Lovecraft and his two aunts, Mrs. Gamwell and Mrs. Clark, residing on Angell Street, Providence, while we of the Eddy clan lived on Second Street in East Providence.

Much of Lovecraft's work had appeared in a tiny amateur publication to which he had introduced us; it was known as *The Tryout*, and was published by C. W. Smith of Haverhill, Mass. Through Lovecraft, we received a copy as often as it was printed, and the more we read of Lovecraft's work the deeper was our conviction that here was genius, unrecognized by most, perhaps, but real, unbridled genius, nevertheless. It was our intention to try to impress upon Lovecraft the importance of getting his work before the public in a larger way, and we had the new magazine dealing in so-called "horror stories," known as *Weird Tales*, in mind. The editor, Edwin Baird, was known to Mr. Eddy through extensive correspondence; in fact, my husband was even then in the throes of composing a weird story of his own, tentatively titled "The Beloved Dead," and he wanted Lovecraft to read the manuscript before he submitted it.

We settled in the tiny parlor at our Second Street home, and lost no time in steering the conversation around to the subject at hand. Lovecraft beamed as we praised his work, or what little of it we had seen. Then he shrugged deprecatingly, chuckled, and said: "I'm afraid you overestimate the value of my work because you, yourselves, enjoy reading my trash—I assure you there's nothing phenomenal about my stories; most of them are the result of a vivid imagination, that's all. By the way, I walked over here and found it most pleasant. I must try it again sometime."

We gasped when we realized that, with the thermometer soaring above 90°, our guest had *walked* from his upper Angell Street dwelling to our East Providence abode—and the strangest thing about it was that he wasn't even perspiring! When we knew Lovecraft better, we realized that he could stand heat in any proportion, but cold, not at all.

We discussed weird stories for hours in the stifling hot parlor, and he read aloud from several of his manuscripts, including one he'd composed at the tender age of fourteen[11]—his natural propensity for writing weird fiction was apparent even then. He told us that the real key to success in writing a "weird tale" was to keep the reader's imagination at fever point, and suggesting terrible things instead of "coming right out" with them. As he discussed the writing of the weird and uncanny, he told us of his story, "The Lurking Fear," a horror serial which was appearing at that time in a small monthly magazine published by a good friend of his,[12]—and of his method of injecting the element of terror in this serial by hints and vague references to the "unknown"—the mounds which sometimes seemed to move; the swollen trees in the cemetery, unnaturally-shaped, with limbs distorted; with vague hints that they fed on buried things; queer sounds and cries in the night; the unexplained disappearance of human beings; and houses which screamed of past madnesses. He closed his discussion by averring that in the terrific power of suggestion lay the secret of success in all weird literature.

When we approached the subject of his submitting his work to the editor of *Weird Tales*, he smiled cryptically. True, he'd allowed his good friend Julius to publish "The Lurking Fear,"—he'd sort of "gotten a kick" (the slang is my own) out of the freakish illustrations an artist had given its characters;[13] but as for trying to market his wares with a modern magazine to which so many writers of various types of "weird" fiction contributed, he was disinterested. He told us frankly that he'd never thought seriously of "commercializing" his work—the artistic side of writing had appealed to him all his life, but the idea of selling his writings appalled him—he shrugged non-committally, folded his manuscripts methodically, and returned them to the well-worn leather brief-case.

The rest of the time was spent in Lovecraft's reading over the manuscript of what was then called by Mr. Eddy "The Beloved Dead," later published in *Weird Tales* under the title "The Loved Dead,"—a story which created a furore among certain readers when it appeared, because it dealt with something then new in the field of weird fiction—the thoughts and feelings of a necrologic individual.[14] The manuscript thoroughly delighted Lovecraft, and he insisted on reading it aloud. He insisted that Mr. Eddy lose no time in submitting it to the magazine, predicting an instantaneous acceptance by its editor. I believe it was his enthusiasm for Mr. Eddy's story that finally convinced him he should likewise submit a few of his own manuscripts to Mr. Baird. That they were accepted at once, everybody who ever read that magazine catering to lovers of the uncanny knows, for time and again Lovecraft's stories have been reprinted by that same magazine, years later, by request of its readers.

After that first visit from Howard Phillips Lovecraft, our friendship was firmly established. Still a self-appointed recluse, at first his personal visits were not too often, but our correspondence was voluminous. When we moved from East Providence, Lovecraft was the first visitor in our new home. As usual, he brought along some manuscripts, among which was his now famous "The Rats in the Walls." He started to read this creepy yarn to us at midnight—and continued, placing special emphasis on certain words as he read, his facial expressions changing as he became so absorbed in what he was reading aloud that it seemed he was actually living the story, making it come alive. The conclusion of the story left us literally gasping! I think it was then we both realized that this man possessed the greatest gift of writing weird stories since Edgar Allan Poe. Not only did his characters live and breathe—the surroundings, too, came to life! I'll never forget that night! Many houses in Providence were gas-lighted at that time, and Lovecraft's face, as seen by the flickering rays of gaslight, while he read aloud his own ultra-fanciful creation, was truly something "out of this world"—ever to be remembered. I shuddered myself to sleep that night!

Many times, Lovecraft would surprise us with a gift of sweets for the children, who were then small—milk-chocolate bars were his favorite—and it seemed he always kept a supply on hand. Once we had cold chicken in the ice-box, and, offering our guest some, at one of our many midnight get-togethers, he surprised us by exclaiming: "To be sure—and don't bother with the silverware; it's lots more fun eating chicken with one's fingers!" Cups of hot coffee were his delight, very well-sugared and with plenty of cream. Cheese, he adored, and we often had cheese sandwiches for our repasts. Fish of any kind he heartily hated—in fact, any sort of sea-food was abhorrent in the extreme to this master of the weird. Many of his most-loved horror tales deal with unnamed monsters of the deep. He had a passion for ice-cream, and could easily consume a quart at a time; chocolate seemed to be his favorite flavor, though he liked all kinds. Danish pastry intrigued him, and at one time he haunted bakeries specializing in pastries of this kind.

Referring to Lovecraft's dread of the cold, there is one night I especially remember. It was late in February and bitterly cold, with the thermometer dropping rapidly. The hour was extremely late; and trolleys had stopped running; we had no 'phone with which to call a cab. Not realizing it was so cold outside, our genial guest declared that the walk home would do him good; perhaps, he added, he might do a little exploring en route—one of his favorite pastimes was discovering quaint little alleys and byways of which he had never before been aware; and usually Mr. Eddy accompanied him on these explorations, long past the midnight hour. Acting on impulse, Mr. Eddy now offered to accompany him part of the way home, and it is fortunate that he did, for a few blocks later Lovecraft, overcome with the biting cold, slumped to the sidewalk, and had it not been for a nearby all-night drugstore, where Lovecraft was taken and revived, the ending might have been different. As it was, he finished the trip home in a cab. That was the last time he ventured out in such extremely cold winter weather.

It was during the hot summer months that Lovecraft expressed the desire to have Mr. Eddy accompany him on a quest to find a so-called "Black Swamp" somewhere, it was said, in the wilds of Chepachet, R. I.—a swamp so overhung by trees that no sunlight ever penetrated it. Always on the lookout for oddities of nature, the idea of seeing such a swamp intrigued Lovecraft to such an extent that he took the whole day off, leaving his writings, as eager as any schoolboy to witness nature's phenomenon. The whereabouts of that swamp—if such a swamp truly exists—is still a mystery—at least, it was never located, and Mr. Eddy almost had to carry Lovecraft back from the rural excursion, at least a mile, to the trolley line, for, unaccustomed to such vigorous jaunts at that time, the writer of tales macabre soon became so exhausted he could hardly move one foot after the other. It was a great disappointment to Lovecraft that the trip was a failure, as far as finding the swamp was concerned; but the rural characteristics of the village delighted him, and found place, I am sure, in many of his later stories.[15]

Lovecraft often told us, though his stories would seem to belie it, that he did not believe in superstitions or superstitious lore. He had a copy of Cotton Mather, and had access to all of the weird literature by past writers. Ambrose Bierce was among his favorites. Lovecraft loved to discuss writings of his contemporaries, and was never loath to sing the praises of a story that he especially liked. Jealousy was an unknown factor, I am sure, in his life. In fact, he enjoyed helping others interested in writing to "make the grade"—many and varied were his revisions, and the world will never know half of what he accomplished in this field. The poems he revised and made salable for others would stretch from coast to coast, and some of them have gained much recognition without any credit going to Lovecraft—he preferred it that way. Lovecraft, in his later years, accepted the job as "ghost-writer" for many prominent people, and they became famous as writers with few even suspecting that behind their fame was the facile pen of H. P. Lovecraft, Esq. He never boasted of this; to him, it was all in the day's work, and many times we helped him type manuscripts that he had "ghost-written"—up to the time of his demise he abhorred typing, because it came under the heading of modernity, I think.

It is common knowledge among his intimates in the writing field that Lovecraft enjoyed being known as "Grandpa Theobald." His letters to us were often thusly signed, and in a church visitor's book he once signed himself "Howard Phillips Lovecraft, Esquire, Gentleman"—this was during a visit to Providence's oldest, quaintest church[16] one week-day, with Mr. Eddy. The steeple especially intrigued Lovecraft and appealed vastly to his imagination, which was always at its best when viewing ancient architecture.

I have never known another human being who shared Lovecraft's affection for cats to so great an extent. I have seen him stoop and pet and console (using a special kind of language cats seemed to understand), a stray, injured feline; and I know that he loved to feed stray cats.

It was a bitter blow to him when his own beloved cat, "Nigger Man," disappeared strangely one night, never to return.[17] After that, his fondness for cats increased—whenever he saw a black cat, he was reminded of lost "Nigger Man," he often told us—he kept his emotions well-hidden from the public eye, but that he possessed the quality of sympathy I have no doubt. I have seen it exhibited in a thousand little ways—although he would have been the last to call himself a sympathetic individual! When he called at our home he loved to sit in a big rocker and let our cats walk all over him. He knew each cat by name, and they knew, and loved, him.

He was especially fond of a calico cat we owned, named "Susie," and when Susie became a mother he actually sent her his "heartiest congratulations!"

Of his marriage to Sonia Greene, not too much is known. He visited us the night prior to his departure for New York, to advise us that he was saying goodbye to Providence, and asking us if we would accept some of the personal furniture he would no longer have any use for. He made no mention at all of his forthcoming marriage. One of these pieces of furniture was a marble-topped bureau, which we still have—another was a folding bed, gone with the years. Both were delivered to us by an expressman the next day.

On the night of his visit to us, destined to be the last for many months, he discussed the fact that "Old New York" with its historic background and many traditions had always appealed to him, and he hoped to be happy there, because from then on New York would become his "adopted state." He was perturbed, however, because he had a "dead-line" to meet—he showed us a freshly-typed manuscript which he had "ghost-written" for no less a personality than the late Harry Houdini, a weird experience of the master magician's in far-off Egypt, scheduled to appear in a forthcoming issue of *Weird Tales*.[18] He told us he hoped in the excitement of leaving Providence on an early morning train, he wouldn't forget and leave the manuscript behind! It was imperative that the manuscript reach the editor by a certain time. Alas—for well-laid plans of mice and men! Taking a "cat nap" while waiting for his train in Providence's Union Station in the "wee sma' hours," the worst happened—the manuscript was lost! The first we knew of it was when a small, frantic statement of its loss appeared in the next morning's *Providence Journal's* Lost and Found column—offering a substantial reward for its return. The manuscript was never found, but fortunately, seeming to have a sixth sense in such matters, Lovecraft had brought the original pen-and-ink copy of the manuscript to New York, and a public stenographer made quick work of it.[19]

The next news we had of Lovecraft was an engraved announcement of his marriage to Sonia Greene. It was a simple announcement, but it took us so completely by surprise that it was several hours before we thoroughly digested the news. The marriage, destined to be short-lived, took place in New York in the spring of 1924. Lovecraft sent us snapshots of himself and Sonia—now dimmed with the passing of the years—and in letters to us he never forgot to include "Sonia sends her love, and hopes some day to meet you." In the snapshots, Sonia Greene Lovecraft appeared as a tall, handsome woman, dark and stately. Lovecraft himself looked completely happy and at peace with the world.

At least one weird story by Sonia appeared in *Weird Tales*, bearing signs of Lovecraft's unmistakable revision, and published when she was still Sonia Greene. If Sonia, too, was a writer, we anticipated a long and happy marriage, but such was not to be—after an interval of several months, during which letters from Lovecraft became few and far between, we began to receive postcards from Lovecraft bearing various postmarks, and we realized he had left New York and perhaps Sonia.

Before Lovecraft's sudden departure from Providence he had been deeply interested in Mr. Eddy's idea of writing a story centered around a character devoid of hearing, speech and sight who lived alone in a reputedly haunted house. Lovecraft's encouragement, suggestions, and compliments as the story progressed resulted in Mr. Eddy's "Deaf, Dumb and Blind" being accepted by the editor of *Weird Tales*, and we were pleased to receive felicitations from Lovecraft upon its publication. He felt honored, he assured Mr. Eddy, because he had been present at its conception, so naturally he felt a fatherly interest. He always considered that story Mr. Eddy's best.

Then, after an interval of several months, our genial friend again dawned on our horizon. He had the same affable smile, as he came to our home, but he had lost much weight since his sojourn in New York. It was good, he averred, to feel the sidewalks of Providence once more under his feet. That he had not lost his genius for writing weird fiction was proven by a veritable masterpiece he turned out, its locale Old New York, and its title "The Horror at Red Hook,"—as creepy a yarn as ever left Lovecraft's pen. Lovecraft had that rare gift of sensing a story in old architecture, peopling old buildings musty with disuse, and "The Horror at Red Hook" surpasses many of his other stories, I think, with its sheer hints and inferences.

Many times we took upon ourselves the task of typing his manuscripts; we experienced no difficulty in deciphering his small chirography, but instead we rather enjoyed having a "preview," as it were, of his latest work. He believed in economizing on paper, and his manuscripts would be written on the backs of old letters, advertisements, or any paper that provided ample space for his needs at the moment. He revised his own stories as he went along, and many times we would have to turn the page of a manuscript upside down, sideways, and search the corners for arrows pointing to words he wished to put in. He had a perfect horror of mistakes, and one of the standing conditions when he sold a story was that he had the privilege, always, of proof-reading his work before it finally was placed in the printer's hands. He never spared himself the job of re-writing a story, no matter what its length, if he noted an error in it.

Although we realized that Howard Phillips Lovecraft had never enjoyed robust health, when news of his death reached us that bleak day in March, 1937, we were momentarily stunned—at a loss for words to console his bereaved aunt, Mrs. Annie Gamwell, who broke the news to us via 'phone. He died at Jane Brown Hospital, and for the benefit of doctors who had attended him he left behind him copious notes on his physical feelings as the end drew near, thinking with his last conscious thoughts of others, as had been his wont. This last gesture paints an eloquent picture, to my way of thinking, of the real Lovecraft—indeed, a gentleman of the "old school"—and of the past he loved.

His funeral was held at High Noon at a funeral home, and, though the little gods of fate seemed to will that we should arrive there too late for the services, we did visit Swan Point Cemetery, with its many tombs, winding lanes and exquisite monuments—and did I imagine it, or did the spirit of our late beloved friend and fellow-writer hover over us as we bowed our heads in reverence and respect to the memory of one of the finest men— yes, and greatest geniuses, who ever walked this earth? A man little-known, perhaps, by the majority, but a man who, to those who came in more than casual contact with him, exemplified all that is fine and good in a fellow human being.

Long may the spirit of "Howard Phillips Lovecraft, Esquire, Gentleman" endure!

I Met Lovecraft

Paul Livingston Keil

> Paul Livingston Keil was an amateur journalist in the New York area. In 1922, he took a celebrated photograph of HPL, James F. Morton, and Frank Belknap Long in front of the Poe Cottage in the Fordham region of the Bronx, as he describes in the following memoir, published in the *Phoenix* 4, No. 6 (July 1946): 149. HPL would later have a brief dispute with Keil regarding aesthetics: in his article "The Omnipresent Philistine" (*Oracle*, May 1924), HPL strongly disagreed with Keil's remarks about censorship as expressed in his amateur journal, *Pauke's Quill*.

One of my most vivid recollections of days gone by in Amateur Journalism, is the first time I met Howard Lovecraft. From the first exchange of correspondence I could tell, that here was a man unique, bright and scholarly. The fact that my home was just a nice jaunt away from Poe's Cottage in the Bronx, New York City, enticed Howard to an afternoon's prearranged visit to wander up to Fordham. He appeared with no less a distinguished companion than James F. Morton, Jr., and another journalist named Long. It was indeed a privilege to become acquainted with Howard, truly a genius; this was in the early '20s.

It is difficult for words to describe Howard as I remember him. I recall that he was "different" in mannerism and ways. He was tall and conservative in appearance—shy and quiet, yet when he spoke, he really said something; each word exact to produce the thought. Being serious, profound and erudite, that one could not help but admire him.

The three stayed at our home for awhile, my mother as hostess fitting in with the gathering, for she was familiar with Poe, his "Raven" and "Bells." Then we visited the Cottage equipped with a camera. I still cherish the pictures taken that day. We browsed in and around the Cottage, with its mementos and historic interest, and the informative comments of Lovecraft and Morton. It is assumed the reader is familiar that Morton, a former head of his class man at Harvard College, was one of the most brilliant men, ever to be active in Amateur Journalism. A true "kindred soul" to Lovecraft in his appreciation of real literature, philosophy and the more cultural things of life.

I remember the many letters, postmarked "Providence, R. I.," from Lovecraft, each a masterpiece. Knowing my interest for the Red Men, his letters were couched and full of Indian lore, every one a literary gem. We met again in Brooklyn; but never since then a man of his profound knowledge. He was a great asset to our movement whose influence can never be erased. To have known him, was of lasting impression and deep respect.

The Man Who Came at Midnight

Ruth M. Eddy

> Ruth M. Eddy was one of the two daughters of C. M. and Muriel E. Eddy. The following memoir appeared in *Fantasy Commentator* 3, No. 3 (Summer–Fall 1949): 71.

Gaslight flickered eerily through the crack in my bedroom door. It was Hallowe'en, night of the supernatural, and long past midnight. I had drifted off to sleep with visions of hobgoblins and Jack-o'-lanterns drifting through my childish mind. Suddenly, as in a dream, I heard a sepulchral voice saying, "Slithering . . . sliding . . . squealing . . . the rats in the walls!"

Half-asleep, half-awake, I lay in the darkness for a moment, and then shouted for my mother as loudly as I could. She came into my room and spoke softly, "Everything's all right, dear. It's just Mr. Lovecraft telling us about the new story he's writing. Don't be afraid. Go back to sleep." Her warm tones were reassuring, and I was comforted as she leaned down to kiss me.

But sleep was impossible, for little as I was then, I lay listening to the strange-sounding story our nocturnal visitor was reading. As I was to find out years later, not only was Howard Phillips Lovecraft an expert writer of weird, spooky and uncanny tales, but he was also something of an actor. He made his fictional characters come truly alive through reciting his manuscripts aloud. And this he did in the wee sma' hours of the morning as my parents listened attentively.

Lovecraft did not like daylight. He preferred darkness, always. Even when doing creative writing at home, if it was daytime he would draw the heavy curtains and write by artificial light. He did not like to leave his house during the day, but he and my father would often explore dark, unlighted alleys after midnight, walking along wharves and dimly-silhouetted bridges on the edge of the swamplands. It is not hard to imagine H.P.L. postulating unknown entities in these dark places, and from such nocturnal jaunts would often come ideas for his future stories.

In case I could stay awake long enough, I would sometimes listen to these tales, drifting off to sleep however before the story had ended. I grew accustomed to his voice, though I never quite got up enough courage to peek past the bedroom door at the reader himself. Yet in later years, as my father and mother discussed this friend of theirs, I could not help feeling that I had really known him, too.

How Lovecraft loved coal-black cats! He always had one near him. Cats sat in his lap while he wrote and they followed him out on his lone midnight explorings, His beloved black cat played a prominent part in "The Rats in the Walls," and when one day this cat disappeared he became heartsick.

I feel H.P.L. would have been astounded, indeed, had he heard his "Dunwich Horror" broadcast two years ago on Hallowe'en.[20] Never a lover of modern days and ways, using even such a common device as a telephone annoyed this gentleman and scholar of a different world! He preferred writing by hand to typing, and my parents often typed his manuscripts to relieve him of a hated task.

The shy and reticent Howard Lovecraft gained encouragement from my father and mother because of their interest and enthusiasm in his work, and soon after that Hallowe'en night he sold his macabre "Rats in the Walls" to a well-known magazine. Not a Hallowe'en has passed since Lovecraft's death in 1937 without my family gathering for the reading aloud of a weird story by our favorite author—now internationally famous as a writer in the genre—although our eloquence cannot compare with his masterful interpretations.

And even though I never saw Howard Phillips Lovecraft, I shall always remember him as the man who came at midnight!

II. Criticism in Lovecraft's Lifetime

A Note on Howard P. Lovecraft's Verse

Rheinhart Kleiner

> Rheinhart Kleiner (1892–1949) was one of HPL's earliest colleagues in the amateur journalism movement; they became acquainted when HPL sent Kleiner the first issue of the *Conservative* (April 1915). Kleiner visited HPL several times in Providence in the late 1910s and saw HPL extensively during the latter's stay in New York (1924–26). After dropping out of sight for about a decade, he came back in touch with HPL in 1936. After HPL's death he wrote numerous memoirs about him. The following article, published in the *United Amateur* 18, No. 4 (March 1919): 76, constitutes the first critical article on any aspect of HPL's work.

Comment occasioned by the verse of Mr. Howard P. Lovecraft, who is a more or less frequent contributor to the amateur press, has not consisted of unmixed praise.

Certain critics have regarded his efforts as too obviously imitative of a style that has long been discredited. Others have accepted his work with admiration and have even gone so far as to imitate the couplets which he produces with such apparent ease.

Between these two opinions there is a critical neutral ground, the holders of which realize how large an element of conscious parody enters into many of Mr. Lovecraft's longer and more serious productions, and who are capable of appreciating the cleverness and literary charm of these pastoral echoes without being dominated by them to the extent of indiscriminate praise and second-hand imitation.

Those who would beguile Mr. Lovecraft from his chosen path are probably unaware of the attitude which he consistently maintains toward hostile criticism. Mr. Lovecraft contends that it gives him pleasure to write as the Augustans did, and that those who do not relish his excursions into classic fields need not follow him. He tries to conciliate no one, and is content to be his sole reader! What critic, with these facts before him, will think it worthwhile to break a lance with the poet?

But even Mr. Lovecraft is willing to be original at times. He has written verse of a distinctly modern atmosphere, and where his imagery is not too obtrusively artificial—according to the modern idea—many of his quatrains possess genuine poetic value.

Many who cannot read his longer and more ambitious productions find Mr. Lovecraft's light or humorous verse decidedly refreshing. As a satirist along familiar lines, particularly those laid down by Butler, Swift and Pope, he is most himself—paradoxical though it seems. In reading his satires one cannot help but feel the zest with which the author has composed them. They are admirable for the way in which they reveal the depth and intensity of Mr. Lovecraft's convictions, while the wit, irony, sarcasm and humour to be found in them serve as an indication of his powers as a controversialist. The almost relentless ferocity of his satires is constantly relieved by an attendant broad humour which has the merit of causing the readers to chuckle more than once in the perusal of some attack leveled against the particular person or policy which may have incurred Mr. Lovecraft's displeasure.

Howard P. Lovecraft's Fiction

W. Paul Cook

W. Paul Cook (1881–1948) was a leading figure in amateur journalism for much of his life. He came in touch with HPL in 1917 and, as HPL frequently acknowledged, was instrumental in HPL's resumption of fiction writing in that year. The following essay—the first critical article on HPL's fiction—appeared in the *Vagrant* No. 11 (November 1919): 38–39, accompanying the publication of "Dagon" in the same issue.

Howard P. Lovecraft is widely and favorably known throughout the amateur journalistic world as a poet, and in a lesser degree as an editorial and essay writer. As a story-writer he is practically unknown, partly because of the scarcity of publications large enough to accommodate much prose, and partly because he does not consider himself a competent story-teller. His first story to appear in the amateur press was "The Alchemist," published in the *United Amateur*.[1] This story was enough to stamp him as a pupil of Poe in its unnatural, mystical and actually morbid outlook, without a hint of the bright outdoors or of real life. His second story, "The Beast in the Cave," published in the VAGRANT,[2] was far inferior in every respect, even in being given a modern setting, which may be counted as against it in Mr. Lovecraft's case. The outstanding feature of this really slight effort was the skill with which an atmosphere was created.

In "Dagon," in this issue of the VAGRANT, Mr. Lovecraft steps into his own as a writer of fiction. In reading this story, two or three names of short-story writers are immediately called to mind. First of all, of course, Poe; and Mr. Lovecraft, I believe, would be the first to acknowledge his allegiance to our American master. Second, Maupassant; and I am quite sure that Mr. Lovecraft would deny any kinship with the great Frenchman.[3]

Mr. Lovecraft with "Dagon" is not through as a contributor of fiction to the amateur press. He will never be as voluminous a fiction writer as a poet, but we may confidently expect to see him advance even beyond the high mark he has set in "Dagon."

I cannot fully appreciate Mr. Lovecraft as a poet—which is saying nothing against him as a poet! In fact, he should perhaps feel flattered! To me, most of his verse is too formal, too artificial, too stilted in phraseology and form. But I can and do appreciate him as a story-writer. He is at this day the only amateur story-writer worthy of more than a polite passing notice.

The Vivisector

Zoilus [Alfred Galpin]

Alfred Galpin (1901–1983) came into contact with HPL in 1918 and worked closely with HPL in the amateur journalism movement. HPL visited Galpin in Cleveland in 1922. In 1921–23 HPL was the informal editor of a series of six columns entitled "The Vivisector," published in Horace L. Lawson's amateur journal, the *Wolverine*. Letters by HPL and Lawson establish that HPL wrote five of the columns and that Galpin wrote the sixth. The following is an extract from Galpin's column, published in the *Wolverine* No. 11 (November 1921): 16–18. The pseudonym is taken from the name of a Greek critic of the 4th century B.C.E. who severely criticised the Homeric poems.

An invitation to criticise the last two issues of *The Wolverine* gives one an excellent opportunity for evil-doing. One might in some cases take advantage of such openness, but this time one can't, because *The Wolverine* isn't that kind of magazine.

It is easily the best contemporary publication of the new typewritten sort, and is likely to remain so unless *Corona* or *Pine Cones* be resurrected. Indeed, if the last two numbers are an indication of those to follow, even these excellent veterans might have to yield first place. So much for praise, now for a little criticism.

"Facts Concerning the Late Arthur Jermyn and His Family," by Mr. Lovecraft, shows another phase of that writer's gloomy but powerful genius.[4] It is perfect in execution, restrained in manner, complete, and marked by Mr. Lovecraft's uniquely effective handling of introductory and concluding portions. The legend is not so powerful as many of Mr. Lovecraft's dreamings have been, but it is unquestionably original and does not derive from Poe, Dunsany, or any other of Mr. Lovecraft's favorites and predecessors. Its affiliations are rather closer with Ambrose Bierce, and I personally should place it beside much of Bierce's best work without fearing for the fame of the United's representative. Mr. Lovecraft is unquestionably a man of distinguished genius in the short story, but he is unfortunate in coming rather late in the line of macabre writers, and in lacking many of those elements of sophistication which are so imperative in our times. For example, his critical faculty is poor and his stories are almost entirely at the mercy of his mood. Moreover, he is singularly lacking in psychological perception, a thing which is essential to immortalize any tale except that of the sheerest and most Shelleyan fiber. As a consequence of this latter lack the plot of the Jermyn tale is a trifle obvious, and its principal character is wooden. But with all these drawbacks Mr. Lovecraft is deserving of a fame much broader than he chooses to seek. For the power and persuasion of his style, and for the gripping, unearthly cast of his imagination, he is as great as any living author in his field and in the range of my acquaintance. He certainly excels Lord Dunsany in directness of narration and the whole realm of the horrible in imagination. If the reader be astonished at this praise, let him read "Polaris" and "The White Ship" for beauty of style, "The Doom that Came to Sarnath" or any of his temple or city fables for luxurious detail, or "Dagon," "The Statement of Randolph Carter," and "Nyarlathotep" for sheer wonder of imaginative power, and then he will merely have scratched the man's personality.

Preface to *The Shunned House*

Frank Belknap Long, Jr.

Frank Belknap Long, Jr. (1901–1994) was one of HPL's closest friends. They had come in touch in 1920 and worked closely in the amateur journalism movement and as professional writers for the pulps. Long and HPL met frequently during the latter's New York stay (1924–26). In 1928 W. Paul Cook wished to publish HPL's "The Shunned House" as a booklet. He asked Long to write a preface; it appeared on pp. [5–6] of the booklet. But *The Shunned House* was never bound or distributed by Cook and did not achieve full distribution until Arkham House sold copies in 1959–61.

The Shunned House is a wonderful story. It is so far removed in theme from our familiar world of radios and politicians and adding machines that it does not touch, at any point, the ancillary stream of modern writing. I can discern in it, here and there, faint analogies to contemporary "terror tales," to the work of Lord Dunsany and Arthur Machen and Algernon Blackwood, but in the main Mr. Lovecraft begins where other writers leave off. *The Shunned House* suggests, somehow, the startling and disturbing excursions of S. H. Hinton into the fourth dimension.[5] Only a mathematician, an inspired mathematician, could write a story like this without an intimate realistic perception of the spheres that lie outside the field of ordinary experience. And Lovecraft is not a mathematician. Has he transcended the critical idealism of Kant by training his imagination to become independent of the space-limitations imposed by our normal forms of perception? I can only propound the question; I cannot answer it. Ben De Casseres[6] says somewhere that there is a profound courage in certain forms of credulity, and I shall continue to believe that Lovecraft is occultly endowed until he convinces me that he isn't by writing a story that doesn't suggest new dimensions of space and time.

The Shunned House would probably be rejected by every editor in America.[7] I question the advisability of commending it further! The fact that Mr. O'Brien has included one of Lovecraft's tales in his 1928 Roll of Honor[8] may afford critical support to those who are wary of acclaiming work that is bizarre and vivid and new, but the discriminating reader will appraise the book for himself with a dash of Emersonian self-reliance, and faring valiantly through its pages of mystery and terror, will rejoice exceedingly.

A Weird Writer Is in Our Midst

Vrest Orton

Vrest Orton (1897–1986) was a resident of Vermont and became acquainted with HPL in late 1925. He hosted HPL at his home in Brattleboro, Vermont, from June 10 to 24, 1928. It was during this time that an unsigned article appeared in the *Brattleboro Daily Reformer* ("Literary Persons Meet in Guilford," June 18) about a gathering of HPL and his colleagues at the home of the poet Arthur Goodenough. Two days earlier, the above article appeared in the same newspaper (p. 2). HPL referred to it as a "puff" (*SL* 2.245). It appeared in the column, "The Pendrifter," operated by Charles Crane.

Dear Pendrifter:

I note with more than common interest your suggestion for the inauguration of a Society for the Detection of Literary People Settling in our Midst. You were especially generous to me in your column and I am very grateful for the kind welcome you extended. I think you have done nobly (with the paucity of data) on the first detection for the Society. Perhaps it may interest you and your readers to know that another subject exists about which research ought to be begun. I refer to Howard Phillips Lovecraft, at present stopping with us in Guilford. There is so much that one can say about Lovecraft that one hardly knows where to begin. First of all he is a writer and an extraordinarily good one and the subject on which he writes is uncommonly interesting, because so few people know much about it. Lovecraft is an investigator, a scholar, an antiquarian and a writer chiefly concerned with the Weird. He has been writing for a good many years but it was only a few years ago that a magazine was started which gave him a chance to publish much of his material. This periodical was *Weird Tales*, and while for many years stories from Lovecraft's pen went without achieving the dignity of print,[9] all because the regular magazines would have nothing to do with the weird, *Weird Tales* has printed a story of his in about every issue and would like to print more. But Lovecraft sees to that by not writing any more often than he feels like writing. The readers of this magazine, who number into many thousands, are kept in a state of unsatisfied hunger for his stuff. Hundreds of them have written letters, and published opinions stating that, in their estimation, H. P. Lovecraft is a writer of weird tales as great if not greater than Edgar Allen [sic] Poe.

And I think they are more than half right. Lovecraft is a very great writer . . . perhaps so great that he will never be appreciated. If he would only turn his pen to tales of romance and profane love, or to fictionalized biography and psychology in the guise of detective-story thrillers (of which there is such a flood) he would become famous over night. But he won't do this. Though writing is his chief source of income, he won't write unless he feels like it and he doesn't give a damn for money. In many ways he is an alien soul and as strange as the grotesque tales which come from his pen.

Lovecraft was born in Providence, in 1892, I believe, though to hear him speak of himself as "the old gentleman" one would fancy he saw light at least as far back as 1850. His favorite complex is one of assuming an advanced age and if any man in these modern times lives and continues, by choice, to live in the 18th century, it is he. There is little in modern life that holds him, while on the other hand, he believes that existence during the 18th century was the most perfect form of civilization ever devised by man. This notion accounts for his antiquarian enthusiasm. If there is a man in this century who knows more about the customs and habits of the Americans of the period from 1700 to 1800, I haven't heard of him. Lovecraft's chief interest is architecture of that time and he is especially interested in the early American buildings of New England. In Guilford and vicinity he has been having the time of his life and has really been in ecstasy over the most delightful examples of early houses he has discovered there.

He is madly in love . . . with New England and won't live anywhere else. Life outside of its borders is misery for him. Two years ago he tried to exist in New York for the sake of his literary labors, but gave it up as a bad job after a few months, though his many friends and acquaintances there exerted the heaviest pressure to make him stop longer. Many of his short stories and poems deal with the sacred soil of New England and he derives ever increasing inspiration from this part of the world.

I confess that I don't understand the depths to which Lovecraft probes into the weird, uncanny phases of the unknown. I have never been a reader of weird tales myself . . . and probably never shall be. But I have read several of his in manuscript, and was struck with such unmitigated horror that I shall undoubtedly never read any more. He is concerned not with the ordinary weird tale which treats of ghosts and "spirits" in lonely graveyards, or the one which has to do with social effects, having the horror explained away by natural means.[10] The weird tale to him must be motivated and shot full of cosmic fear and it must produce in the reader a profound sense of dread and of contact with unknown powers, never to be explained away or understood. The oldest and strongest of all emotions is fear, but by fear Lovecraft means a cosmic fear, not the simple physical kind. His stories have more in them than the mere mundanely gruesome, secret murders, the bloody bones and the clanking of chains in the dark. These are the obvious paraphernalia of lesser writers with other ideas. Lovecraft investigates more deeply. What interests him, so he states, is the terrible conception of the human brain which can amount to a malign and particular suspension or defeat of those fixed laws of nature which laws are the only safeguard against the assaults of chaos and the demons of unplumbed space. With this almost inconceivable and unthinkable philosophy, he probes into things far beyond the ken of the average writer. And from these eerie journeyings come stories that are at once so charged with pure horror and so productive of that tragic cosmic fear itself, that a person with anything less than a strong determined mind had better not read . . . them especially at night.

Like Poe, Lovecraft's fame was first acclaimed abroad rather than in his own country and there publishers are getting out books of his stories where the demand for tales of this kind is keener and wider.[11] And like Poe, he will, I haven't the slightest doubt, set a mark for writers to shoot at for a long time. Some say he is greater than Poe as a writer of the weird . . . I don't know, but I do know that his stories strike me as having been written by a man far more profoundly interested in the subject of the weird than was Poe. Poe's output was not wholly in that field . . . indeed many of his tales were tales of ratiocination, a phase that Lovecraft leaves to the writers of the prosaic mystery story. If the devilish fear of the cosmic unknown affected Poe, it is not as apparent as it is in the stories that Lovecraft writes. I do not say he is a greater writer than Poe, for in some departments he is not. But I do say that as a scholar and research worker in the one subject of the weird from his point of view, and a writer on that subject exclusively, H. P. Lovecraft is the greatest this century has ever seen or maybe will ever see.

The Sideshow

B. K. Hart

> Bertrand Kelton Hart (1892–1941) was the literary editor of the *Providence Journal* during the 1920s. In his column, "The Sideshow," in November 1929, he printed a list of what he considered the best horror stories ever written. HPL found this list so tame that he submitted his own list, as well as those by August Derleth and Frank Belknap Long. Hart published these lists in his column of November 23 and 25. The following extract appeared in his column of November 30 (p. 10), when he stumbled upon a copy of T. Everett Harré's *Beware After Dark!* (1929) containing HPL's "The Call of Cthulhu."

We have been talking a good deal lately about ghosts, and revenants, and the weird things which do or do not happen over the borderline of fact, and consequently I have been paying more than usual attention to books that touch on the theme. And when I stumbled on a new one called "Beware After Dark" (which is a collection of strange tales selected by Mr. T. Everett Harré) I was greatly pleased. It is a good book in its kind. The Arthur Machen story of the white powder is here, and Benson's "Negotium Perambulans," and Andreyev's "Lazarus," and many more lately recommended in this column. But what startled me wide awake and brought back the two-headed dog and the white morning rain over the broken back of Waterman Street Hill, was a passage that leaped to my eye the moment I opened the book.

> "The manuscript was divided into two sections, the first of which was headed: 1925—Dream and Dream Work of H. A. Wilcox, 7 Thomas Street, Providence, R. I."

We always tend to shy a little at a familiar label, caught in the bat-wing flight of print, but this was so precisely the house in which I had lived, and so much the place for a ghost to happen in a book called "Beware After Dark!" that I fancy I gasped. We do not look for our everyday neighbors in works of fiction, in any case, and least of all do we expect to find them haunted.

Now, mark how well the author achieved verisimilitude in this tale. Henry Arthur Wilcox[12] is a name with an accurate Providence timbre to it. He had been (and what more plausible) a student at the Rhode Island School of Design, and lived alone at 7 Thomas street, rather a dark and puzzling fellow, who was looked upon as eccentric. "Even the Providence Art Club, anxious to preserve its conservatism, had found him quite hopeless." Presently we see him conferring with "George Gammell Angell, professor emeritus of Semitic languages at Brown University:" and before long Professor Angell is (as the tabloids might phrase it) strangely dead to city street. Skillful that! And disconcerting. I do not mind discovering my mystery-story victims strewn ten thick upon the London Embankment or down the mean streets of Liverpool; and you have only to murmur Hammersmith to adduce for me the linked vision of a corpse and a Scotland Yard inspector. But when you drop your snarled skein of horror and death into my own dooryard I begin to grow a little nervous about the business. ... The tale (as strange a thing as ever I set eyes upon!) is entitled "The Call of Cthulhu" and it implies, entirely without my consent, that the whilom tenant of my old chambers used to toss in his dreams and hear vast abysmal voices summoning him from a terrific void in the world's heart.

Linked to those once-pleasant rooms, where birch-wood generally flamed on a cheerful hearth, I must now believe there stretches a ghastly, eldritch chain sending in a voodoo-like pool of carking horror far down in the antipodes. . . . I won't have it. My own little ghost shadows, slinking home to the sun in the healthy dawn, are quite enough for Thomas street, and I reject these sinister brutes from the other side of the beyond, cluttering up the traffic with their gargantuan bulk.

Yet they have a power over me, as the old people used to say, because there is something more than a chance connection between the Thomas street devils and The Sideshow. I had only to turn to the title-line to find it out. And there, to be sure, sailed the name of one of our most engaging contributors—indeed the one who set us all off on this ghost hunt—Mr. H. P. Lovecraft. . . . He is, by the by, widely recognized as a skillful writer of weird tales. Mr. E. J. O'Brien, in "The Best Short Stories of 1929" gives the laudatory three-star rank to his yarn, "The Dunwich Horror," and other large distinctions have befallen him. . . . Personally I congratulate him upon the dark spirits he has evoked in Thomas street, but I shall not be happy until, joining league with wraiths and ghouls, I have plumped down at least one large and abiding ghost by way of reprisal upon his own doorstep in Barnes street. . . . I think I shall teach it to moan in a minor dissonance every morning at 3 o'clock sharp, with a clinking of chains.[13]

Or would it be better to have it prowl through the cellar, murmuring "Hushhushshsh" the livelong night?

What Makes a Story Click?

J. Randle Luten

> Little is known of J. Randle Luten, author of the following article, published in the *American Author* 4, No. 4 (July 1932): 11–13. HPL saw the article and was pleased with its references to himself and to Clark Ashton Smith, but was dismayed that he was linked with the pulp hack Otis Adelbert Kline.

> I have no reason to expect that any one will believe my story. If it were another's tale, probably I should not feel inclined to give it credence myself. I tell it herewith, hoping that the mere act of narration, the mere shaping of this macabre day-mare adventure into words will in some slight measure serve to relieve my mind of its execrable burden. There have been times when only a hair's breadth has intervened betwixt myself and the seething, devil-ridden world of madness; for the hideous knowledge, the horror-blackened memories

which I have carried so long were never meant to be borne by the human intellect.

Now that is what is meant by a good beginning. Start something. In a horror tale like "The Gorgan [sic]," written by Clark Ashton Smith, it is necessary to give the readers some hint of the horror to come. In my humble opinion this is a splendid opening paragraph. It was taken from the story mentioned above and by the author also mentioned above, and found in *Weird Tales*, April issue this year.[14]

In writing a story, bear in mind that the first few paragraphs—in fact the first paragraph—has a great deal to do with selling your story. If your opening is not right, make it so; because no matter how well written your story is, it has an awful handicap to overcome if that first paragraph isn't up to snuff. You may have a wonderful plot, you may have emotion, you may have appeal in your story—but it has to have a catchy opening to sell to the "pulps."

In writing, "What Makes a Story Click," naturally the first thing to consider, is the beginning of a story. Here is another opening paragraph taken also from *Weird Tales*, same issue, written by H. P. Lovecraft, titled, "In the Vault."

> There is nothing more absurd, as I view it, than that conventional association of the homely and the wholesome which seems to pervade the psychology of the multitude. Mention a bucolic Yankee setting, a bungling and thick-fibered village undertaker, and a careless mishap in a tomb, and no average reader can be brought to expect more than a hearty albeit grotesque phase of comedy. God knows, though, that the prosy tale which George Birch's death permits me to tell has in it aspects beside which some of our darkest tragedies are light.

There you are, isn't that a good opening? Mr. Lovecraft gives his readers a nice morsel to chew on, and prepares you for a nice horror tale.

And a third, taken from "The Earth Brain," by Edmond Hamilton in *Weird Tales*, April issue:

> Landon and I had not seen each other for two years before that day when New York knew fear. That day is remembered yet, with its sudden and unexpected earth-tremor that shook the island shortly after noon, swaying proud towers and shaking windows to fragments and loosing a storm of panic-stricken cries that could not drown the long, grinding roll of shifting earth beneath.

Consider yourself. You are an average reader; you pick up a magazine and begin a story. If the first paragraph starts slow or begins with some lengthy description of a house or room, or describes some uninteresting scene; you nine times out of ten will turn to another story, or might throw the magazine down in disgust. *Publishers and editors know this.* Therefore, we must create interest in the first paragraph in order to sell our stories.

Here is one of my own, patterned a bit after Edgar Allen [sic] Poe:

> They say I am insane—that I am mad, but why do they say this? The malady has quickened my senses—not dulled them. It's true that the hideous macabre happenings of the past seven days have been a great strain on my mental powers; and it's true that my formerly dark hair has turned to silvery white in the space of an hour; but I contend that I am not mad. Harken! and see how healthy—how placidly I can narrate the entire story.[15]

Does that arouse your interest? It's not perfect, I know, but it contains the thing necessary to have a good opening.

Then, after you have started your story satisfactorily, you must continue to be interesting and hold your readers' interest. Sometimes it is best to write your story, then select your opening. When you do, remember this: try to have your opening as close to your climax as possible. Then you can have a "flash back," if you wish and describe your setting and your characters. Or, after you open your story and create interest, then you can use a few words describing setting, characters, etc. Ponder over these openings though, and be sure that your story opens well.

We now have our story opened, what next? Be interesting. How? By having suspense. Cumulate this very necessary suspense. Dangle the threat of disaster in the eyes of your readers. Increase suspense with no let-down until your climax is reached, unless you have a few words of explanation. And make them few, too.

How do we handle this thing called suspense? What is it? Suspense is the withholding of data—important data—from your readers. If it is a love story, do not let the reader know whether the heroine is going to love the hero or not, or vice versa. Let this knowledge be the climax. Or, if the story opens with a problem confronting the main characters and the problem isn't whether they love each other but how they (or possibly one) will secure their freedom, so they can be married, don't let the reader have any idea of how this problem will be solved until the climax, then surprise him with a novel twist.

Another method of creating suspense is action. Keep the reader in doubt as to the outcome of the hero, whether he will overcome odds and win out or not. Maybe the hero is driven by Fate, maybe he has a great problem to solve, and you have no love interest in your yarn; then you hold suspense by having the villain win for a time and by making it look as if the hero will never win. Then in the climax everything comes out all right.

There would be no suspense if you let your readers know ahead of time how it's going to turn out and that the hero is going to win.

In horror tales the suspense is created by piling horror upon horror. Make it appear that the hero hasn't a chance to come out on top. Sometimes make it appear that he will lose his life as well. Then you can be interesting—can create and hold suspense—by arousing the curiosity of your readers about your story and make them read to see how such a terrible, hideous situation can be overcome. In my opening previously described I have appealed to the readers' curiosity. They will want to see if the hero is mad, and also to see what made him have a reason to be in this condition, then what thing or creature caused his hair to turn white.

Here is suspense from one of my stories:

> The boney plate had indeed pressed against the dura mater. Quickly the surgeon's eyes diagnosed the entire condition present. He could, by removing part of this bone, and giving treatment to the rest, possibly restore this man his life. On the other hand he could apparently remove the pressure but still leave enough to kill.
>
> It was certainly a temptation to Dexter. Here, with one stroke he could remove the barrier to his and Irene's happiness. How easy it would be to bungle this operation. No one would blame him. What a wonderful chance. Then too, his scalpel could press, oh so easily, that soft tissue and—.
>
> The overhead lights flickered on his keen knife, the chromium steel instruments glistened on the circular glass table, the patient coughed, a deep lung cough, the anesthetist twisted a dial on his ethylene gas machine, and the brain surgeon began to operate.

How did you like that? Isn't that suspense? The reader doesn't know whether Dexter will kill this man or not. Of course, he does not, because the hero should be above reproach; but I like to show the gray side of a man's character as well as the white side. Haven't we all a gray side?

The suspense is held in some stories by increasing the complications, by making the main problem have some side angles that have to be solved. The way you work it or in the manner you use makes little difference just so you withhold the important knowledge from your readers until the climax. Then let them have it, and write "END."

II

Another important thing about a story is the manner in which the author describes scenes, describes characters, and describes his action. It is necessary to say more than "Marlee had eyes," or that the surgeon examined the patient. Put more feeling into it. Like this: Marlee had alluring eyes of blue, the blue of azure heavens or the blue found on the soft petals of a delphinium. And this: The surgeon ran his slender, tapering fingers along the thigh of the injured man, carefully he examined the bruised member for signs of a fracture.

This is known in writers' parlance as "glamor." You must have "glamor" words or your story will be flat, will have no kick. Glamor is the thing in the story that is remembered by the reader, even after the story is finished and the magazine laid aside. Make them remember your stories. Make them talk about your stories. Put glamor in it until they will be telling all their friends about such and such a story written by such and such an author. It's glamor that moves the reader, makes him grit his teeth in rage, makes her shed a tear and mumble a soft prayer for the hard-pressed hero or heroine. It's glamor, I repeat, that has the readers so intensely interested in the outcome of the story; has them so worked up that they can't stop to eat, can't stop to attend the baby, can't stop for anything until they have read the last line of that story.

The next time you read a story that you think is good, stop and analyze it and look for the "glamor" words. Also see just how many adjectives the author used. Read some of Edgar Allen Poe's works: he is a master of *glamor*.

In love stories "glamor" words are used describe the sweetness of the heroine, the manliness of the hero, and the terrible situations they may be thrown into. In a horror story it is simply the judicious use of adjectives. However, all "glamor" words are not adjectives; some may be nouns or adverbs, or the glamor may consume an entire sentence or paragraph as this:

> I have investigated many clues of the spectral, the ghastly, the bizarre, and many mazes of terror from which others would have recoiled with caution or trepidation. . . . But now I could wish that there were one lure which I had not followed, one labyrinth which my curiosity had not explored.

In the quotation above, taken from "The Gorgan" by Mr. Smith, we find almost an entire paragraph devoted to glamor. Let me define this word "glamor" for you as I see it. "Glamor" words are those words, sentences, or phrases that give the reader the actual feeling of the story, imparts to the reader the author's feelings as he felt them—*in short, "glamor" words are words of emotion.*

Here is a paragraph from H. P. Lovecraft's story, showing glamor and how it creates emotion:

> As he remounted the splitting coffins he felt his weight very poignantly; especially when, upon reaching the topmost one, he heard that aggravated crackle which bespeaks the wholesale rending of wood. He had, it seems,

planned in vain when choosing the stoutest coffin for the platform; for no sooner was his full bulk again upon it than the rotting lid gave way, jouncing him two feet down on a surface which even he did not care to imagine. Maddened by the sound, or by the stench which billowed forth even to the open air, the waiting horse gave a scream that was too frantic for a neigh, and plunged madly off through the night, the wagon rattling crazily behind it.

That is the stuff that contains *glamor*, and it is the function of glamor to give emotion. They work hand in hand. "Glamor" words produce emotion; emotion creates suspense; suspense grips the reader and makes your story salable.

Below is a paragraph from "The Earth Brain" by E. Hamilton. Notice the "glamor" words and the emotion they produce, and then observe the suspense reached:

> The Earth-Brain flamed pure crimson instantly, the crimson of leaping hell-fires and raging holocausts, the red of a superhuman, stupendous wrath. Colossal anger emanated from it at the same moment like a wave of destroying force, and as that cosmic wrath swept through me I knew that I had committed blackest sin against the universe in daring to attack the brain of the living earth-body upon which dwelt I and all my tiny race!

In writing a story, after you have visioned your scenes, after you have used your quota of "glamor" words and produced the necessary emotion, after your suspense is created, glance back over your work and see if you have dangled the threat of disaster sufficiently before the eyes of your readers. For this is important. You must insert a few words here and there that will let your readers know that all is not well with the hero; and though it appears that he has won, still as Al Jolson expresses it: "You ain't seen nothing yet."

When you introduce your characters in your story, give them characterization, so that the reader will have no difficulty in recognizing them again, if he should run across any of them later. Let your reader see your actors plainly—make them live before his eyes. Take this character of an old man from "The Gorgan":

> Nor were his garments uncommon, aside from the fact that they too were excessively old, and seemed to exhale an air of greater antiquity than was warranted even by their cut and fabric. It was not these, but the man's visage which electrified all my drowsy faculties into a fascinated and awestruck attention. With the mortal pallor of his deeply wrinkled features, like graven ivory, with his long, curling hair and beard that were white as moon-touched vapor, with his eyes that glowed in their hollow sockets like the coals of demon fires in underworld caverns, he would have made a living model for Charon, the boatman who ferries the dead of Hades across the ebon silence of the Styx.

Can't you just see that old man? Certainly you can. Mr. Smith arranges his words so that readers will have no trouble recognizing this character when he appears later.

Last but not least, get your setting right. Don't ramble around, touching gently here and there. Bear down and make a few words do the work of a hundred. The average reader isn't the least bit interested in long-drawn-out settings.

Read some of Dickens' works, if you're different. He has nice description, if you like that type. In novels, you may use more description of places or things; but in short stories it's fatal. Usually a paragraph or two should suffice. Here is an example taken from Poe's "The Fall of the House of Usher."

> ... and at length found myself, as the shades of the evening drew on, within view of the Melancholy House of Usher. I knew not how it was; but, with the first glimpse of the building, a sense of insufferable gloom prevailed my spirit. I say insufferable, for the feeling was unrelieved by any of that half-pleasurable, because poetic, sentiment, with which the mind usually receives even the sternest natural images of the desolate or terrible. I looked upon the scene before me—upon the mere house, and the simple landscape features of the domain—upon the bleak walls—upon the vacant, eye-like windows—upon a few rank sedges—and upon a few white trunks of decayed trees—with an utter depression of soul which I can compare to no earthly sensation more properly than to the after-dream of the reveller upon opium.

You won't soon forget that house, after reading that! Of course, we can't all be a Poe, but we can try to pattern some after the master.

Edgar Allen Poe is one of my favorites. I read and reread his works continually. He could handle glamor, emotion, suspense, and climax like no other writer. That is possibly the reason the French immortalized him—he was the originator of the modern short horror stories. So far, no one has equalled him. There is a place for someone at the top of the ladder, someone with a vivid imagination, a ready flow of words, and a fine sense of balance; when this writer arrives, Poe will have an equal. Who will it be?

III. Comments from Readers

A. *Weird Tales*

H. Warner Munn,[1] of Athol, Massachusetts, writes: "I am indeed delighted that Lovecraft is to be a steady contributor. *Weird Tales* discovered him, I believe; and if it had never done anything else, that would be sufficient reason for its continued existence. You are doing a great work in publishing stories that the great ultraconservative magazines might refuse."

[5, No. 3 (March 1925): 164.]

... H. P. Tead, of Decatur, Illinois, writes: "In the February issue 'The Statement of Randolph Carter', by H. P. Lovecraft, so far outshines all the other stories that there is simply no comparison whatever. The author may well be proud of this. It is worthy of Poe, the master, and if it had been printed as one of his hitherto unpublished tales, I doubt if anyone could have told the difference."

Howard Anderson (we have mislaid the envelope telling what city he is from) votes for Mr. Lovecraft's story, but adds: "He should go further into the story and explain the mystery." The very thing that Mr. Anderson thinks is a defect is praised by another reader, Ward Motz, who writes: "The best of this was that Mr. Lovecraft left something to the imagination. I believe that is one failing in most stories: they go too far. Personally I would rather have a little left for my imagination."

[5, No. 4 (April 1925): 165.]

"Having read your July number," writes H. S. Farnese,[2] of Los Angeles, "I vote for 'The Stranger from Kurdistan'. Stories with a personal devil are always interesting; hence the popularity of Goethe's *Faust*. And Lovecraft, who wrote 'The Unnamable', scores a hit, as usual.[3] In telling a weird story the style of Mr. Lovecraft can hardly be beaten. Keep him busy."

[6, No. 3 (September 1925): 417.]

Writes August Derleth, Jr.,[4] of Sauk City, Wisconsin: "As to the January issue, my first vote goes unreservedly to 'The Tomb', by H. P. Lovecraft. The sheer beauty of words, without considering the excellent theme, is enough to merit the tale first place. Mr. Lovecraft, in my estimation, is a second Poe. . . ."

[7, No. 3 (March 1926): 421.]

E. Hoffmann Price,[5] in a letter to the editor, thus sums up the genius of Lovecraft: "To paraphrase the Moslem: *There is but one Lovecraft, and the unnamable is his God.* In his utter unreality and impossibility, he is like a non-Euclidean geometer who, though working on physically impossible axioms, reasons truly from them and produces theorems, and subsequent Q.E.D.'s, which are as true as if they actually were true; or as one who reasons of the inconceivable fourth dimension and by self-consistent hypotheses and logic deals logically with impossibility. It is this self-consistency, lacked by many horror-mongers, that makes Lovecraft more unusual than Poe; for Poe kept one foot on earth, whereas Lovecraft swings boldly into the unreal, pinions fully spread. We listen to the music of Erich Zann, we follow Randolph Carter to his sepulchral doom, we live in tombs, we attend strange festivals where the waiting guests read *The Necronomicon* . . . unreality made real."

[7, No. 4 (April 1926): 556-57.]

Ray Cummings,[6] himself an author of prominence, writes in a letter to the editor: "Who in blazes is H. P. Lovecraft? I never heard the name before. If he is a present-day writer—which I can not imagine he is—he deserves to be world-famous. I read 'The Outsider' and 'The Tomb'.[7] No need of telling you they are masterful stories. Quite beside their atmosphere—all those fictional elements which go to make up a real story—I felt, and still feel, looking backward upon my reading of them—somehow *ennobled*, as though my mind had profited (which indeed it had) by the reading. Never have I encountered any purer, more beautiful diction. They sing; the true poetry of prose."

Yes, H. P. Lovecraft is a living writer, and he resides in Brooklyn.[8]

August Derleth, Jr., of Sauk City, Wisconsin, writes: "If Lovecraft's 'The Outsider' does not get first place I shall be disappointed in the readers of *Weird Tales*. That story is worthy of Poe, and, if I may say so, I believe it to be better than any work of Poe, and I have read every bit of Poe except his letters. I can not find words to express my enjoyment of that superb tale. As I was engrossed, my sister at the piano played Rachmaninoff's *Prelude in C Sharp Minor*, and its majesty was an excellent parallel to the story.[9] Give us more, many more, by Lovecraft, please!"

[7, No. 6 (June 1926): 858.]

Writes J. Vernon Shea, Jr.,[10] of Pittsburgh: "It might be interesting to you to know that you have young readers as well as old. I am just a boy of thirteen, but I am in the opinion that *Weird Tales* is the best magazine ever published. Such writers as Eli Colter, Seabury Quinn, H. P. Lovecraft, Robert S. Carr and Edmond Hamilton deserve special mention for their excellent work. I can never forget 'The Outsider', by Lovecraft. It was the weirdest, most thrilling and most eery tale I have ever had the good fortune to read."

[8, No. 4 (October 1926): 573.]

The Rev. Henry S. Whitehead,[11] himself an author of note, writes: "Congratulations on the March issue. I think Lovecraft has struck twelve with 'The White Ship'. It is one of the finest things of its sort I have ever seen. It is literature."

[9, No. 5 (May 1927): 711.]

"Lovecraft's story in the October issue, 'Pickman's Model', breathes the eeriest, most paralyzing and yet most realistic atmosphere of horror I have ever encountered anywhere, fiction or fact," writes Jack Snow,[12] of Dayton, Ohio. "Most weird tales are fantasies pure and simple, told in a manner that is momentarily convincing. But Lovecraft's tales make you halt in the middle of a downtown business street and remark uneasily to yourself: 'Why, that might happen!' Lovecraft is the realist of weird fiction."

Max F. Myers, of Lewistown, Pennsylvania, writes to The Eyrie: "Mr. Lovecraft deserves paeans of praise for his latest, 'Pickman's Model'. It is my estimation of a weird tale in every sense of the word. I believe that his technique is unparalleled by any of the authors who contribute to your magazine (my apologies to Mr. Quinn). 'Absence makes the heart grow fonder.' Perhaps that is why I went into ecstasies of joy and whooped with delight when I found Lovecraft's name on a story on the October issue."

[10, No. 6 (December 1927): 726.]

Edmond Hamilton, author of 'The Time-Raider',[13] writes: "The other day I reread Lovecraft's 'The Outsider'. It's surely the best thing *Weird Tales* ever published. If some literary detective had found it among Poe's papers it would have been acclaimed as his greatest work, without a doubt."

[11, No. 1 (January 1928): 136.]

R. E. Howard[14] writes from Texas: "Mr. Lovecraft's latest story, 'The Call of Cthulhu',[15] is indeed a masterpiece, which I am sure will live as one of the highest achievements of literature. Mr. Lovecraft holds a unique position in the literary world; he has grasped, to all intents, the worlds outside our paltry ken. His scope is unlimited and his range is cosmic. He has the rare gift of making the unreal seem very real and terrible, without lessening the sensation of horror attendant thereto. He touches peaks in his tales which no modern or ancient writer has ever hinted. Sentences and phrases leap suddenly at the reader, as if in utter blackness of solar darkness a door were suddenly flung open, whence flame the red fire of Purgatory and through which might be momentarily glimpsed monstrous and nightmarish shapes. Herbert Spencer may have been right when he said that it was beyond the human mind to grasp the Unknowable,[16] but Mr. Lovecraft is in a fair way of disproving the theory, I think. I await his next story with eager anticipation, knowing that whatever the subject may be, it will be handled with the skill and incredible vision which he has always shown."

[11, No. 5 (May 1928): 711–12.]

Jack Snow writes from Piqua, Ohio: "Just a short note to tell you how greatly I appreciated Lovecraft's 'The Call of Cthulhu'. Such stories do not require an ordinary 'thank you'; they go through life with the reader, coloring and enhancing his world, and raising it from its mundane sordidness to fantastic heights of beauty and poesy from which no man nor thing can topple it."

[12, No. 1 (July 1928): 138.]

J. W. Meek, of Jackson, Mississippi, writes to the Eyrie: "It has been my pleasure to read your magazine *Weird Tales* from your first issue to your issue of this month, and during this time in no issue have you printed a story that has been as interesting, weird or breath-taking as H. P. Lovecraft's story, 'The Lurking Fear'.[17] Weird tales, ghost-stories and other supernatural stories have been my hobby for years, and during this time I have made a collection of what, in my opinion, have been the best stories. Most of these stories come from your magazine *Weird Tales*, others from Poe and other writers of this nature; and I certainly intend to add to this collection 'The Lurking Fear'. The thing that impressed me most was that Lovecraft actually gave a description of the Thing; he did not say as the usual run of stories do that 'no pen could describe it' or that 'it was too horrible for words'."

"'The Lurking Fear' by Lovecraft is his best so far," writes Paul Hendrickson of Lancaster, Ohio. "I like his ability to keep one uncertain as to whether the plot will end in some far abyss, or in the way it eventually did."

[12, No. 2 (August 1928): 280.]

III. Comments from Readers

A. V. Pershing of St. Paul, Indiana, writes to the Eyrie: "I have just finished 'The Dunwich Horror' by the great H. P. Lovecraft.[18] I am a graduate of Indiana University and have taught physics in the high schools for six years. During this time I have read stories by some 'real' authors; for instance, I have read all of Shakespeare's plays, and many of Poe's works. I say that Lovecraft has an uncanny, nearly superhuman power of transporting one bodily to scenes of his unparalleled 'horrors' and forcing upon us the exquisite pleasure of 'living' the story, so that he (the reader) experiences actual meetings with the shadowy demons of Older Earth. The bare remembrance of such matter-of-fact acquaintances with the gibberish 'terrors' of his pen freezes my brain, the while my thoughts scatter and flee panic-stricken to the crumbling recesses of ancient hyper-space where laughing, screeching demons of all the crystallized filth and anguish of a universe obscenely chant the orgies of the insane existence we term 'reality.' Some day I hope to purchase a classic, containing all of Lovecraft's works so far published in *Weird Tales*. I like best a *weird Weird Tales*.[19] Again I say that surely Lovecraft is as great a writer as ever lived. Where does this genius live and how old is he?"

Writes Jack T. Whitfield, of Penn Yan, New York: "I have just finished reading about the best story I have ever read in the three and a half years I have been reading your extraordinary magazine. To me H. P. Lovecraft has outdone himself in 'The Dunwich Horror'. It held me more deeply than any story I have read for some time. Since I can not find words to express my appreciation of this story, let it suffice that I find it utterly enthralling. . . ."

"I note with interest and some amusement," writes Bernard Austin Dwyer[20] of Kingston, New York, "the frequently expressed opinions as to who is *Weird Tales'* best writer—as if there could be any question! Lovecraft is of course so far above the others that there can be no comparison. I will make exception in favor of Wandrei: he possesses real artistic feeling, and a sense of color and audacity of imagination seldom equaled. Clark Ashton Smith is a genius, as impossible to duplicate as are the faery fantastical forests traced by the frosts on winter mornings. I wish I could see much more of Smith's work. But excepting these two there is nobody who deserves mention in the same breath with Lovecraft. Lovecraft never descends to anticlimax—never starts 'in a wild weird clime'[21] and ends in one's own back yard—no; with every word the reader feels the horror more engulfing—the terror of abysmal outer spaces, and unguessed chasms of infinity. I regard him as the greatest weird writer living today. 'The Outsider'—'The Picture in the House'—'The Rats in the Walls'—'The White Ship'—and last, but by no means least, 'The Dunwich Horror'! I can not find words sufficiently to declare my admiration of his virginity of conception—the weird, the outré, unhackneyed, fully satisfying depth of colorful imagery and fantasy—as strange, as terrible, and as alien to the land of our everyday experiences as a fever-dream. Lovecraft, I am sure, will in after days be noticed as one of the very greatest writers of the weird and the grotesque that ever lived. Indeed I consider him as equal to Bierce and Blackwood, and at times equal to Poe—'The Outsider', for instance. . . ."

[13, No. 6 (June 1929): 851–52, 854.]

E. L. Mengshoel, of Minneapolis, writes to the Eyrie: "It was with a certain amount of satisfaction that I learnt in your last issue that Lovecraft's 'The Dunwich Horror' had been given the majority of votes for the best story in the April number. Satisfaction, because I would myself have given that one my vote, if I had voted, and, moreover, I find cause to be less pessimistic about the literary taste and imaginative faculties of the average reader of your magazine. *That* story was worthy of a Poe. In fact, I have never read anything from Lovecraft's pen that was not something out of the ordinary, something rendered in a vivid, fascinating manner by a genius of extraordinary invention and powerful imagination. He very nearly persuades even a matter-of-fact person to take his yarns for facts. By the way, I would like to ask him if there has not really existed an old work of writing named the *Necronomicon*, which is mentioned in 'The Dunwich Horror'. On the whole, the W. T. is growing more and more indispensable to me at least. It is a refreshment compared to the mass of literary farce that we are treated to in the other magazines."

[14, No. 2 (August 1929): 148, 150.]

Genevieve W. Fisher, of Vineland, New Jersey, writes to the Eyrie: "What I like best in your magazine is Lovecraft's stories. He is by far your best writer; his style and his English are wonderful, as shown in his latest story, 'The Dunwich Horror'. Hope we have more like that. I don't remember whether Lovecraft wrote 'The Lurking Fear' or not, but I remember that as one of your best stories published, especially in its remarkable descriptions. . . ."

[14, No. 3 (September 1929): 294.]

A. V. Pershing, of Indianapolis, writes to the Eyrie: "I have read several of the finest stories in the new September issue, but I have only just now gorged myself with '*the*' perfect horror tale: 'The Hound', by H. P. Lovecraft.[22] Although I am still dazed, as my recovery from the frigid embrace of this charnel nightmare is not yet complete, I wish humbly to thank Mr. Lovecraft for his power to loose one from the chains of the commonplace to roam with sweet horror amid the shadowy throngs which grope their tortured ways through the endless corridors of Eternity—without place, without time, without purpose—free from the mirage of present-day actuality."

[14, No. 5 (November 1929): 716.]

J. Wasso of Pen Argyl, Pennsylvania, suggests that the admirers of H. P. Lovecraft's stories get together and form an H. P. Lovecraft club. "I have a dandy name for it," he writes. "Come on, let's show them how much we think of Lovecraft, master of weird tales."

[15, No. 2 (February 1930): 148.]

"I was delighted with 'The Stranger from Kurdistan' in the December issue,"[23] writes N. J. O'Neail,[24] of Toronto, "and hope you will soon reprint 'The Outsider', which is now nearly four years old.[25] And we haven't heard from H. P. Lovecraft in ten months, except for one reprint. Hope he'll have something to offer soon; to say 'something good' would be redundancy. I was very much interested in tracing the apparent connection between the characters of Kathulos, in Robert E. Howard's 'Skull-Face',[26] and that of Cthulhu, in Mr. Lovecraft's 'The Call of Cthulhu'. Can you inform me whether there is any legend or tradition surrounding that character?[27] And also Yog-Sothoth? Mr. Lovecraft links the latter up with Cthulhu in 'The Dunwich Horror' and Adolphe de Castro also refers to Yog-Sothoth in 'The Last Test'. Both these stories also contain references to Abdul Alhazred the mad Arab, and his *Necronomicon*. I am sure this is a subject in which many readers besides myself would be interested;[28] something which could be reviewed in a series of articles similar to those written by Alvin F. Harlow."[29]

[15, No. 3 (March 1930): 292, 294.]

Dale V. Simpson, of Marion, Ohio, writes to the Eyrie: "It is my wish to express my belated appreciation of your magazine and the authors who furnish its marvelous stories. I say 'marvelous' advisedly; at least, to me they seem so. An oasis in this desert of commonplace literature, in a manner of speaking. (Somehow this phrase does not seem quite original with me, but it expresses my meaning.) I purchased the first copy which appeared on the news stands, and have never missed more than one or two issues since. I *think* (and it certainly takes considerable thinking to decide) that H. P. Lovecraft is my favorite author. I wish his tales might appear in every issue. And my choice of all the stories which have appeared in your magazine since its birth is his 'Dunwich Horror'. This prevented me, for days, from giving full attention to my work. Always have horrors which might lurk in deep, dark caves underground, or dim-lit caverns under the sea, fascinated me. As a child I would scream with terror if allowed to look into a deep well; yet at the first opportunity I would return to torment myself by again gazing into the dark depths. But 'The Dunwich Horror' transported me, upon the wings of imagination, to the uttermost depths of vast caverns in the bowels of the earth—caverns which are swept by foul, moaning winds laden with the breath of the grave and which contain cosmic cesspools wherein the corruption, filth and evil of millions of centuries have accumulated; from there I traveled, in an instant, to far-off worlds or places where only a brief glimpse of unnamable horrors and formless, space-filling alien entities send me scurrying and screaming (mentally) with terror back to my warm fireside. I ask you, what need have I of an interplanetary vessel when I can read such stories?"

[15, No. 4 (April 1930): 436, 438.]

A letter from Bernard Austin Dwyer, of Kingston, New York, is so interesting that we quote it in full: "Having yesterday purchased—as soon as it was out—and last night read the most of *Weird Tales*, I feel impelled to offer a few random ideas and criticisms.

"*Weird Tales* is to me 'the magazine irresistible,' never being on the stalls more than a day before I have it. The well-known—and well-loved—red cover is something I can not pass by. The magazine offers an excellent evening's entertainment. Nearly all of the stories are good—not Lovecraft, of course, but one can not expect all to equal this giant of literary fantasy. Lovecraft, apart from the unguessed, startling originality of his climaxes, has a quality of tone, a sheer, eery atmosphere of his own, that is at once inimitable and unapproachable. When one reads Lovecraft, one enters into a dream-world in all verity—one tiptoes timidly amid a million shadowy horrors—beastly phantasms of an unguessed midnight potency. There the evil charms and machinations of the Other Gods in the Elder World surround one, and one shudders at the mystic horrors hidden behind the snowy peaks of unknown Kadath in the cold waste, or peering from beneath the aged and rotting gambrel roofs of archaic Arkham or Kingsport cottages. No—they can't all equal Lovecraft—but because the sun shines supreme, one doesn't deny light to the lesser luminaries."

[15, No. 6 (June 1930): 724.]

III. Comments from Readers

A letter from H. P. Stiller, of New York City, says: "I have been a reader of your magazine from the first issue printed, something like seven years ago, I believe. I have always experienced a taste for the outré in fiction, which has always been gratified in its pages. One of the greatest authors undoubtedly is H. P. Lovecraft. Stories like 'The Dunwich Horror' are classics and should be preserved for posterity. I would suggest them offered in a book—and would they sell![30] Let me suggest that you reprint one of Lovecraft's early masterpieces, namely: 'The Rats in the Walls'. I would wager that it would get first choice in the monthly readers' vote. Please let us readers know through the Eyrie whether Mr. Lovecraft is working on a new story or not; he has been absent for a number of months, and every new copy arouses in me a forlorn hope that, perhaps, your pre-showing for the month ahead contains his name. I'm still hoping! By the way, my choice for April's best story is Whitehead's 'The Shut Room'."

[15, No. 6 (June 1930): 731-32.]

"Much has been debated on who is your best author," writes Charles Rush, Jr., of New York City. "I think H. P. Lovecraft easily takes that degree. For sheer freezing horror and excellent craftsmanship, he is hard to beat. From 'The Silver Key' to the latest reprint, 'The Rats in the Walls', he has held a standard unsurpassed by any of your other authors, with the possible exception of Seabury Quinn's 'Restless Souls', Edmond Hamilton's 'Crashing Suns' and Robert E. Howard's 'The Moon of Skulls'."[31]

[16, No. 5 (November 1930): 584.]

"Keep the magazine weird by all means," writes Harold Farnese, of Los Angeles; "not too many mechanical stories, aviation, etc.; a modern atmosphere usually lacks the thrill of things unknown, unless penned by a master hand. Speculative stories of other planets, however, should be welcomed by your readers. H. P. Lovecraft's poems are very fine and play a good second to this author's inimitable stories. His style of building up a weird and eldritch atmosphere has yet to be equalled by other writers."

[18, No. 1 (August 1931): 142.]

"I must congratulate you upon the June-July issue of *Weird Tales*," writes J. Vernon Shea, Jr., of Pittsburgh, in a letter to the Eyrie. "It was truly one of the most superb you have yet issued. Judged from any standard, the stories were undeniably good. Of course, the story that leads them all is 'The Outsider', still to my mind the greatest weird story ever written. What a sensation, like that of greeting a long-lost brother, it was to encounter it again! ..."

[18, No. 2 (September 1931): 148.]

Anthony Amato, of Ridgeley, West Virginia, writes to the Eyrie: "I simply had to tell you how much I enjoyed the August issue. You certainly deserve a lot of praise for the wonderful collection of stories contained this month. The one that stands out foremost, that really is a weird tale in the fullest sense of the word, is 'The Whisperer in Darkness'. What a story! Mr. Lovecraft almost convinces the reader that he is relating a true story. Believe it or not, I can feel the shivers racing up and down my back even now, as I write this letter."

Writes J. Vernon Shea, Jr.: "'The Whisperer in Darkness' stands out as indubitably the finest weird tale of the year. It once more proves the superiority of H. P. Lovecraft over all other weird tale writers, and is a fit companion to 'The Outsider', 'The Dunwich Horror', 'Pickman's Model', 'The Rats in the Walls', and 'The Call of Cthulhu'. What a splendid climax it has, and with what shuddery horror it insinuates itself forever into our memories! Yet I must protest against the accompanying illustration for somewhat spoiling the effect of that climax."[32]

[18, No. 3 (October 1931): 292.]

"Congratulations on your August issue," writes Robert Leonard Russell, of Mount Vernon, Illinois. "It is as good as any you have published yet. I liked all your stories in this issue and especially 'The Whisperer in Darkness', H. P. Lovecraft's supreme tale of outré horror. I most certainly hope that Mr. Lovecraft will write more stories soon, say four or five a year, and perhaps a sequel to the 'Whisperer'...."

[18, No. 3 (October 1931): 296.]

"The August *Weird Tales* is certainly a distinguished number, containing as it does 'The Whisperer in Darkness' with its blood-freezing and apocalyptic hints of outer horror," writes Clark Ashton Smith in Auburn, California. "I was glad to see August W. Derleth's little story, 'Prince Borgia's Mass', and I also liked very much the tender and exquisite 'Old Roses', by Stella G. S. Perry."

[18, No. 3 (October 1931): 298.]

A letter from Howard J. Duerr, of Buffalo, says: "I have been a reader of *Weird Tales* almost *ab inito* [sic], and never have I failed to be pleased with it. Where else can I find such writers as Ray Cummings, Edmond Hamilton, H. P. Lovecraft, or my two favorites—E. Hoffmann Price and Robert E. Howard? One of the features of the magazine I have always liked best has been its poems, some mediocre, some good, and others, such as H. P. Lovecraft's sonnets, exquisite."[33]

"Your September number was unusually interesting," writes Duke Williamson, of Springfield, Massachusetts. "The most unusual tale is probably Smith's 'Voyage to Sfanomoë'. The story is exquisitely worded, written in a classic style of which the author is a master. In my opinion, it is fully competent to stand with his 'The End of the Story', 'Sadastor', and 'The Last Incantation'.[34] Of course the most powerful tale is that chilling masterwork by H. P. Lovecraft. Before you read a page of a Lovecraft story you are engulfed in a whirlpool, as it were, of deep mists, eery whispers and deadly foreboding which continues and rises until the very last page, when the climax shatters all and leaves the reader breathless. The above may seem foolish; but Lovecraft's superb tales are so powerful that they affect me for days. By no means secondary are the vivid and brilliant descriptions with which Mr. Lovecraft paints his backgrounds; one could actually hear those swirling, trickling brooks, those buzzing voices, and the wind in the trees, through the magic of the author's words."

[18, No. 5 (December 1931): 580, 582.]

In a letter from New Brighton, New Zealand, G. W. Hockley writes to the Eyrie: "I must say a few words in reference to the high quality of the verse in the magazine. Lovecraft's series, *Fungi from Yuggoth*, contained some masterpieces of outré poetry. 'Antarktos' is surely one of the weirdest pieces of verse ever written, conveying in a few lines chill suggestions of unthinkable antiquity. . . ."

[19, No. 4 (April 1932): 436.]

E. L. Mengshoel, of Minneapolis, writes to the Eyrie: "The majority of your readers being against reprints, I cheerfully join the minority; for, as Henrik Ibsen says in his play, *An Enemy of the People*, 'The majority are always wrong.' But reprint something not so generally known, then. And just now I recall one voice for the *Necronomicon*. Well, why not? It certainly would be interesting to know what those mysteries are about, as they have been referred to quite often in your stories by Lovecraft and others. . . ."

[20, No. 5 (November 1932): 716.]

A letter from John W. Bennett, of Milwaukee, says: "I have just finished reading H. P. Lovecraft's 'The Dreams in the Witch-House' in your

July issue. I'm still shivering. Allow me to say it is a masterpiece of weird fiction. Lovecraft very, very closely approaches the ultimate, shuddery horror of Poe or Blackwood."

[22, No. 3 (September 1933): 390.]

In a letter to the Eyrie, Robert Bloch,[35] of Milwaukee, says in part: "Your new issue is superb—the best in some time. Lovecraft scores heavily. Yessir, Grandpa Cthulhu's new story takes the cake—real writing, real background, real horror. Second place goes, of course, to the second-best writer, Clark Ashton Smith.[36] His infusion of color into prosaic plots is true literary achievement. Outside of Quinn's and Hamilton's stuff, WT is, as ever, O. K., as long as Lovecraft, Smith, Howard, Long, Wandrei and Price continue to provide you with thrilling, unearthly stories to jolt the jaded reader out of commonplace monotonies."

[22, No. 3 (September 1933): 393.]

Alexander Ostrow, of New York City, gives us a sidelight on H. P. Lovecraft. "I have just finished reading your August number," he writes to the Eyrie. "All the stories were so equally excellent that I hesitate to cast my favorite stories ballot. In all the time I have been reading *Weird Tales* I have never cast a ballot for the same reason, although when Howard Philip [sic] Lovecraft appears in any issue, there is no question as to which story is *the* best. Your readers might be interested in knowing that not only is Lovecraft a master of weird fiction, but that he is also an authority on Shakespeare. I have in my possession and have seen elsewhere a variety of essays on the works of Shakespeare by Mr. Lovecraft when he was active in the affairs of the National Amateur Press Association."[37]

[22, No. 4 (October 1933): 517.]

G. W. Hockley writes from New Brighton, in far-away New Zealand: "I must write just a few lines in appreciation of the July *Weird Tales*. The good old magazine is consistently excellent, and the July issue certainly rang the bell. It was especially welcome for the reappearance of the one and only H. P. Lovecraft. 'The Dreams in the Witch-House' is in a class by itself, and shows that this peerless weird-story writer is as good as ever he was. It is the best story in your magazine since the same author's 'Dunwich Horror' of 1929. Full marks must also be given to Hazel Heald for that eery tale, 'The Horror in the Museum', which ranks next to Lovecraft's story as the most engrossing bit of horror-fiction you have published for a long time. . . ."

[23, No. 1 (January 1934): 134.]

III. Comments from Readers

A Bouquet for Mrs. Heald

Bernard J. Kenton,[38] of Cleveland, writes: "How can any discriminating reader find merit in other fantasy magazines when *Weird Tales* adds a new Poe to its columns every month or so? Of the recent writers, Hazel Heald strikes my fancy most, for whenever did anything so strikingly horrible as 'The Horror in the Museum' appear in print? Even Lovecraft—as powerful and artistic as he is with macabre suggestiveness—could hardly, I suspect, have surpassed the grotesque scene in which the other-dimensional shambler leaps out upon the hero. 'Winged Death'[39] (Heald) makes life a living joy for the amateur criminologist. It is my prediction (verified at least in fiction such as 'Winged Death' and 'The Solitary Hunters')[40] that the man of exceptional intellect will turn to crime when legitimate channels of amassing wealth are unnavigable; compared to them, Al Capone will look like a kid stealing milk bottles. C. L. Moore, author of 'Shambleau', looks good to me and if he [sic] falls no lower than half the level in 'Black Thirst' that was reached in 'Shambleau', I shall be satisfied."[41]

[23, No. 6 (May 1934): 654-55.]

A Slap on the Wrist

Henry Kuttner,[42] of Hollywood, California, writes: "Here's a letter of comments and criticism, inspired chiefly by 'Through the Gates of the Silver Key' in your July issue. I wonder if it has not occurred to you that sheer thorough explanation of the weird may rob a subject of weirdness. It seems to me that mystery is an essential of the weird, and when, in such a story as Lovecraft's, the author tries to cover Heaven and Hell, humans and non-humans, explaining everything in one colossal sweep, the story falls flat and becomes more preachy than interesting or weird. Little need be said about the surprizing ending of the yarn. Lovecraft at one time could supply a good ending, but now he is getting trite as hell. It is a bad example of a forced surprize ending that he has on that story. Lovecraft's earlier stories, 'The Hound', 'The Rats in the Walls', 'The Call of Cthulhu', 'The Dunwich Horror' and one of the best, 'The Horror at Red Hook', were far more truly weird than his later stories, which go past the weird and mysterious, and, throwing a cold light of scientific reason onto non-human affairs, result in a science-fiction story. If you will bring to mind Lovecraft's best stories (not his most successful ones), you will find that mystery, not calculating science, provided the fillip of true weirdness. That is why C. L. Moore seems to me a better writer than Lovecraft—the *present* Lovecraft. . . ."

[24, No. 3 (September 1934): 398-99.]

The Music of Erich Zann

Robert Nelson,[43] of St. Charles, Illinois, writes: "I was deeply disappointed to see no note of comment whatsoever on H. P. Lovecraft's 'The Music of Erich Zann', which appeared in the reprint section for last November. This is one of the finest of eery short stories ever written, and is included in at least one of our leading anthologies.[44] Few know and can realise the terror and anguish and sadness and unnamable visions which the power of music can evoke. All of this is ably suggested in 'The Music of Erich Zann'. And rereading this tale, the suggestions grow and mount on one, with the result that the entire aspect becomes something of a very serious nature. 'The Dark Eidolon' by Clark Ashton Smith seems to me even to surpass his 'The Colossus of Ylourgne'[45]—a magnificent living piece of work."

[25, No. 3 (March 1935): 399.]

Like a Lovecraft Masterpiece

John Malone, of Jackson, Mississippi, writes: "How does Hazel Heald do it? 'Out of the Eons'[46] was like a masterpiece by H. P. Lovecraft. Hardly any of the horror was pictured, most of it was suggested, until the climax, when the revelation came! . . ."

[25, No. 6 (June 1935): 778.]

Reprint Lovecraft's Stories

Donald A. Wollheim,[47] of New York City, writes: "Why not reprint all of Lovecraft's earlier works? I am sure that your readers would appreciate them greatly; 'Hypnos', for instance, and 'The Moon Bog', and the others. I agree with Paul Brown who bemoans the loss of some of your eery atmosphere. By all means employ Hugh Rankin more. He is the one artist able to depict the undepictable. See his illustrations to 'The Lurking Fear', 'The Space-Eaters',[48] and the 'Dunwich Horror', for example—those dim, half-seen horrors beyond form or cognizance. No one else seems able to do that. Rankin apparently has a patent on it."

Out of the Eons

Lewis F. Torrance, of Winfield, Kansas, writes: "'Out of the Eons' was the most remarkable, the best, the greatest, et al, narrative it has ever been my good fortune to read in *Weird Tales*. It seems to have that indefinable something that science-fiction has been lacking. Yours for more Hazel Heald."

[25, No. 6 (June 1935): 780.]

In Praise of Mrs. Heald

B. M. Reynolds,[49] of North Adams, Massachusetts, writes: "The April number was a treat. I cannot say enough in praise of the work of Hazel Heald. She is veritably a female Lovecraft. Her 'Out of the Eons' is a masterpiece. . . . I almost expected that Mr. Lovecraft himself would stroll into the museum and take a hand at deciphering the hieroglyphics on the scroll and cylinder. Let's have more like this from Mrs. Heald. . . ."

[25, No. 6 (June 1935): 782.]

Based on Fact?

Charles H. Bert, of Philadelphia, writes: ". . . I would like to mention an unknown fact about 'The Outsider' by H. P. Lovecraft. It may interest the editor and readers to know that this story is based upon cold fact! Yes, cold fact! While most readers consider 'The Outsider' the finest piece of literature to appear in the pages of *Weird Tales*, have they ever thought it was possible? Very few have. But have you heard of the 'Mystery Child of Europe', Kaspar Hauser? For eighteen years Kaspar Hauser was in solitary confinement, and never saw the light of day until he came to this age. You see, he was abducted when he was a small child, and placed in solitary confinement, in a dark room, for eighteen years. He escaped accidentally and was found wandering near Anspach, Bavaria, seemingly from nowhere. What must have been his thoughts of the outside world during his incarceration! Strange, indeed, they must have been. How had he acted when he saw the light of day? Lovecraft's character in 'The Outsider' is amazingly similar to Kaspar Hauser. Perhaps Lovecraft is familiar with the tragic history of Hauser. Judging from his works, Lovecraft must be a scholarly person. So, 'The Outsider', the wildest flight of imaginative fancy ever written, surpassing the best of Poe's, is fact! Truth is stranger than fiction, you know. I'm ending this letter with a plea for the return to your pages of that incomparable little man: Jules de Grandin."

[25, No. 6 (June 1935): 784.]

Admirer of Lovecraft

Emil Petaja,[50] of Milltown, Montana, writes: "I have just completed reading two issues—the last issues of WT, and should like to express my opinions of them. . . . But why on earth (or the universe, for that matter) don't you get some new tales by the Prince of Fantasy—that great classic weird writer who will never be equaled—H. P. Lovecraft? When I recall 'The Strange High House in the Mist' and 'The Outsider', I can't help wishing I could recall some of the great thrills I felt in first perusing these masterpieces. But I'm sure *anything* Lovecraft wrote would be wonderful—and most welcome! Why not try to get him to write a long story—something forceful and colossal and magnificent; bringing to life eon-dead civilizations brought to earth from the outside—with its setting perhaps—say in the Antarctic?"[51]

[26, No. 2 (August 1935): 270.]

Lovecraft's Literary Art

Henry Kuttner, of Beverly Hills, California, writes: "Just got the January issue, and was especially delighted with two of the stories in it. . . . And, of course, 'Dagon', by Lovecraft, with its extraordinary paragraph describing the undersea horror darting to the monolith, 'about which it flung its gigantic scaly arms.' That one paragraph has an effect of weirdness comparable to the flight of the terrified whippoorwills at the death of the monster-man in 'The Dunwich Horror', and the daemoniac celebration beneath the church in 'The Horror at Red Hook'. How about reprinting HP's 'The Moon-Bog', and his other tale about a derelict U-boat that reached sunken Atlantis? . . ."[52]

From a French Reader

Jacques Bergier,[53] of Paris, France, writes: "As one of your numerous European readers, I compliment you on having the finest fantastic magazine I have ever read. You have published some of the best stories of this kind, such as: 'Through the Gates of the Silver Key' by Price and Lovecraft, 'Dust of Gods' and other stories by Moore, 'The Gorgon' by Smith, 'The Night Wire' by Arnold,[54] and many others. I wish to thank you for many hours of entertainment, and also to make some suggestions. By all means, give us more stories by H. P. Lovecraft. He is the only writer of today who is really *haunted*. Some of his stories, such as 'Pickman's Model' and 'The Rats in the Walls', surpass even Poe, Blackwood and Machen."

[27, No. 3 (March 1936): 380-81.]

More Stories by Lovecraft

B. M. Reynolds, of North Adams, Massachusetts, writes: ". . . By the way, Mr. Editor, when, if ever, are we going to have any more tales by Lovecraft? Apparently, Robert Bloch has been trying to pinch-hit for Lovecraft for you, but he is an easy out. I'm sure no one can fill Lovecraft's shoes with most of us readers. We miss his Elder Gods, and how!"

[28, No. 3 (October 1936): 383.]

In Praise of H. P. Lovecraft

Henry Kuttner, of Beverly Hills, California, writes: "Congrats on several counts: the forthcoming Finlay cover; the December cover, unusual and attractive; the Lovecraft story. As usual, the Lovecraftian tale tops all others in the issue, and the only wonder is why HPL doesn't write, and you don't run, more stories of this nature. Lovecraft remains, as always, supreme in his ability to write of the utterly unearthly in a disturbingly convincing manner. The Dweller in Providence avenged himself effectually on Bloch for his double demise in 'The Dark Demon'[55] and 'The Shambler from the Stars'!"

[29, No. 2 (February 1937): 254.]

H. Warner Munn, author of 'The Werewolf of Ponkert',[56] writes from Athol, Massachusetts: ". . . Lovecraft's Elder Gods have spawned a fertile progeny; the *Necronomicon* has suggested a long shelf full of unhallowed tomes. . . . I need say little of my pleasure at finding Lovecraft active again. It seems like old times returned. . . ."

[29, No. 4 (April 1937): 507.]

Lovecraft Reprints

Robert Bloch writes from Milwaukee: "I raise my raucous voice again to request, along with other readers, a reprinting of 'The Picture in the House', by you-know-who. Also his 'The Unnamable', 'The Statement of Randolph Carter', the 'Call of Cthulhu', 'The Horror at Red Hook'; these were gems, and are now unobtainable. The success of 'Pickman's Model' should be a good criterion of how avidly these reprints would be welcomed.[57] To think that H. P. wrote those magnificent yarns along in the early 1920's and can still turn out top tales like 'The Thing on the Door-Step'! Amazing. But please print 'The Picture in the House'. It's a honey."

[29, No. 4 (April 1937): 508-9.]

Sad indeed is the news that tells us of H. P. Lovecraft's death on March 15, in the Jane Brown Memorial Hospital in Providence, Rhode Island. He was a titan of weird and fantastic literature, whose literary achievements and impeccable craftsmanship were acclaimed throughout the English-speaking world. He was only forty-six years of age, yet had built up a following such as few authors ever had. As a child he was a prodigy. He learned the alphabet at two years of age, and early developed a liking for old-fashioned and fantastic books. Always a weak and nervous child, he managed to stick out four years in high school at the cost of a breakdown which kept him from college and put him virtually out of the world for a number of years. About 1920 his health began of itself to effect that mending which specialists for thirty years had sought in vain to bring about; and shortly afterward he began traveling, visiting new places and meeting old friends whom he had contacted through his wide correspondence. He had a masterful command of several languages;[58] and, as E. Hoffmann Price once remarked, "There is scarcely an artistic or cultural subject on which H. P. Lovecraft cannot learnedly hold forth, and with an unfailing hold on the attention of the listener." As for his hobbies, let us quote Price again: "His hobbies? This is not a catalogue; let me short-circuit that by saying that the range must be from architecture to zoology." Between 1917 and 1936 Lovecraft wrote forty-six stories, each of which is a *tour de force* in itself. He invented the Lovecraft mythology (the *Necronomicon*, Abdul Alhazred, etc.), which has been adopted by many other writers of weird fiction. With all his studies, his capabilities, his wide knowledge, and his vast intelligence, H. P. Lovecraft was a kindly, generous human being, modest as to his own work, and ever ready to lend a helping hand to others. He carried on a voluminous correspondence with over seventy-five weird fiction enthusiasts, and endeared himself to all of them with his kind patience and generosity. His death is a serious loss to weird and fantastic fiction; but to the editors of *Weird Tales* the personal loss takes precedence. We admired him for his great literary achievements, but we loved him for himself; for he was a courtly and noble gentleman, and a dear friend. Peace be to his shade!

An Unfillable Void

Lorne W. Power, of Windsor, Ontario, writes: "The passing of that outstanding author, Howard Phillips Lovecraft, leaves a void which can never be filled. He was nothing less than a genius, and the greatest writer of weird fiction since Poe. His realistic method of treatment and uncanny ability to breathe life into his creations could give the most hardened reader shudders. The best of his works were printed in *Weird Tales*, and I suggest that these be published in book form. Such a volume would prove a 'best-seller,' judging by the immense popularity of the author. I, as well as thousands of others, will miss 'Abdul Alhazred' and his *Necronomicon* more than words can convey, and though others may try to take his place, they can only succeed in calling up memories of the deceased."

A Staggering Blow

Manly Wade Wellman writes from New York City: "The death of H. P. Lovecraft is a staggering blow, I am sure, to your magazine and to fantasy fiction in general. I had hoped to meet Mr. Lovecraft, and mourn my ill luck in not doing so; I can say, at least, that he was my early inspiration and constant study in this field, as he must have been for many younger writers. His death and that of Robert E. Howard, so close together, leave a gigantic gap in the ranks of WT writers—it's going to be a grim job to close up and march on. Again let me express my shocked feeling of sorrow and loss at the passing of this consistently fine artist."

Death of a Master

Robert Leonard Russell, of Mount Vernon, Illinois, writes: "The morning paper brought the shocking news—Howard Phillips Lovecraft is dead. The greatest modern writer of weird fiction has passed on at the age of forty-six, in the very prime of his life. I feel, as will many other readers of *Weird Tales*, that I have lost a real friend. Lovecraft made a place for himself that can never be filled by another. His monstrous *Necronomicon* with the dread Cthulhu, Azathoth and the other Elder Gods struck a new note of weirdness. A Lovecraft story was always by far the best in any issue. I was eleven years old when I read his 'The Silver Key', and I have not missed a Lovecraft yarn since. One of my ambitions—never achieved however—was to meet the master himself and talk to him. And now the pen that gave us 'The Dunwich Horror', 'The Hound', 'The Whisperer in Darkness', 'The Thing on the Door-step', and many another tale of shuddery horror writes no more. We shall miss him."

From Mrs. Heald

Hazel Heald writes from Newtonville, Massachusetts: "I want to express my sorrow in the passing of H. P. Lovecraft. He was a friend indeed to the struggling author, and many have started to climb the ladder of success with his kind assistance. To us who really knew him it is a sorrow that mere words cannot express. His was the helping hand that started me in the writers' game and gave me the courage to carry on under the gravest difficulties. But we must try to think that he is 'just away' on one of his longest journeys and that some day we will meet him again in the Great Beyond."

From Robert Bloch

Robert Bloch writes from Milwaukee: "Now that Lovecraft's gone it's strange; I don't think so much about his imaginative genius, and pre-eminence as WT's first and finest author. I just remember what he meant to me personally—you know how I wrote him a fan note so long ago; how he got into a correspondence with me, encouraged me to write, helped, criticized. If it weren't for him I'd never have hit WT or any other magazine. And there are so many others that owe him a similar debt of gratitude. I wonder what they'll all do now—the fan magazines that depended on him for support and encouragement, the many aspiring correspondents that looked to him for help and advice, and all the others that knew and so greatly admired him. He was a great writer, but an even greater friend; a real New England gentleman of the old school. I think we ought to count ourselves proud to have known him. Of course there ought to be a memorial volume, with stories chosen by the readers. That's the smallest tribute one can pay. But there's an end of the world—the world of Arkham, Innsmouth, Kingsport; the world of Cthulhu, Yog-Sothoth, Nyarlathotep, and Abdul Alhazred; the finest world of fantasy I know."

From Seabury Quinn

Seabury Quinn writes from Brooklyn: "Lovecraft, whom I had the pleasure of knowing personally,[59] was both a scholar and a gentleman, and his writings disclosed both his scholarship and his gentility, as well as a genius which has not been observable since the death of Poe and Hawthorne. We who knew him personally shall miss his quiet humor and his always-interesting conversation; thousands of those who had never met the man will join with us in deploring the loss of his contributions to a field of literature which he had made peculiarly his own. God rest his soul."

[29, No. 6 (June 1937): 762-64.]

Death of H. P. Lovecraft

Kenneth Sterling,[60] of Cambridge, Massachusetts, writes: "I am sure you must be deeply grieved at the passing of Howard Phillips Lovecraft. A contributor to *Weird Tales* since its inception, he has always been considered one of the leading writers of modern weird literature, and was, in my opinion, the pre-eminent creative artist in this field. His vivid, powerful style, unsurpassed in producing and sustaining a mood of horror, is well known to you and your readers. His decease leaves a gap which can never be filled. But it is a far more severe loss to those of us who had the infinite pleasure of a personal acquaintance with the inimitable 'Ech-Pi-El.' His generosity and magnanimity won the love and respect of all who knew him. He possessed a supreme intellect—one which I have never seen exceeded—and I have come in contact with many prominent professors at Harvard University. He had an incredible store of knowledge—he was versed in virtually every field of learning. In addition to this great erudition, he had an acutely analytical mind—his thinking was keenly logical and free of all bias and closed-minded narrowness. Contrary to what one would be led to expect from his fiction, Lovecraft was a confirmed materialist and iconoclast, as expressed in innumerable letters and articles. His conversation was transcendently brilliant, outshining even his excellent writings. He was a man of great vigor and sincerity, and had great influence on his circle of friends, many of whom are noted authors in the fantasy field and other types of fiction. I think it would be most fitting if H. P. Lovecraft were remembered as a scholar and thinker as well as an author.[61] In closing, let me urge you to reprint many of Lovecraft's fine stories and poems, and if possible, to have his works published in permanent book form."

From Clark Ashton Smith

Clark Ashton Smith writes from Auburn, California: "I am profoundly saddened by the news of H. P. Lovecraft's death after a month of painful illness. The loss seems an intolerable one, and I am sure that it will be felt deeply and permanently by the whole weird fiction public. Most of all will it be felt by the myriad friends who knew Lovecraft through face-to-face meeting or correspondence: for in his case the highest literary genius was allied to the most brilliant and most endearing personal qualities. I—alas!—never met him, but we had corresponded for about seventeen years,[62] and I felt that I knew him better than most people with whom I was thrown in daily intimacy. The first manuscript of his that I read (probably in 1920)[63] confirmed me in the opinion of his genius from which I have never swerved at any time. It opened a new world of awesome speculation and eery surmise, a new imaginative dimension. Since then, he has written scores of masterpieces that extend the borders of human fantasy and conquer fresh empires amid the extra-human and ultra-terrestrial infinities. Among these, I might mention 'The Outsider', 'The Call of Cthulhu', 'The Colour out of Space', 'The Rats in the Walls', 'The Dunwich Horror', 'Pickman's Model' and 'The Dreams in the Witch-House' as being special favorites. However, there are few tales of his that I have not read and re-read many times, always with that peculiar delight given by the savor of some uniquely potent distillation of dreams and fantasy. Leng and

Lomar and witch-ridden Arkham and sea-cursed Innsmouth are part of my mental geography; and dreadful, cyclopean R'lyeh slumbers somewhere in the depths. Others will venture into the realms that the Silver Key of his mastery has unlocked; but none will read them with the same wizard surety, or bring back for our delectation essences of equal dread and beauty and horror."

From Edmond Hamilton

Edmond Hamilton writes from New Castle, Pennsylvania: "I just heard the news of H. P. Lovecraft's recent death. This is quite a shock, coming so soon after the death of Howard. While I never met either of them, I have been appearing with them in *Weird Tales* for so long that I had a dim feeling of acquaintance. I think I read every one of Lovecraft's stories from 'Dagon', years ago. It is too bad that he is gone—there will never be another like him."

From Henry Kuttner

Henry Kuttner writes from Beverly Hills, California: "I've been feeling extremely depressed about Lovecraft's death. Even now I can't realize it. He was my literary idol since the days of 'The Horror at Red Hook', and lately a personal friend as well. The loss to literature is a very great one, but the loss to HPL's friends is greater. He seemed, somehow, to have been an integral part of my literary life—and the shock was more severe because I had not known that his illness was serious."

From Earl Peirce, Jr.

Earl Peirce, Jr.,[64] writes from Washington, D. C.: "The news of Lovecraft's passing, although not the shock of surprize, is nevertheless the shock of an irreparable loss, not alone to WT, but to his admirers and acquaintances the world over. I shall always regret that I never had the good fortune of meeting him personally, but I am truly grateful for the impulse which prompted me to write to him a few months ago, and that I have two letters in his own hand. What most impressed me were his sincerity and genuineness, which qualities were not alone in making him unique among modern writers. You have my sympathy, for this must be a hard time, but I imagine it is a feeling of pride for you to know that so many of his stories originally appeared in *Weird Tales*. Unlike many other men of genius, Lovecraft was fortunate enough to be living at a time when his work was recognized as outstanding. With the passing of time this recognition will become more universal and his work will take its proper place in the world's great literature."

Bruce Bryan, of Washington, D. C., writes: "Lovecraft had a rare faculty for beginning with something commonplace and building up an overwhelming aura of horror that left his readers hanging onto the ropes. In that sense, I can't think of anyone who could surpass him. He had a knack of delving into man's subconscious, untranslated fears—putting them into an appreciable form, giving them appealing names and personifying one's own, inmost, half-comprehended, even personal nightmares."

[30, No. 1 (July 1937): 122-24.]

Harold S. Farnese, of Los Angeles, writes: "Reading your magazine habitually, I sometimes wonder whether you ever realized how great a contributor you had in H. P. Lovecraft. Whether you ever gauged the fineness of his stories, the originality of his genius? Of course, you published them, alongside of others. You sent him his cheque, and that was that. But has it ever occurred to you that in Lovecraft you had the greatest genius that ever lived in the realm of weird fiction?"

[30, No. 1 (July 1937): 125.]

In Memoriam

Mrs. Hazel Heald writes from Newtonville, Massachusetts: "A brain like H. P. Lovecraft's seldom was found—uncanny in its intelligence. He was ever searching for more knowledge, gleaning by endless hours of study a richer and fuller understanding of people and of life. Being a great traveler, he reveled in the study of old cities and their hidden lore and would walk many miles to inspect some historic spot. He was a real friend to all who knew him, always ready to give his valuable time to aid some poor struggling author—a true guiding star. He was very partial to dumb animals, especially cats, signifying that interest in several of his tales. He would step out of his way to pat some forlorn alley cat and give it a friendly word, and the kittens of a neighbor furnished him unbounded enjoyment. He was an ardent lover of architecture and all the fine arts, and a day spent in a museum with him was time well spent. By endless hours of toil he worked far into the night giving the world masterpieces of weird fiction, sacrificing his health for his work. Lovecraft was a gift to the world who can never be replaced—Humanity's Friend."

[30, No. 2 (August 1937): 248.]

The Master of Weird Fiction

N. J. O'Neail, of Toronto, writes: "It was with a shock like that of a physical blow, that I read yesterday (in the June issue of WT) that the Master of weird fiction has passed from us. It seemed impossible that death could ever touch even the mortal clay of Howard Phillips Lovecraft. As Wordsworth wrote of Milton: 'Thy soul was like a star, and dwelt apart; thou hadst a voice whose sound was as the sea, pure as the naked heavens, majestic, free.'[65] It is with no disparagement to many able writers that I say that *Weird Tales* can never be quite the same to me again. It and Lovecraft were almost synonymous, to my mind; his work dominated every issue in which it appeared, and his spirit pervaded the pages, even when his pen was not represented there. My first move, usually, in opening a new copy of *Weird Tales*—and I still have every issue of the last eleven years—is to look for the reprint story, in the hope that it may be one of Lovecraft's. My next glance is at the schedule of contents for the following number, hoping to find his name there. Then, before reading any of the stories, I turn to the Eyrie; there it was, yesterday, that I read the staggering news. To attempt to name Lovecraft's best work would be a mere grouping of individual tastes, in a field of super-superlatives, for he never wrote a second-rater; nothing was allowed to leave his hands until it had the polished perfection of a cameo. To me, some of his earlier and shorter stories stand out even more vividly than his overpowering later work. For instance, 'The Music of Erich Zann', a masterpiece of abstract horror; 'The Outsider', a classic, of course, of the outré; 'The Festival', 'Pickman's Model', and 'The Lurking Fear', the last of these a particular stand-out because of its potential reality. While some writers exhaust the dictionary in their efforts to picture the horror with which they are dealing, Lovecraft's technique was far superior, for he gave the impression always of striving to conceal or to minimize horror, instead of painting it in rainbow colors and in circus poster type. . . . Lovecraft's passing is not a case of 'The King is dead; long live the King!', for there is no heir-apparent to succeed to the crown. There are several younger writers—one woman in particular—who show marked promise, and who, I believe, acknowledge that they owe much in encouragement and inspiration to H. P. L. They are not Lovecrafts; they may never be; but the fact that their work demands comparison with his, and appraisal by the standard of perfection which he set, is in itself a high tribute. Mrs. Heald, Mr. Bloch and Mr. Kuttner are facing a challenging future."

III. Comments from Readers
Evaluation of Lovecraft

Paul S. Smith, of Orange, New Jersey, writes: "Lovecraft was gifted with a remarkable imagination and was the possessor of one of the most perfect and striking English styles that I have ever encountered. If you ever publish a book of Lovecraft's stories I earnestly hope you will include 'The Rats in the Walls', which I consider to be his masterpiece. And more than this, I think it is the best weird story I have ever read, and this is saying a great deal. Among Lovecraft's other outstanding stories I would mention 'The Dunwich Horror', 'The Lurking Fear', 'The Whisperer in Darkness', 'The Hound' and 'The Thing on the Door-Step'."

[30, No. 2 (August 1937): 250-52.]

A Tribute to Lovecraft

Robert W. Lowndes, of Stamford, Connecticut, writes: "Being, in all likelihood, one of the last followers of H. P. Lovecraft's magnificent work in the fantasy field to enter into correspondence with him,[66] it may seem somewhat strange for me to say that it is as though I had lost a beloved friend of many years' acquaintance. Yet this is the case, and those who knew him far better than I did can understand my feelings: there is consolation of a sort in the thought that if I, who knew him but through the media of two letters and a few of his tales, am grieved with the knowledge that there can be no more friendly, wise, generous, and inspiring letters from him, what must be the feelings of those who had been corresponding with him regularly over a period of years, or who knew him personally? As he himself wrote of Robert E. Howard, only a few short months ago,[67] weird and fantastic fiction will be terribly impoverished by his passing; as E. Hoffmann Price wrote of Howard, the personal loss of H. P. Lovecraft to those who knew him, and those who corresponded with him, dwarfs all else into insignificance. How well recalled is the first Lovecraft tale I read (in my first issue of *Weird Tales* at that—October, 1931): 'The Strange High House in the Mist'. Then, a gradual but steady increase in my little fund of tales and novelettes from his pen until he rose to undisputed supremacy in my affections. I often dreamed of meeting him some day; hoped to write to him. . . . I finally ventured a letter. What a moment it was for me when I saw a letter in return! His first paragraph assured me that I need have no hesitation in writing to him; then, after putting me at ease, he launched forth into discussion of the several points I had raised, in that friendly, acute, and understanding way which others know so much better than I do. He had the unique faculty of making a worshipper feel that what one wrote to him was as interesting as what he had to offer in reply. *Weird Tales* has printed the majority of Lovecraft's published works, I believe, but he is not well-known outside of the circle of *Weird Tales* readers and fantasy enthusiasts. Can we readers hope that eventually someone will collect all of his works and publish them in a single volume? What a treasure for the lovers of the weird and the fantastic that would be! An even greater treasure would be a compilation of his masterly, though enormous, correspondence; yet what splendid reading his letters would make, even though they ran to a number of volumes! Yet, great as these are, they can go but a little way to approach the greatest treasure of all for those who were acquainted with him: the man, Howard Phillips Lovecraft himself."

[30, No. 2 (August 1937): 253-54.]

H. P. L.

Samuel Gordon writes from Washington, D. C.: "Spinoza's tomb carries an inscription which runs something like this: 'Here lies a man who was closer to God than any other mortal.' If there ever lived a man who was apparently closer to the essence of the weird in nature than Lovecraft was, I do not know of him. He seemed to see a world far from the commonplace; a world with hidden meanings and innuendoes; a cosmos peopled with demons and gods older than the first star. And who can definitely say that Lovecraft saw but illusions? In these days of stark realism, of wars and rumors of wars, of cracked politics and politicians, of 200% Americans and enemies that bore from within, it was more than relief to turn to a Lovecraft story; it was a rare treat and a positive delight. He may have written from a sense of belief; or half-belief, or with his tongue in his cheek. But, regardless, he will always live in the thoughts of those to whom he brought such pleasurable escape from what, for want of a better term, we call reality. I, for one, will miss Lovecraft and his stories."

[30, No. 2 (August 1937): 255-56.]

The Genius of Lovecraft

Francis Flagg[68] writes from Tuscon, Arizona: "The death, at a relatively early age, of Howard P. Lovecraft has undoubtedly robbed weird literature of one of its master writers. Lovecraft and I had corresponded over a number of years on such subjects as monarchism, socialism, communism, materialism, religion, and incidentally, literature. Of Lovecraft's standing as a writer of great and unique talent there can be little question. His weird tales are comparable to Poe's and superior to O'Brien's. There seems to be a tendency to separate Lovecraft the materialist from Lovecraft the weird artist and thinker, as if the man's brain had been contained in two compartments, but indeed this is wrong. Lovecraft was never more the materialist than when he was the weird artist. There is a psychological reality in many of his tales that could only have been set down by a materialist thinker. This was true of Poe; and a study of Lovecraft's writings (comparing them to the products of contemporary weird writers) will reveal that this is true of him also. Lovecraft is dead, and it is with a keen sense of loss and real grief that I realize his brilliant letters will never come my way again."

[30, No. 3 (September 1937): 378.]

From a French Enthusiast

Jacques Bergier, of Paris, writes: "Over a year has elapsed since I last wrote to you. *Weird Tales* still remains 'the unique magazine' and has printed some astounding tales during that year; such as Moore's 'Lost Paradise', Lovecraft's 'Haunter of the Dark', Williamson's 'Ruler of Fate', and Howard's 'The Hour of the Dragon'.[69] I deeply and sincerely mourn the passing of H. P. Lovecraft. I believe that Lovecraft was one of America's greatest writers, an equal to Poe. I believe that recognition of this fact will come after a lapse of years, as with Poe. Such tales as 'The Music of Erich Zann', 'The Dreams in the Witch-House' and 'The Temple', as well as his cycle of the Elder Gods and strange civilizations, and the extraordinary 'Through the Gates of the Silver Key', will remain, marking a writer of extraordinary power, to be placed with Poe, Wells, Machen and Blackwood. The passing of Lovecraft seems to me to mark an end of an epoch in the history of American imaginative fiction, an history that begins with Poe, continues with Bierce's *Can Such Things Be?*, Chambers' *The King in Yellow*, Merritt's 'The Moon Pool', and then the era of fantastic story magazines of which only *Weird Tales* and a science-fiction magazine now continue to print real fantasy. I think that many of the stories published in this last year—and among them, almost all of Lovecraft's—were great and will endure. And in spite—or perhaps because—of my scientific training I sometimes think that perhaps Lovecraft had a glimpse across 'undreamable abysses,' of facts about the structure of the universe that science will one day discover...."

[30, No. 3 (September 1937): 382.]

Save the Necronomicon!

Elaine McIntire, of Malden, Massachusetts, writes: ". . . But! what in tarnation is 'The Terrible Parchment'?[70] Is our friend Wellman trying to put my pet book *Necronomicon* on the spot? Well, he'd better not try! I'm up in arms! I like to think that there is such a thing. It gives me something to think about coming home alone late at night along dark streets. What about it, readers? Are we going to let it pass? . . ."

[30, No. 4 (October 1937): 504.]

The Dead Masters

Reginald A. Pryke, of Kent, England, writes: "Since way back in 1925 we (that means three of us) have been your loyal followers and admirers. In the days of Senf's covers, monthly Jules de Grandins, Henry S. Whitehead and Dunwich Horrors, into Rankin's era with his clouded, evil, misty illustrations, bursting into Howard's pulsating epics, Depression days and bi-monthly issues—terrible time of famine—and so into the present day. *Per ardua ad astra!*[71] You have a record to be proud of, a future to encourage you to even greater efforts, and a spirit to take the sad blows Fate has dealt you unflinchingly. A moment to think of The Fallen. . . . And Lovecraft: Let the men who knew and loved him as a friend pen his obituary. I, who only knew him through his matchless pen, bid farewell to an artist who knew how to play upon man's sense of fear as Kreisler plays upon his violin. Those long, brooding, almost somnolent opening paragraphs of his, almost devoid of conversation—somehow, Lovecraft's pen seemed to falter when he attempted to put words into a personal mouth—impersonality was his keynote. With a sense of nightmare, barely glimpsed, the reader's eye fled from paragraph to paragraph, almost chased or driven, until the grotesque climax was attained, the spell broken, the pursuit lifted, leaving him weakened yet strangely exhilarated. Fear, like fire, is cleansing. Whitehead, Eadie, Howard, Lovecraft. Each in his own field such an undisputed master that the loss seems unbearable. Each, of course, has his disciples. Robert Bloch, for instance, seems a fit proselyte of Lovecraft, who, with experience, may yet equal his master, but no disciple can fill the place of his teacher in the mind and heart of any who knew that teacher's genius. . . ."

Donald A. Wollheim, of New York City, writes: ". . . Wellman's Necronomiconic is a honey. But it won't end *Necronomicon* tales. I, for one, want to see the Necro grow bigger and bigger. It was one of the factors contributing to the making of WT's vivid and unique personality."

The Terrible Parchment

Joseph Allen Ryan, of Cambridge, Maryland, writes: "Wellman's short, 'The Terrible Parchment', was especially interesting to me; for I believe I was on hand when the idea for the tale was born. Otto Binder, Julius Schwartz, Mort Weisinger and I (as usual, I was the small frog in the big pond) were standing at the corner of West 48th Street and Broadway in New York City last summer, chewing the rag a bit before departing on our various ways. The conversation drifted to *Weird Tales*, and to H. P. Lovecraft and the *Necronomicon* in particular. Mort glanced at the near-by news stand and remarked: 'Suppose you went over to that stand and asked for a copy of the *Necronomicon*, and the fellow handed it to you. What would you do?' None of us knew exactly what course he would follow under the unusual circumstances. Otto remarked: 'Pay for it, I guess.' Mort digested this for a moment or so, then continued: 'That would make a good plot for a story—for some fan magazine, that is. You would explain that Lovecraft's readers had thought so much about the mythical *Necronomicon* that their combined thought-force materialized it.' As Weisinger knows Manly Wade Wellman quite well, it may be that the idea got around to the latter, who developed it into a short for WT. How about it, Manly?"

[30, No. 4 (October 1937): 507-9.]

In Appreciation of Lovecraft

David Markham, of Metlakatla, Alaska, writes: "Lovecraft, unlike most people, left behind a monument built with his own hands—a slender but remarkable shaft which will for countless years regale and thrill many with its haut-relief of pictured Arkham. Peace to his ashes; death must be an ecstatic adventure for such a man. And in that far bourn may he finally encounter and slay Tsathoggua, rend Cthulhu piecemeal, and silence for ever the maunderings of the mind-touched Alhazred who flung the *Necronomicon* into an already troubled world."

[30, No. 5 (November 1937): 639-40.]

J. Vernon Shea, Jr., of Pittsburgh, writes: "The October number is another good issue. I read 'The Shunned House' with a feeling of sadness, for the many references to Providence made it seem like a post-delayed letter from H.P.L. The story is not quite of his best, for it has the over-slow approach and the lingering on technicalities that marked some of his last work; nevertheless, the culmination is startling, and the artistry veritably impeccable. I doubt if any of your writers will ever quite attain the high standard of Lovecraft at his best...."

[30, No. 6 (December 1937): 764.]

Charles H. Bert writes from Philadelphia: "... I felt a sort of spiritual affinity with 'Polaris' by H. P. Lovecraft. I am an amateur astronomer myself, and know those heavenly bodies cited by friend Lovecraft well."

[31, No. 2 (February 1938): 254-55.]

Bernard Austin Dwyer writes from West Shokan, New York: "... Next, I will mention a very short poem—*Lost Dream*, dedicated to our departed master Lovecraft, by Emil Petaja.[73] May I express my appreciation of how that little poem coincides with one's impressions of the works of Lovecraft? 'One fumbles in his scarlet cloak; I see his slender fingers move—he turns a key. ...' A silver key, of course. Congratulations to Mr. Petaja for his splendid little poem...."

[31, No. 3 (March 1938): 380-81.]

Teotihuacan

E. Hoffmann Price writes from Redwood City, California: "Hardly had I read a page of 'The Diary of Alonzo Typer'[74] when I suspected a hand from the grave: the certain touch of H. P. Lovecraft. Long before I reached the middle, I came to passages that I will wager none but HPL could have written. The last paragraph on the right half of page 160 was a dead giveaway. It conclusively proved HPL's writing. HPL and I discussed Shamballah at great length; I seriously doubt if any other writer in your pages ever made a reference to it. I am certain that the (authentic) *Book of Dzyan* never occurred in any of the works of your other authors. It is quite conceivable that someone may have run across that ponderous mountain of lore which is suggested by Shamballah in *Dzyan*, I admit. But all told, it sounds too much like HPL in its very presentation; I must either believe that HPL's ghost is walking, that William Lumley is, like the Dalai Lama, an incarnation of a previous master, or that this yarn is one of those oddly-named 'collaborations'. ... If William Lumley wrote that yarn without consultation with HPL, he has succeeded in a feat I had deemed utterly impossible: writing a story that is more like Lovecraft than Lovecraft himself! Whatever its history, I was glad to see it in print. The references to Shamballah reminded me of many a letter HPL and I exchanged, and of our own collaboration, a few years ago. Now here is a challenge to one or more of Lovecraft's followers: The Old Master had pondered, for some time before his death, on this matter of a weird story whose locale was to be the Valley of Teotihuacan—'the dwelling of the gods'—in the now bleak and desolate expanse of country somewhat north of Lake Texcoco, nearly forty minutes' drive from Mexico City. I had sent HPL photos, data, personal impressions and reactions to the pyramids and crypts of the valley. We had even planned, whimsically of course, to have Robert E. Howard join us in one expedition to Teotihuacan: I to be chauffeur, R. E. H. swordsman and gunner, and HPL to be necromancer for the party. And whenever I see their names it reminds me of a plan that was really not impossible, up until that tragic day in June of 1936 when R. E. H. went on an exploration unaccompanied by any of his friends. This whole issue, I might say, reminds me of the dead that have no equals among the survivors: Lovecraft, Howard, Whitehead. Like the Valley of Teotihuacan, the February issue is a memento of dead giants. Well, what valiant acolyte of HPL will fictionalize the mysterious Valley of Teotihuacan? Me, I am not equal to the task, though I have had quite a handful of Mexican adventure yarns in print since my jaunt south. Many wishes for a happy and prosperous 1938."

[31, No. 4 (April 1938): 506.]

H. Sivia writes from Palestine, Texas: ". . . I liked especially Kuttner's time-machine yarn[75] and Lumley's 'The Diary of Alonzo Typer', which is strangely reminiscent of Lovecraft's style. . . ."

[31, No. 4 (April 1938): 507-8.]

J. Vernon Shea, Jr., writes from Pittsburgh: "Far and away the best story in the February issue is 'The Diary of Alonzo Typer', the finest tale in months. I don't recall ever having seen the name of William Lumley before, and yet from internal evidence he would seem to be a Lovecraft protégé. He needs to learn only not to overcrowd his details, and to be a little more careful of his style. His story has a convincing touch of outsideness. . . ."

[31, No. 4 (April 1938): 509-10.]

A Tribute to Lovecraft

Jeffrey St. John Casserley writes from Klamath National Forest, Oregon: "It is strange, indeed, that I, who have been a reader of your unique magazine for nearly fourteen years, and who during that period enjoyed the splendid writing of H. P. Lovecraft, should for the first time, moved by the untimely passing of that master of the outré, undertake to express my humble appreciation now that it is too late. . . . In my opinion, Lovecraft ranked first among the five great masters of the realm of the unknown, and I think that you may agree with me when I state that Dunsany, Poe, Machen and Blackwood acknowledge no peers in the English language in their field save only Lovecraft. Oddly enough, the man's very name was indicative of the quality of his work, for if ever a man loved an inimitable style and was satisfied only with the finest of polished craftsmanship, that man was he whose passing leaves a place which can never again be filled. We say that he is dead; but surely his personality can never be obliterated, nor his memory fade. His work lives on, while perhaps by now he knows the answers to all of that which he so splendidly endeavored, as much as mortal man can, to bring to the world."

[31, No. 5 (May 1938): 639.]

Lovecraft

Paul S. Smith writes from Orange, New Jersey: "I was greatly pleased with Lovecraft's story, 'The Doom that Came to Sarnath', which appeared in the June issue. It is so beautifully written that it seems like a poem in prose. Would that the author was still with us: I find it very difficult if not impossible to believe that there will ever be another Lovecraft; but if William Lumley can maintain the high level of excellence he has shown in 'The Diary of Alonzo Typer', I think he will at least prove to be a worthy successor to the late master. This story and 'The Horror in the Museum' by Hazel Heald are, I think, the most Lovecraft-like productions you have published. . . ."

[32, No. 2 (August 1938): 253.]

Robert Black writes from San Antonio, Texas: "I have been reading your magazine for years—always in deepest appreciation. But this is my first letter. First, let me draw a great tide of maledictions onto my head by criticizing the dead master, Lovecraft, and his story, 'The Doom that Came to Sarnath'. All I can say is that he must have been reading some of Lord Dunsany's books before writing that—it has all the Dunsany touches and quirks—not like Lovecraft at all. . . ."

[32, No. 4 (October 1938): 509.]

Dunsany and Lovecraft

E. Hoffmann Price writes from Redwood City, California: "In the October Eyrie, Robert Black writes, re HPL's having read Lord Dunsany, and expecting maledictions from outraged HPL fans. They should not be outraged. When I saw HPL in 1933, he outlined his literary studies one night as we hoofed it through the older streets of Providence, Rhode Island, passing by the house of the widow who had, years ago, numbered Poe among her admirers.[76] This led to extensive discussion of Poe's influence on HPL's work; we sat in HPL's 'private graveyard,'[77] whose dramatic lighting, a blend of mist and arc-light and incredible shadows, was as striking as the maestro's word-pictures. Well—to cut short these recollections of HPL, I will say that he frankly admitted the strong influence of Lord Dunsany, just as strong as that of Poe. He said that his career had been a succession of such influences and that at the time he was laboring to turn out what he termed 'a less derivative' type of story. Thus, Mr. Black's observation is accurate, and just. No one was ever more frank and honest than HPL. And, I am sure, none of his admirers can justly be outraged at the idea that he, like most of us in this business, was influenced by Lord Dunsany and others."

[32, No. 6 (December 1938): 759.]

A Veritable Proteus

E. Hoffmann Price, of Kurdistan and points west, writes: "Derleth's interesting yarn in the March issue[78] is a colorful tribute to his late master, HLP [sic]. The sage of Providence did what very few accomplish: start a school of mythology! And Derleth, I think, has more of the real touch than any other of the disciples. Amazingly versatile, Derleth. A veritable Proteus. Somehow, it struck me that HPL's yarn, 'The Quest of Iranon',[79] symbolized his own career. This is hard to explain, but that was the reaction. It left me with the conviction that that beautiful bit of writing was rightly kept until after his death, and then published as an epitaph. Perhaps I have this idea because of his oft-repeated statement to the effect that the longer he worked and studied, the further he was from his aim as a writer; an estimate that no one shared with him."[80]

[33, No. 5 (May 1939): 151-52.]

Lovecraft's Works

Thomas O. Mabbott[81] writes from New York City: ". . . I do not know if Lovecraft or Howard was the greater loss, but as Howard was younger, the potential loss was worse. By the way, is there no chance of a collected edition of Lovecraft? He deserves one."

[34, No. 2 (August 1939): 157.]

Ray Douglas Bradbury[82] writes from Los Angeles: ". . . Lovecraft again proved his wizardry of words by chilling me with a draft of 'Cool Air'. I knew what was coming—but what a splendid build-up he gives us in his tales. No poetry this month. My only complaint on the issue. How about some more verse by Lovecraft? To me he is the Poe of poetry."

[34, No. 5 (November 1939): 123-24.]

Lovecraft Autographs

Willis Conover, Jr., writes from Cumberland, Maryland: "You will forgive me if I register my complete, unadulterated disgust at the so-called 'fan group' for permitting an unbelievable state of affairs to exist. The Lovecraft Memorial Volume[83]—ah, what a fine, noble thing it is for Messrs. Derleth and Wandrei to gather the writings of the beloved HPL for presentation in book form! We, the loyal fans of this late great one, rejoice and cry Hosanna! Nuts. There's a better word, but you won't find it in print. The 'fans' are generous with words, but when it comes to actually supporting the venture, every fist hides itself in a pocket. August Derleth and Donald Wandrei have worked on this volume for two years, confident that HPL's followers would back them up when the time came. Well, the time has come, and what's happened? About *one-tenth* of the money necessary to pay for publication has been received! If all the Lovecraft fans came through, there would be no difficulty in putting out this book, plus succeeding volumes of selected letters, etc. Derleth says he and Wandrei are going ahead anyway with the publication—but I don't doubt that their faith in the dependability of the fan group is as shaken as mine, and as is the faith of every *real* friend and follower of H. P. Lovecraft. The kindly, erudite Lovecraft is dead—but we who profess to be his fans are handing him another, a more complete, more final death. Not only are we slurring his memory, we are killing his chances for literary immortality. If we of his own circle do not accept him, who can believe that the world will? No additional 'inducement' should be necessary; but to the first five persons, and then to the tenth, fifteenth, twentieth, twenty-fifth, and thirtieth, who mention this letter in sending their subscriptions ($3.50 per copy) to August Derleth, Sauk City, Wisconsin, for the Lovecraft volume, I will mail a specimen of H. P. Lovecraft's own handwriting—his signature—either as an autograph to be kept with the book, or as an individual treasure, the personal mark of a man who deserves some small return for what he put into life. Lovecraft gave me these ten autographs just before he died to dispose of as I wished, and I am disposing of them in this manner. Derleth will forward those names and addresses to me.[84] Whether or not you receive one of the prize autographs, you will be the possessor of the first great monument to H. P. Lovecraft: the complete volume of his choice stories, some of which you may not have read elsewhere, and may never read elsewhere."

[34, No. 6 (December 1939): 120-21.]

The Lovecraft Tradition

August Derleth and Donald Wandrei, co-discoverers of *The Case of Charles Dexter Ward*, tell here of Lovecraft's working methods—and they put his story together.[85]

"When I first visited Lovecraft in Providence in the summer of 1927, he showed me among other things the ms. of a long story which he had just written. This was *Ward*. He had spent months writing it, but he simply refused to type it over for submission to magazines. He hated to typewrite anything, even a letter. The length of that particular story made the task seem superhuman, for him. At the time I was just learning how to operate a typewriter; I therefore proposed to gain experience by practising on his story. He agreed with alacrity, and I brought the ms. back to St. Paul with me.

"Then I discovered the full magnitude of what I had let myself in for. The story was written in longhand on the reverse side of letters he had received, some 130 or 140 sheets of all sizes and colors.[86] He didn't believe in margins or 'white space.' Every sheet was crowded from top to bottom, from left edge to right, with his small, cramped handwriting. That was his original draft; you can imagine what happened when he got through revising, words and sentences crossed out or written in, whole paragraphs added, inserts put on the back of the sheet where they got tangled up with the letters from his correspondents, and the inserts themselves rewritten with additional paragraphs to be put in the insert which was to be put in its proper place in the story. Lovecraft's handwriting was not easy to read under the best of circumstances; he had his own peculiarities of spelling, often used Latin and Greek phrases, and often used coined words of his own. These made the problem of deciphering his complex puzzle-pages even more difficult. All in all, working after my classes at the U., it took me four months to get through the labyrinth.

"My typescript was doubtless loaded with errors. When he received it, he may have decided that it would take as much time and trouble to correct my typescript as it would to retype it.[87] At any rate, there is no evidence that he took either step, or that he ever sent the story to any editor in any form.

"After Lovecraft's death, when we were collecting all the Lovecraft stories, published and unpublished, we located *Ward* in the possession of R. H.

Barlow and secured its loan. When the package came, there were the pages I had typed many years ago, but, to our consternation, only the first thirteen pages; and there was the original ms., but, to our greater consternation, less than half of it. After much correspondence, we decided that the rest of the ms. had been lost beyond any hope of recovery. Thus it was that *The Outsider and Others* was published over a year ago without this major Lovecraft story. Recently, however, we received from the same source the remainder of the ms. which had somehow been separated and mislaid. We at once were able to verify it as the complete ms. And by this time we had a typist skilled in reading Lovecraft's handwriting; even so, it took another two months to prepare a fresh typescript and to proofread it minutely.[88]

"That *Ward* should be published first in *Weird Tales* is natural and fitting.[89] The great majority of Lovecraft's tales appeared originally in *Weird Tales*; and to many of us who have read the magazine since its first issue the word *Lovecraft* and *Weird Tales* are almost synonyms. It was chiefly through *Weird Tales* that Lovecraft won recognition as being preeminent in his field, and, by his creation of the 'Cthulhu' mythology, came to exert a broad influence on other writers. *Ward* is one of the earliest stories in which he used the 'Cthulhu' mythology.

"After his first tales, there began to develop in his later ones a curious coherence, a myth pattern so convincing that readers began to explore libraries and museums for certain imaginary titles of Lovecraft's own creation. Probably the best known of these imaginary titles is the *Necronomicon* of the mad Arab Abdul Alhazred. 'Yog-Sothoth' and 'Cthulhu' were two of the entities or Old Ones in his mythology which were often used by other writers. It was in 'The Call of Cthulhu', originally published in *Weird Tales*, that this Cthulhu Mythology first became fully apparent. Lovecraft himself wrote in a letter, '—all my stories, unconnected as they may be, are based on the fundamental lore or legend that this world was inhabited at one time by another race who, in practising black magic, lost their foothold and were expelled, yet live on outside ever ready to take possession of this earth again—' In later stories in *Weird Tales*, like 'The Dunwich Horror' and 'The Whisperer in Darkness', he continued to develop the Cthulhu Mythology around the mysterious and terrible Old Ones who live on outside, and the secret rites and suppressed magic books that are the only surviving links to them.[90]

"It will indeed be a pleasure to see *The Case of Charles Dexter Ward* in print in the magazine where H. P. L. would most have wanted to see it published—thus rounding out the Lovecraft tradition and the Cthulhu mythology."

III. Comments from Readers

Any Lovecraft Photos in Existence?

Robert Rosen writes from the Bronx, New York:
"I have been a reader of WT for some seven years, and in that period I have had the pleasure of reading the superb creations of H. P. Lovecraft. His passing has left an unfillable gap in the ranks of creative fantasy literature, and it has been my unquenchable desire to secure a photograph of this great man. If you can in any way assist me in the securing of same, I will be in your gratitude always."

If anyone happens to know of any HPL pictures—how about letting us know? We could tell readers about it in the next issue—so that anyone who wanted a picture would know where to get hold of one.

[35, No. 9 (May 1941): 120-21.]

Where You Can Get a Photo of Lovecraft

From 2530 N. Oakland Avenue, Milwaukee, Wisconsin, Harold Gauer writes:
"I note an inquiry in the *Eyrie* about photos of H. P. Lovecraft. August Derleth once sent me a small picture of Mr. Lovecraft which I copied and enlarged for use on the dust jacket of *The Outsider*. I still have the negative and some 4 × 5 prints can easily be made from it. According to Mr. Derleth, it is practically the only photo available...."[91]

[35, No. 10 (July 1941): 122, 124.]

Outstanding Service

"You are performing an outstanding service in making 'The Shadow over Innsmouth' available to that part of Lovecraft's public which finds it difficult to afford a copy of *The Outsider and Others*; and that is a large part, believe me," writes August Derleth from Sauk City, Wisconsin. He goes on to say that the Lovecraft collection will soon be out of print—and that:

"'The Shadow over Innsmouth'[92] has never before seen publication in any magazine, or in any general form whatever, with the exception of once having been produced in book form in a privately printed and extremely limited edition.[93] This tale is one of the best, the most exciting of the longer tales belonging to the Cthulhu Mythology. Reference to it was made in at least two of my *Weird Tales* stories ('The Return of Hastur', 'Beyond the Threshold'[94]), which more than anything I can say testifies to the powerful hold it has upon the imagination of its readers. The precise place of 'The Shadow over Innsmouth' in the Cthulhu Mythology is not certain, but Donald and I have placed it between 'The Whisperer in Darkness' and 'The Shadow out of Time'. It was written before 'The Haunter of the Dark', 'The Dreams in the Witch-House', and 'The Thing on the Doorstep', and only *At the Mountains of Madness* apart from 'The Shadow out of Time' followed it in the Cthulhu Mythos.[95] That means that it followed closely in sequence upon some of the most successful of Lovecraft's stories—'The Dunwich Horror', 'The Call of Cthulhu', and 'The Colour out of Space'. It is a dark, brooding story, typical of Lovecraft at his best."

[36, No. 3 (January 1942): 125.]

"I should make it clear that I am *not* claiming that the mantle of Lovecraft has fallen upon my shoulders. It is only that, having worked with HPL's materials and works for so long in connection with Arkham House, I am at least heeding his admonition to develop the vein he opened. 'The Trail of Cthulhu' is one result, and 'The Dweller in Darkness' (to appear in an early issue of *Weird Tales*) is another.[96] If *Weird Tales* fans like these efforts, they need only say so, and there will be others. . . . *Weird Tales* bought my first story back in 1925, and for a while was my only market. I was 15 then, and 16 when the story was published ('Bat's Belfry' in the May, 1926 issue). Since then I have contributed to the magazine regularly . . . and as long as there is a *Weird Tales*, I hope it will continue to carry my work in its pages. I have always had for the magazine the strongest imaginable feeling of loyalty."

August Derleth

[37, No. 4 (March 1944): 107.]

Collectors' Items

Here is an interesting point made by Jack Snow whose yarn, "Seed", appears in this issue of *Weird Tales*.

"Bible of all alert book dealers in the United States, Great Britain and many other lands, *Publishers' Weekly*, features a section wherein book dealers may advertise for rare and out-of-print books wanted by their customers. . . .

"The above is a preamble to an incident which will delight H. P. Lovecraft's many readers and admirers. For in the July 7, 1945, issue of *Publishers' Weekly* a New York book dealer listed among books he is searching for *The Necronomicon* and Ludvig Prinn's *The Mysteries of the Worm*—mythical volumes invented by Lovecraft and mentioned in a number of his most popular stories.[97] Certainly these are the two rarest of all out-of-print books—they have never been in print! August Derleth, Robert Bloch and Henry Kuttner will particularly enjoy this since they have carried on the Lovecraft mythos by mentioning volumes in their stories in *Weird Tales*...."

[39, No. 3 (January 1946): 92.]

"The letter by Robert Paulive certainly calls for an answer in the pages of *Weird Tales*, so here is my contribution to same. I have been reading Lovecraft's stories ever since I discovered a book of them eight years ago, when I was ten years old; he is my favorite author, and the wonderful mythology he created is my favorite subject matter in a fantasy story.

"The Lovecraft or Cthulhu Mythos is a series of stories by Lovecraft and several of his fellow-writers, having a similar background and based on a pantheon of Elder Gods and demons created by Lovecraft. August Derleth, in his biography of HPL, says that the Cthulhu Mythos was in turn based on varied characters, places, and situations from several stories of early writers—Ambrose Bierce, Poe, Arthur Machen, and Robert W. Chambers. Lovecraft created the *Necronomicon* of the mad Arab Abdul Alhazred, and included passages and fragments of it in many of the stories of the series; he also wrote of the shadow-haunted and cursed towns of Arkham and Innsmouth, where much of the action of the Mythos takes place, and of the hidden places of the earth where ancient evil waits, watchful and ready to spring forth upon the world—Irem, the City of Pillars; R'lyeh, where dead Cthulhu lies sleeping; Ya-N'thlei [sic]; and the hidden Plateau of Leng."

Robert E. Briney,[98]
Wilmette, Ill.

"H. P. Lovecraft was born in 1890. He was early attracted to books (he wrote practically all his life); some people claim he read every book in his grandfather's huge library, and remembered everything in it.

"Early in his writing career he started writing weird tales; first he imitated the style of Lord Dunsany and then started developing his own oft-imitated style. This style describes the mysterious and terrible actions of the gods which Lovecraft names the Old Ones. Some of the most important of these Old Ones are Cthulhu, high-priest of the gods; Azathoth, shapeless Ruler of the Universe; Nyarlathotep, messenger of the gods, and many others. The *Necronomicon*, by the 'mad Arab Abdul Alhazred', together with other books, figures importantly in the Lovecraft circle lore. The general atmosphere of Lovecraft in his stories is one of morbid preoccupation with the thought of nearing doom; but hints are made of a great obscene rejoicing to come when the gods wake from their timeless sleep beneath the seas and become as powerful as they ever were. The Cthulhu cult meets to pray for the coming of this rising of the gods. Naturally, none of these cults or books or gods ever existed (I hope!) but Lovecraft describes them vividly indeed.

"Lovecraft died in Providence, his home town, in 1937, in his forty-seventh year. Writers of the Lovecraft group still carry on his tradition and make his memory and his writings known the world over."

Steven Nickman,
Ventnor, N. J.

"In regards to Mr. Paulive's query in the March, '52, issue of WT: The volume known as the *Necronomicon* is, alas, the fertile creation of the late and without a doubt, great master of horror fiction, H. P. Lovecraft. The Cthulhu Mythos is a great part of his imaginative conception of a hideous world of 'might-have-been.' As are the fabulous towns of Arkham, Dunwitch [sic], Kingsport, and dreaded Innsmouth.

"Perhaps it should be explained that Lovecraft wrote two distinct types of fantasy: the regional and grimly realistic tales of cosmic horror typified by such tales as 'The Dunwich Horror' and 'The Shadow out of Time'; the other type were his 'Dunsian' [sic] pieces like 'The Cats of Ulthar' and the short novel, *Dream-Quest of Unknown Kadath*."

Leif Arjen,
Rockford, Ill.

"The chronology of Lovecraft's *Necronomicon* was so convincing that many a book dealer has been called on to supply a copy! Lovecraft also created as supplements to his *Necronomicon* the *R'ley* [sic] *Text*; the *Book of Dzyan*,[99] and many more."

John Gatto,[100]
Uniontown, Pennsylvania

"Although the characters, books, places, incidents, names, etc., etc., that are used in the Cthulhu stories are fictional it is interesting to observe that both Bob Michael of the Werewolf Bookshop and book agent Philip C. Duschnes have at one time or another advertised as having for sale copies of the *Necronomicon*—Mr. Michael's edition was priced at $999,999.00 (that's right—nine hundred ninety-nine thousand, nine hundred ninety-nine dollars) while Mr. Duschnes wanted only $375 for his copy. In the face of such contradictory evidence I can only refer Mr. Paulive to any

competent and comprehensive biography of Howard Phillips Lovecraft—
and let him make his own decision!"

           Irving Glassman,
           Brooklyn, N. Y.

[44, No. 4 (May 1952): 91-93.]

 "You will undoubtedly receive many letters from old readers telling Mr. Robert Paulive of New York about the *Necronomicon* and the so-called Cthulhu myth. Is it not about time for *Weird Tales* to print the truth about one of the greatest myths fostered in modern times? Namely, that the *Necronomicon* and all that it implies is merely a product of H. P. Lovecraft's fertile imagination? Or don't you dare?

 "You see, *I have seen and handled a copy of the* Necronomicon! It was in 1927 in, of all places, Honolulu. It was 'owned' by a dubious Levantine character whom I met under equivocal circumstances. He permitted me to examine it for nearly half an hour. The volume was in quarto, and had obviously been rebound many times, the current binding of blackish green leather being cracked and broken. It ran to something over 400 pages, but the contents were in deplorable condition. Many sheets were missing, many mutilated, and all were brittle with age.[101] They were scrawled over with comments in many languages. Enough remained of the title page to show that the volume was printed in London in 1632.[102] I take it to have been one of a very small private edition, probably adapted from Wormius (as H. P. L. calls him). The book was poorly printed in heavy black letter, and was in Latin. Though not very fluent in that language I could make out enough to convince me that it was the real thing. The *Necronomicon*, as near as I could tell in the short time it was in my hands, appears to be divided into three main sections: 1. A history of magic and demonolatry on this planet; 2. A symposium of relations between the earth and other spheres and dimensions, such as 'Yuggoth', and 3. A terrible miscellany and collection of spells, formulae, and incantations.

 "I know perfectly well that H. P. L. was quite familiar with the *Necronomicon*, and no doubt owned a copy, or had access to one. I particularly looked for the original of one of his direct quotations from it, and found it in Section 2:

   "'Mortuus non credite illud quin latet aeterno
   Quum per saecula mira Mors etiam pereat.'[103]

 "This is as close as I can get to remembering the Latin after all these years. Well, the Levantine offered it to me for $300. He obviously wanted to get rid of it for some reason, but would not come below that price, which was cheap enough in all conscience. But I was broke in those days. I implored him to hold it for a week, and spent the time begging, borrowing, and stealing until I had made up the sum. But my man did not keep the appointment, and I never saw him again. Some time afterwards I learned that he had sailed hurriedly for China a few days after I met him.

"Yes, the *Necronomicon* does exist . . . and the implications stemming from its existence have often cost me my sleep at night. . . .

"My best wishes for the continued success to *Weird Tales*, which I shall continue reading so long as you publish it. Should you publish this letter in the 'Eyrie' please withhold my name and address, for a good many reasons, some of them—well, psychical. Neither do I wish to be deluged by letters from people to whom I can give no more information than I have given above. Nor will I, for any consideration, dispose of my complete file of *Weird Tales*."

Sincerely yours,
"An Old Reader,"
Bountiful, Utah

[45, No. 5 (July 1952): 93-96.]

"Though a regular reader of *Weird Tales*, it is seldom that I look at The Eyrie. However, I did happen to notice the inquiry by R. Paulive, published in the March issue. While on the subject of *The Necronomicon*—Manly Wellman told me once that one time in New York he happened to notice a small, dingy second-hand bookshop located in the cellar of an old, decrepit building. Being a book-collector and not being in a hurry at the moment, he went down the rickety stairs and into the place—dim, musty, and vaguely forbidding in its atmosphere. Old volumes of no possible interest to anyone were jumbled on shelves and standing on the floor in disorderly heaps. A glance told him that nothing was there that he wanted, and he was about to leave, when an old crone appeared, and asked 'Was there something you wanted?' Feeling obliged to have some justification for being in the shop, he said, "Have you a copy of *The Necronomicon*?' To Manly's consternation, she answered, 'Certainly,' and hobbled over to the dimmest and dustiest corner of the room and began pawing along shelf-backs. After a few moments, during which Manly didn't know whether to wait or to run, she said 'Humph! It was here just a few days ago, but it must have been sold.'

"It is a good story, and incidentally get Manly to do some more John Thunstone stories for you—and us, his readers."

J. H. Stewart Jr.,
Wichita, Kansas

[45, No. 5 (July 1952): 96.]

III. Comments from Readers

The Other Side Speaks—and Most Convincingly

"I have read with interest, and some amusement, the reverent letters sent by inveterate readers of H. P. Lovecraft in response to your request. However, with some misgivings and the suspicion that I shall not be very popular, I dissent from the general adulation, and admit that I do not greatly admire either the literary style of Mr. Lovecraft or the 'Cthulhu Mythos.' Amid the general acclamation, I feel called upon to submit my minority opinion, hoping to induce, thereby, a more critical attitude toward a seeming folk-hero of fantasy writing.

"Excepting some stories, and I by no means intend a blanket indictment of all of Lovecraft's work, I think that his style is prolix, affected, turgid, and labored. It is full of obvious and ill-concealed strivings for effect—'posing,' it might be called. Lovecraft apparently lacked the ability to tell a plain tale and tell it straight. He lacked the clarity and objectivity of a writer such as Ambrose Bierce, who evoked horror by a direct, clear, impeccable prose and added to its effect by a matter of fact detachment.

"Not even the most enthusiastic followers of Lovecraft, in Sauk City or elsewhere, can claim for him reticence and detachment. These two qualities, in my mind, are necessary for a good 'ghost story,' and Lovecraft lacked both completely. He always indicated the feeling supposed to be evoked in the reader with the use of the adjectives 'terrible,' 'horrible,' etc., on every page, and his style is so difficult to follow in many cases that one is often at a loss to know what is supposed to have taken place.

"As for the Mythos: A ghost story, like any other, should be credible enough to evoke in the reader 'the willing suspension of disbelief.' While perhaps one does not have to believe in ghosts to write about them, although it certainly helps, the writer must be able to suspend his own disbelief to make his story ring true, and Lovecraft utterly failed in this. All of the devices such as the invention of mad Arabs and the *Necronomicon* cover an obvious lack of sincerity, and, I fear, set the indelible and undesirable mark of the hack upon much of Lovecraft's work. And, if this be true of the master, how much more so of the pupils and imitators, who have attempted to perpetuate the 'Mythos.' In the majority of his stories, Lovecraft utterly failed to convince me of the possible reality of his elder gods and whatnot, undersea kingdoms, and other assorted unworldly flora and fauna. I am no sceptic: I am morally certain of the possibility of preternatural invasion of man's affairs, and am not at all hesitant to say so in print. Perhaps hence derives my enjoyment of well-written ghost stories, so that I feel that your efforts in the direction of exploring the Mythos are as hollow brass and tinkling cymbals, and, frankly, pretty much a waste of print. Better concentrate on getting some authors with a discipline in grammar, a sense of balance, and a real ability to write. August Derleth has this; it is frequently wasted on imitations of Lovecraft.

"I remain a loyal subscriber."

Joseph V. Wilcox
Albion, Michigan

[44, No. 6 (September 1952): 6.]

"I feel that last issue's letter from Joseph V. Wilcox contra H. P. Lovecraft contained enough misleading and opinionated matter to warrant a rebuttal in your pages.

"Mr. Wilcox objects to Lovecraft's style as 'affected, turgid, and labored.' That is to say, it was complex and dense. So was that of Poe. Lovecraft belongs among writers who cultivated a special manner consciously. As time passes, such writers tend to refine their style until an almost esoteric effect is produced. This makes for difficult reading, but if the style is warranted by the effect, it is certainly permissible. I feel that in the main Lovecraft justified his mannerisms by employing them skillfully and controlling them judiciously.

"If H. P. L. 'lacked the ability to tell a plain tale and tell it straight,' so did Machen, Conrad, Faulkner, and Dickens, to name just the first to come to mind. Neither clarity nor objectivity is necessary in the dream-like effect Lovecraft sought.

"Similarly, 'reticence and detachment' are not necessary for 'a good ghost story' (I can't think of a single true ghost story in Lovecraft's work). Reticence and detachment are earmarks of a *certain kind* of horror story; not of all. Lovecraft felt emotional involvement, and wrote that way. Concerning the Mythos and its genuine contribution to fantasy, I can only say that to me it rings true as an admirable feat of the creative imagination. In the midst of one of H. P. L.'s stories I momentarily share his superb escapist dream of an awesome cosmos of veiled, implacable forces and unknowably vast patterns. This is the highest praise I can offer this artist.

"*Weird Tales* has pioneered in presenting three unique talents of the first rank: Lovecraft, Derleth, and Bradbury. Each has his special strengths and weaknesses, each his special admirers. Though my preference is probably clear, I hope I do not overvalue my favorite to the point of undervaluing others."

James Wade[104]
Chicago, Illinois

[44, No. 7 (November 1952): 8.]

"With your kind indulgence and permission, I should like to defend what Mr. Wade was pleased to call my 'misleading and opinionated matter' in my letter (Sept. '52 *Weird Tales*) *contra*, as Mr. Wade says, the late and quite possibly great H. P. Lovecraft.

"In such a rejoinder, one runs the risk of saying nothing more than one said the first time, and I trust that I shall escape this particular pitfall.

"In the first place, Mr. Wade, in admitting that Mr. Lovecraft's prose was 'complex and dense,' with which I would be the last to quarrel, equates these terms with my 'affected, turgid, and labored.' If Mr. Wade has a dictionary at hand, which the general literary excellence of his letter would lead me to assume, he will very soon discover that to say that style is 'affected, turgid, and labored,' is *not* at all to say that it is complex and dense. One may be affected, turgid—which means bombastic or pompous—and labored, which means forced, not easy or natural, without being either complex or dense, although Lovecraft was certainly both.

"The reverse is equally true. The style of the late Nathan Cardozo was somewhat complex, syntactically, but it was certainly not turgid, labored, nor affected; it was natural to him, and was a joy to behold.

"I will stick by the requirements of reticence and detachment. You are not going to scare me by beating me over the head with 'eldritch' adjectives, or by telling me that Yog Shoggoth [*sic*] and his pals are the most awful, the most horrendous, the most damnable things on the face of the earth, or off it. If you can't convey your idea otherwise, it is not at all worth conveying.

"When Lovecraft was good, he was very, very good. I have never denied that he was. But when he was very, very good, as a general rule, he was writing more traditional stories: 'In the Vault', for example, as others, better critics than I, have observed before me. Incidentally, that particular story is very close to a 'true ghost story,' and so, in a lesser way, is 'The Terrible Old Man'.

"Well, undoubtedly Mr. Wade is of the same opinion still. *De gustibus.* And, incidentally, I shall continue to read W. T., despite the opinion of another of your letter writers that I have no business doing so."

Joseph V. Wilcox
Albion, Michigan

[44, No. 8 (January 1953): 8.]

B. *Astounding Stories*

Page Mr. Lovecraft!

Dear Editor:

The cover, as usual, is good. The interior illustrations are all right, but the artist who illustrated *At the Mountains of Madness* lacks the imagination of the others.[105] Schneeman should have illustrated this. Marchioni is unbelievingly improved, and Schneeman is fine. Wesso is far below his old standard.[106]

May I, Mr. Lovecraft, criticize the first installment of your serial? It is only because it is a fine story that I consider it worthy of the time to criticize. Invariably, in reading a story of this type I compare it with Merritt's *Moon Pool*, which is, of course, the perfect story in so far as perfection can be attained by mortals.[107]

In your story compared, not to the usual standard, but to perfection, I find a few faults: a lack of attention to detail and too much repetition; too many specific references to Necronomicon. Could you not have suggested the occult and the mystic in other ways? This is fault of all your stories. But *At the Mountains of Madness* was really good because you are an exceptional master of words, and of the mystic mood. . . .—L. M. Jensen, Box 35, Cowley, Wyoming.

[17, No. 2 (April 1936): 155.]

"Strange City" Again!

Congratulations are certainly in order—for two reasons. . . .

The second reason for congratulations is the coming of H. P. Lovecraft. *The Colour out of Space* holds a treasured place in my memory. Now the author is again turning to science-fiction and the result should be as great as occurred in the case of C. L. Moore. . . .—Donald Allgeier, 724 East Grand St., Springfield, Missouri.

Van Loren Is Promising. We'll Watch Him.

At the Mountains of Madness would be good if you leave about half the description out of it. . . .—Carl Bennett, Jodie, West Virginia.

[17, No. 2 (April 1936): 157.]

III. Comments from Readers

Astounding Thrives in a Crucible of Reader Opinion

Here's a hand for H. P. Lovecraft! At the Mountains of Madness is bound to be up to Lovecraft's usually high literary level, and it looks like a good story as well. Welcome, Mr. Lovecraft! . . .–L. A. Eshbach,[108] 209 West Greenwich St., Reading, Pennsylvania.

[17, No. 2 (April 1936): 159-60.]

Lovecraft Again

It was Lovecraft's name on the February issue which brought your magazine to my attention. As I make it a practice never to start a serial until I have all the parts I cannot pass judgment on this story yet. . . .–Harold F. Bensom, 56 Harris Avenue, West Warwick, Rhode Island.

[17, No. 3 (May 1936): 155-56.]

The Music Goes Round–

At the Mountains of Madness is one keen yarn. Let's hope it keeps it up. That first illustration rather gave one the feeling that the mountains were on an entirely different plane than the figures—rather a different set of dimensions as it were. . . .–Lyle Dahlbrun, 601 Benton Ave., Rock Rapids, Iowa.

[17, No. 4 (May 1936): 157.]

In the June Issue

All congratulations on the publication of H. P. Lovecraft's At the Mountains of Madness, one of the finest novels it has been my pleasure to read, irrespective of its excellence as an Astounding story. Don Wandrei tells me that Astounding Stories has another of H. P. Lovecraft's coming up; publication of Lovecraft's work is a signal step in the increasing excellence of the magazine.–August W. Derleth, Sauk City, Wisconsin.

A Veteran Speaks

The featured serial At the Mountains of Madness, by H. P. Lovecraft, is certainly a spellbinder and I do not intend to miss any of the installments. I believe it is one of the most fascinating stories that I have read, because of the realistic style of writing. . . .–Gene Pigg, 1909 N. 48th St., Seattle, Washington.

[17, No. 3 (May 1936): 158.]

Containing a New Suggestion

Seeing Lovecraft in the February issue caused me to excavate the September, 1927, issue of the first science-fiction magazine from my files and to read *The Color out of Space* over again for the nth time. I have never seen a more beautifully written story in a science-fiction magazine than that was. I am eagerly awaiting the rest of his latest story so that I can read it in continuity. . . .—Oliver E. Saati, 1427 Logan Ave., North, Minneapolis, Minnesota.

Opposed to Adventure

Congratulations on the splendid February number. All the stories were fine, although I thought *Cones*[109] was spoiled by the poor ending. If the rest of *At the Mountains of Madness* is as good as the first part, it will be a winner. . . .—Cecile Phazaton, 5 Hove Park Villa, Hove, Sussex, England.

[17, No. 3 (May 1936): 160.]

There's Always Room for Improvement

. . . And the February with the first part of *At the Mountains of Madness*! Truly that story will make history. Lovecraft, while lacking in ability to create vivid characters is excelled only by Edgar Allen [sic] Poe in creating a desired mood in his readers. His masterful description and his repetition of certain themes casts an almost hypnotic trance upon the reader which persists long after the story is finished. . . .

And then came April! The cover alone is enough to compensate for the worst story ever written. But no such compensation is necessary. Every story in the April issue is slated to become a classic. Lovecraft even supersedes his first two parts of *At the Mountains of Madness*, and in the same issue we have Binder and his *Spawn of Eternal Thought*, which ranks with the best, even in this, the first part, which in most serials is a bit dry. . . .—James L. Russell, 1126 Clement Ave., Charlotte, North Carolina.

[17, No. 4 (June 1936): 156.]

A Request for More Realism

Many thanks for the excellent serial by H. P. Lovecraft, and I hope that Astounding will print many more. What about a sequel to *At the Mountains of Madness*? . . .—Duane W. Rimel,[110] Box 200, Asotin, Washington.

III. Comments from Readers

We Like Opinions

At the Mountains of Madness would have been very good if Lovecraft hadn't overdone it by describing the walls and murals, etc. The ending was altogether boring and not up to average. Please, let's not have another such failure going under the alias of a serial. . . .—Gene Noguere, 3021 Laconia Ave., New York, New York.

On Artists and Imagination

How can any one say that Howard Brown has no imagination? His illustrations for *At the Mountains of Madness* gave that story a distinct air that made Lovecraft's superb style all the more enjoyable. . . .—Lew Torrance, 1118 Fifth Ave., Winfield, Kansas.

[17, No. 4 (June 1936): 157.]

He Says the 1936 Issues Are Better

I have purchased the April issue of Astounding Stories and, although I haven't read a single story, the illustrations seem to show the stories at least up to par. I have been keeping up with *At the Mountains of Madness* and I hope the ending is as interesting as the first part of the story. . . .—Calvin Fine, Box 441, Kilgore, Texas.

[17, No. 4 (June 1936): 157–58.]

On Lovecraft and Merritt

As to the perfection of *Moon Pool* I beg to differ. In my opinion, *Skylark of Space* by Smith[111] far outranked Merritt's work. However, Mr. Jensen has chosen an apt comparison. Merritt and Lovecraft are the outstanding contemporary fantastic authors. It is only fitting that the former's work be used as a yardstick by which to measure the latter's.

I personally prefer Lovecraft to Merritt, but I concede the superiority of *Moon Pool* over *At the Mountains of Madness*. The latter story really calls for a sequel, dealing with the Starkweather-Moore Expedition. . . .—Alan J. Aisenstein, 891 Academy Rd., Woodmere, New York.

We Do Try to Please

I am glad to see the conclusion to *At the Mountains of Madness* for reasons that would not be pleasant to Mr. Lovecraft.—Robert Thompson, Upper Darby, Pennsylvania.

Bricks in Plenty

I hope you take the inclosed "Irish confetti" in the spirit in which it is given. It has to do with the March and April issues which, to put it mildly, were far below your average.

First, why in the name of science-fiction did you ever print such a story as At the Mountains of Madness by Lovecraft? Are you in such dire straits that you must print this kind of drivel? In the first place, this story does not belong in Astounding Stories, for there is no science in it at all. You even recommend it with the expression that it was a fine word picture, and for that I will never forgive you.

If such stories as this—of two people scaring themselves half to death by looking at the carvings in some ancient ruins, and being chased by something that even the author can't describe, and full of mutterings about nameless horrors, such as the windowless solids with five dimensions, Yog-Sothoth, etc.—are what is to constitute the future yarns of Astounding Stories, then heaven help the cause of science-fiction. I know that it is your policy to print more of the whimsy type of science-fiction than of the type having science as a base but, at least, you don't have to wish this bunk on us. . . .—Cleveland C. Soper, Jr., 381 N. Firestone Boulevard, Akron, Ohio.

[17, No. 4 (June 1936): 159.]

Comprehensive Review

At the Mountains of Madness was praised by many but it didn't click with me at all. It dragged horribly and the absence of conversation spoiled it. Why such long discussions about things unfamiliar to most of us? Lovecraft may be good, but that story didn't raise him in my estimation. . . .—Cameron Lewis, 268 Shepherd Avenue, Kenmore, New York.

[17, No. 5 (July 1936): 156.]

We Can't Have Sequels to Everything

At the Mountains of Madness was rather dry, although a pretty girl and the appearance of the Elders would have made it an excellent story for a weird magazine. . . .—Harold Z. Taylor, 777 Luck Avenue, Zanesville, Ohio.

[17, No. 5 (July 1936): 158.]

Including Another New Idea

I have always considered you to be the perfect editor. Your acceptance of *At the Mountains of Madness* makes me all the more sure of my decision. It's the quality of story that those who rave of the "good old days" are looking for. *At the Mountains of Madness* is a story that can be read and re-read with greater enjoyment at each reading. Plenty of material for a sequel. I'm glad to know that another Lovecraft story is on schedule soon. . . .—Jack Darrow,[112] 3847 North Francisco Avenue, Chicago, Illinois.

[17, No. 5 (July 1936): 159.]

Page Stanton Coblentz!

The Shadow out of Time: Absolutely magnificent! I am at a loss for words. 'Twas one of the best tales I ever read. As much an improvement over *At the Mountains of Madness* as the auto over the horse. It started with a lot of description that I didn't like at all, but the middle and end were superb. Part of it actually sent chills up my spine, which a story seldom does. This makes Lovecraft practically supreme, in my opinion.—Cameron D. Lewis, 268 Shepherd Avenue, Kenmore, New York.

Piqued at Lovecraft

It's spring up here in the North, but there is cold winter in my heart because I have at least two bricks to throw at Astounding. I am a good-natured fellow, I hear, but I got mad when I read such trash as *At the Mountains of Madness*.

That was bad enough; but when I began to read *The Shadow out of Time* I was so darned mad that I was tempted to leave the story unfinished. However, I got through it somehow. I couldn't make sense out of either of Lovecraft's stories. So, please, for the love of me, cut out such stories in the future. . . .—Peter Ruzella, Jr., 23 Woodlawn Avenue, Massena, New York.

Lovecraft Again

I've just finished the June issue of "our" magazine and was duly impressed—perhaps not very favorably with *The Shadow out of Time*. I don't claim to be an authority on the subject but this type of story seems to me to belong in a fantastic magazine along with *The Chrysalis*.[113] I think Mr. Robert Thompson was a little off when commending the latter story as a marvelous piece of work.

I also think that Cleveland Soper, Jr., has the right slant on *At the Mountains of Madness*. In my opinion, it was drivel. Lovecraft is out of place in Astounding. In fact, it took me over two days to read his story, *The Shadow out of Time*. The word "horrible" began to pall on me. "Hideous" was another word of great repetition. I don't like to pan people but I think I'm justified in this case. . . .—Andy Aprea, Jr., 310 East Forty-fourth Street, New York City, New York.

And Again—but Favorable

Say, what's the matter with your readers' literary tastes, anyhow? Lovecraft's *At the Mountains of Madness* is perhaps the best-written story ever to find its way into Astounding's pages, yet I notice that a great number of fans have violently slammed it in your last two or three issues.

I can understand some fans' aversions to it, since it is more of the weird type of story than the truly scientific; but when it is condemned as being poorly written—well, all I can say is that these are the so-called fans, the type that revel in the stories written in the Van Lorne[114] disconnected style, who have pulled science-fiction and its followers way down in the estimation of prominent literary critics. . . .—Corwin Stickney, Jr.,[115] 28 Dawson Street, Belleville, New Jersey.

Well, I Read It!

I'm fed up with Lovecraft and this is the worst yet. I think *The Shadow out of Time* is the height of the ridiculous. I was disgusted and horror-stricken with that page of hideous monsters. . . .—James Ladd, 2700 Hershell Street, Jacksonville, Florida.

One for Writers to Read

You say that you want opinions. All right, I'll dissect the June issue—and tell you just what I think of it.

The Shadow out of Time: I don't know whether I liked it or not. Lovecraft's stories are too tedious, too monotonous to suit me. I finish one of his works with the feeling of having wasted my time. Still, on the other hand, there is something about them that "gets me." Memories of the "Old Ones" and the "Great Race" shall linger with me for a long time.

If Lovecraft could only create real characters and action to go with his superb, but lifeless fantasy, he would put out some classics. But things being as is, don't give us Lovecraft too often, editor: we shall tire of him quickly. . . .—O. M. Davidson, Jr., Box 24, Ged, Louisiana.

[17, No. 6 (August 1936): 154–55.]

Sequels Again

I would like to know where Mr. Soper, Jr., gets the idea that the April issue is far below par. Perhaps to him *At the Mountains of Madness* was a little unreasonable, but to me the magazine as a whole was very, very good. . . .—Calvin Fine, Box 441, Kilgore, Texas.

A General Discussion

Lovecraft's *The Shadow out of Time* was very disappointing. Like his *At the Mountains of Madness*, the yarn was all description and little else. Lovecraft is a master when it comes to describing things—there's no doubt about that. But a story has to have more than just description to click. . . .— Charles Pizzano, 11 Winthrop Street, Dedham, Massachusetts.

The Quarterly Again!

The Shadow out of Time is the best story in the issue. It is much better than Lovecraft's other novel, *At the Mountains of Madness*. Maybe it is because it is shorter. Yes, I guess that's what it is. . . .—John V. Baltadonis, 1700 Frankford Avenue, Philadelphia, Pennsylvania.

After a Year

Your June issue is a top-notcher—not a bad story. *The Shadow out of Time* is very good. . . .—James Taurasi,[116] 137-07 32nd Avenue, Flushing, Long Island.

Science-fiction and Fantasy

I have meant to write you ever since the end of *At the Mountains of Madness*, which was too poor for further comment. . . .

The Shadow out of Time was good, but I think Lovecraft dwells too much on fear and horror. . . .—Richard Rhein, Evanston, Illinois.

Science-fiction Doesn't Have to be Scientific

I snatch time from an early lunch to begin a letter of loud damn and faint praise—the damn being for your reading audience in general, the praise for H. P. Lovecraft for being a craftsman and an artist, quite regardless of whether or not he is a scientist. I can't understand the more or less general condemnation of his stories. Is it that they are not scientific? Neither are a good half of the stories printed in the last three issues. . . .

Lovecraft refuses to add the usual space ships and disintegrators to his tales; therefore, he does not write science-fiction. All right, he doesn't! But his stuff is worth admitting to the magazine on literary merit alone.

You have only three or four authors who could qualify as authors *only*, not merely as authors of science-fiction, and Lovecraft is one of them. His stories stand rereading better than almost any others you have printed.

Lovecraft does much the same thing in his stories that Tschaikowsky does in his music—his climaxes are obvious, yet you always get a kick out of them. In my own case, at least, his description is so convincing that I wonder: Is this man chiseling his stories out of fresh, uncut granite, or is he merely knocking away the detritus of some age-old carving? His lore has all the somber ring of truth. You get the general idea. I like Lovecraft. . . .—W. B. Hoskins, 65 N. Pleasant Street, Oberlin, Ohio.

[17, No. 6 (August 1936): 156-58.]

Curiosity Is Aroused

Lovecraft's *At the Mountains of Madness* is a humdinger: I think it deserves a sequel. I'd like to know about the delightfully horrible things "over in them thar hills." Also, another expedition could destroy the monster and discover some of the wonderful lost race still existing. . . .—Leslie A. Croutch, Parry Sound, Ontario, Canada.

[17, No. 6 (August 1936): 160.]

IV. Criticism from the Fan World

H. P. Lovecraft, Outsider

August Derleth

> The following appears to be the first article on HPL by August Derleth (1909–1971) to be published after HPL's death, although "A Master of the Macabre" (see below) was probably begun earlier. It appeared in the little magazine *River* 1, No. 3 (June 1937): 88–89, and contains the first known citation of the spurious quotation "All my stories, unconnected as they may be . . ." The article was reworked into the introduction to *The Outsider and Others* (1939).

> "As for the proper course for a young writer—I would say that it is to forget all about time and place, to assimilate all that is soundest throughout the literature of his ancestors, and to express what he has to say in that manner which his background-knowledge impels him to regard as most powerful and artistic. That is what I have tried to do. . . . There is no question but that realism must form the groundwork for any first-rate piece of writing, no matter how far from reality the author may push any one line of development. Unless the writer knows how to describe and vivify the every-day scene around him, he will never know how to describe and vivify anything. But although he must begin at home, there is of course no obligation for him to stay there."[1]
>
> —H. P. Lovecraft

He is dead now: on March 15th, in his forty-seventh year: and I doubt whether there is often aroused by any one man's passing so spontaneous a grief among all who knew him—not alone for the qualities of the man but for the curious position he held in the world of contemporary letters. About his life there is little to say save that he was born, his constant ill health made him virtually a recluse, and he died. About too many writers there is even less to say. But in the comparatively short period of his major writing—scarcely two decades—he gradually assumed a position unique among his fellow writers as the outstanding American exponent of the macabre tale. And at the same time, to those to whom he wrote, he became a correspondent without equal, a letter-writer who might have sprung full-bodied from eighteenth century England.

Because of his early ill health, H. P. Lovecraft became an omnivorous reader; he read everything upon which he could lay his hands; and out of that voluminous reading grew his lasting respect for the manners and customs of the eighteenth century. "Indeed," he wrote on one occasion, "the eighteenth century is the key to my whole personality. I was born two hundred years too late, and never feel quite at home for lack of a powdered periwig and velvet small-clothes."² Not only did he unconsciously make an effort to conduct himself as he might have done had he lived two centuries earlier, not only did he surround himself with eighteenth century objects, but his prose, his poetry, and above all his letters took on a leisureliness which sets them distinctly apart from all others. His enforced seclusion lent to him a perspective more farsighted than he might otherwise have had; thus he was able in his correspondence to take a long view of present-day phenomena, and whether he wrote of Mussolini, of Poe in Providence, of Proust, of proletarian literature, of the cinema, he maintained an absolutely impartial point-of-view, as if, indeed, he were writing from a vantage point two centuries removed. And gradually there grew up around him a circle of correspondents, most of whom he had never seen, a circle which can be likened only to a literary salon, a transplanting of a past phenomenon into a contemporary mould.

From Greek mythology and the *Arabian Nights*, from Poe, Baudelaire and Dunsany, he derived his admiration for the weird. He had already in his teens edited an amateur journal of astronomy and had early been caught in the fascination of outside spaces, and not much later he became affiliated with the United and National Amateur Press Associations, groups of young editors and writers who preceded the little magazines and reviews in point of time but strove to serve much the same ends, save with a more journalistic bent. At about this time he began to write; already having tried his hand with moderate success at eighteenth century versification, he now began to construct fantasies, dream-fabrics which he later saw bore some resemblance to the work of Lord Dunsany, with which he was not then familiar. From pure fantasy, Lovecraft went on to terror and horror, and presently he was writing such remarkable tales as "The Outsider," "The Rats in the Walls," "The Music of Erich Zann," "The Colour out of Space," "The Whisperer in Darkness," and "The Dunwich Horror," two of which appeared on Edward J. O'Brien's Roll of Honor, and all of which were listed at various times in both O'Brien and O. Henry Memorial volumes, as were many others of his stories.³

After a time there became apparent in his tales a curious coherence, a myth-pattern so convincing that after its early appearance, the readers of Lovecraft's stories began to explore libraries and museums for certain imaginary titles of Lovecraft's own creation, so powerful that many another writer, with Lovecraft's permission, availed himself of facets of the mythos for his own use. Bit by bit it grew, and finally its outlines became distinct, and it was given a name: the Cthulhu Mythology: because it was in "The Call of Cthulhu" that the myth-pattern first became apparent. It is possible to trace the original inception of this mythology back through Robert W. Chambers' little-known *The King in Yellow* to Poe's *Narrative of A. Gordon Pym* and Bierce's "An Inhabitant of Carcosa"; but in these stories only the barest hints of something outside had appeared, and it was Lovecraft who constructed the myth-pattern in its final form. In his stories then he merged fantasy with terror, and even his poetry took on certain symbols of the mythos, so that presently he was writing: ". . . all my stories, unconnected as they may be, are based on the fundamental lore or legend that this world was inhabited at one time by another race who, in practising black magic, lost their foothold and were expelled, yet live on outside ever ready to take possession of this earth again . . .", a formula remarkable for the fact that, though it sprang from the mind of a professed religious unbeliever, it is basically similar to the Christian mythos, particularly in regard to the expulsion of Satan from Eden and the power of evil.

Lovecraft himself had no very high opinion of his work. "The only thing I can say in favour of my work is its sincerity,"[4] he wrote not long before his death. He was himself aware of its faults and limitations; he knew better than anyone else how insidiously the commercialism of pulp requirements affected his tales; he made no effort to widen his scope, though in his thousands of letters are embodied many an essay, formal and informal, including some fascinating whimsies, such as his fanciful biography of "Ibid." Of his work only so long ago as 1931, he wrote: "it is excessively extravagant and melodramatic, and lacks depth and subtlety. . . . My style is bad, too—full of obvious rhetorical devices and hackneyed word and rhythm patterns. It comes a long way from the stark, objective simplicity which is my goal . . ."[5] But if anything, this is, despite its sincerity, evidence of his excessive modesty.

His record of publication is not large—some fifty titles chiefly in *Weird Tales*, and anthology representation in Dashiell Hammett's *Creeps by Night*, and T. Everett Harré's *Beware After Dark*, among others. He was published abroad, ranging from *The London Evening Standard*[6] to the *Not at Night* anthologies of Christine Campbell Thomson. His closest successors to his unofficial title of master of the macabre were among his best friends: Clark Ashton Smith, and the late Henry S. Whitehead. His only equal was Edith Wharton—Gertrude Atherton, Irvin S. Cobb, Dubose Heyward, and some few others having done too little in the field for all the excellence of what they had written. His only book is the badly printed and bound *The Shadow over Innsmouth*, published in April, 1936.[7]

Now that he is dead, there are signs of awakening interest in his work. Neither his prose nor his poetry will ever attain the status of world recognition, but his genius will be recognized, his work will be appreciated by that comparatively small but widespread public who read Machen, de la Mare, Dunsany, Blackwood, and Montague Rhodes James, and, as the years pass, it will become more evident, all questions of merit aside, that H. P. Lovecraft was a literary outsider in his time.

I salute not only his curious genius, but his magnificent spirit, as a writer, he stands among the best in his field, however limited that may be; as a man, he had no contemporary equal, for even as Oliver Alden was the last puritan,[8] so Howard Phillips Lovecraft was the last gentleman.

A Master of the Macabre

August Derleth

> The following apparently began as a review of the Visionary Press edition of *The Shadow over Innsmouth* (1936), but metamorphosed into a memorial article. It first appeared in *Reading and Collecting* 1, No. 9 (August 1937): 9–10.

It is a sad and ironic commentary on the reading public and publishers in general that the first book by an American writer who is a master of the macabre with every right to be placed among Shiel, Blackwood, James, Machen, and de la Mare should have been issued by an obscure publisher, that, moreover, it should be incompetently proofed and badly printed, and that the title chosen from among the available works should not be the best, even though it is a horror tale of a high order. But whatever the Visionary Publishing Company did not do, it succeeded in creating a Literoddity which will be long sought after by students and lovers of the macabre in fiction, when it published in April, 1936, H. P. Lovecraft's *The Shadow over Innsmouth*, illustrated with woodcuts by Frank Utpatel.

Howard Phillips Lovecraft, one of the last members of a family that had been in America four centuries, died March 15 of this year in Providence, Rhode Island, at the age of forty-six; at that time he had been writing for publication for over twenty years. But until the Visionary venture of last year, he had achieved nothing beyond magazine publication and inclusion in anthologies, among them T. Everett Harré's *Beware After Dark*, the well-known Christine Thomson *Not at Night* series, and Dashiell Hammett's *Creeps by Night*. When the first of his manuscripts came to the desk of Edwin Baird, then editor of *Weird Tales*, the editor waved it aloft with loud hosannas and sent it post-haste to press as the kind of material for which he longed but seldom received. Thus began, inauspiciously enough, Lovecraft's introduction to a wider reading public than the amateur press journals in which his work had previously appeared. *Weird Tales*, under Baird's editorship and under that of his successor, Farnsworth Wright, has published more stories by H. P. Lovecraft than all other magazines together, including among them many a title long since enshrined in the memory of his devoted readers—"The Outsider," that haunting graveyard tale which might have been written by Poe; "The Rats in the Walls," the most memorable horror narrative I have ever read; the often-reprinted "The Music of Erich Zann"; and most of the tales comprising what is loosely referred to as "the Cthulhu mythology" of Lovecraft's creation: an entire mythos of legendary gods and evil forces from outside, touching only occasionally upon this everyday world of ours; this he built up from a few hints deriving originally from Poe's *Narrative of A. Gordon Pym*, and Bierce's "An Inhabitant of Carrosa," and, just prior to Lovecraft's literary beginnings, further elaborated by Robert W. Chambers in that writer's little-known volume, *The King in Yellow*. In one of his letters, Lovecraft says: ". . . all my stories, unconnected as they may be, are based on the fundamental lore or legend that this world was inhabited at one time by another race who, in practising black magic, lost their foothold and were expelled, yet live on outside, ever ready to take possession of this earth again . . .", which will be recognized as being basically similar to the Christian mythos regarding the expulsion of Satan and the constant power of evil. In another letter, he adds, "All my tales are based on the fundamental premise that common human laws and interests and emotions have no validity or significance in the vast cosmos-at-large. . . . Only the human senses and characters have human qualities. These must be handled with unsparing *realism* (*not* catchpenny romanticism), but when we cross the line to the boundless and hideous unknown—the shadow-haunted *Outside*—we must remember to leave our humanity and terrestrialism at the threshold."[9]

Despite the fact that the bulk of Lovecraft's tales saw the light of day in pulp magazines, he was not without recognition in his lifetime. It is significant that many a contemporary writer has borrowed facets of his mythology for use; some critical acclaim has come to him by way of his anthology appearances; and Edward J. O'Brien gave many a star to his stories, triple-starring "The Colour out of Space" and "The Dunwich Horror," two of his finest tales, which appeared almost a decade ago. The

O. Henry Memorial Prize collections have likewise listed Lovecraft titles year after year.

The Shadow over Innsmouth, while not representative of Lovecraft's best work, is yet eminently worthy of notice. It is the tale of a traveler's being drawn to shunned Innsmouth on the Massachusetts coast, and of what an unearthly horror he finds to send him fleeing in terror for his life. But that is not all; the mounting crescendo of frightful horror is not enough, for the tale ends with a shocking anti-climax all along subtly hinted at but never quite revealed. The narrative is told in the first person, as are the majority of Lovecraft's stories. It begins prosaically enough, and yet almost immediately there becomes apparent a sinister undercurrent. The actual visit to Innsmouth discloses a strange air not so much of desertion as of secret, nocturnal habitation, and the aspects of the citizens do not reassure the narrator; they were "repellent-looking," they had an odd "fish-like odor," they seemed to be suffering from some strange infliction, and had what the narrator comes to term "the Innsmouth look." Then the scene stirs to life, the sinister undercurrents well forth, the narrator's odd fear and loathing crystallize into tangible horror, and, after listening to an incredible narrative from an old native, he finds confirmation on every hand, finds himself unable to escape Innsmouth by the regular channels, and is at last forced to flee for his life with an unspeakable horror at his heels. But he escapes, he comes free, he awakes from his terror-induced swoon to a "gentle rain," and the reader has just time to draw a breath of relief before the shocking revelation of the anti-climax bursts upon him.

Lovecraft himself had no very high opinion of his work. Perhaps those publishers who requested sight of his stories are in part responsible; certainly a careless editor can too easily fail to recognize the merit that a fellow craftsman cannot escape seeing. He had become inured to being told that the public will not buy short stories; he had read often enough about publishers' reluctance, the trend of the times, the fickle public. One of the largest American publishers offered to publish a collection if Lovecraft could guarantee that a first edition would be sold out.[10] Any reader of his stories could have assured that without hesitation, but Lovecraft could not. The publisher had made a tactical error, and Lovecraft recalled his manuscript. Since then, he had sent his collection to no one, and hesitated to respond even to the urging of his closest friends.

There is now in preparation a comprehensive collection of the writings of H. P. Lovecraft, and a first volume, *The Outsider*, including the bulk of his short stories and his masterly study, "Supernatural Horror in Literature," may appear before the year is out. A second omnibus, to follow next year, will contain his best poems and various prose pieces, and finally, a third, *Selected Letters*, will certainly establish him as a letter writer perhaps without equal in our time. Until these books appear, a slightly wider audience may know what hint of an unknown, unexplored fund of macabre tales lies behind *The Shadow over Innsmouth*.

Disbelievers Ever

R. W. Sherman

Almost nothing is known of R. W. Sherman. The following, one of the first articles on HPL to appear in the fan press, first appeared in *Amateur Correspondent* 2, No. 2 (September–October 1937): 11.

(Dedicated to the Late H. P. Lovecraft)

How ironic is the attitude of humans towards genius of any kind! Subjected to the ridicule and whims of narrow-minded people, the great inevitably go to their death long before the time appointed. Whether directly or indirectly, public sentiment will always play an important part in the life of any man—especially in the lives of those who openly and without recourse to hypocrisy present their unorthodox themes to skeptical eyes.

Such a man was the late H. P. Lovecraft. Throughout the course of his entire literary career he found himself wedged between two factions—a group of enthusiastic followers who worshipped his very name, and a clique of vehement scoffers who seemed to achieve delight in the berating of this master. Which one was the more irritating remains a moot question. His admirers, spurred on by his kindly, intelligent aid in their own endeavors, succeeded only in unearthing further troubles to place upon his already bowed shoulders; while his critics reeled blast upon blast of biting criticism of his works across the editorial desk.

Always strife. Always trouble and hardship. And suddenly, with serpentine swiftness, death intervenes.

For a while there is a stunned silence, a cessation of activities. Lovecraft's followers are stricken by the appalling suddenness of the disaster; in the minds of his critics there is great mental conflict regarding the advisability of continuing on their past course. Unwillingly, forced by their consternation, they once again peruse the works they had so bitterly condemned. And, fighting through wave after wave of weakening resistance, the seed of the genius of the man takes root in their minds. They read further with greater concentration, and the seed begins to sprout. In a flash, the implanted idea has grown to maturity, and they are overcome by many bewildering emotions.

They arise, shaken in soul. In a moment their course, as they see it, is set. In a vain endeavor to cover up their blind criticism, they glibly sing his praises and raise fantastic monuments to his greatness. Too late they have seen the light; and the thought most appropriate for their behavior lies in the last lines of Felix Kowalewski's poem, "Death of the Artist":

> "O Muse of Art, what bitter irony!
> Alive they hound, but dead they worship me!
> 'Tis my poor name floats up in cadenced song!"[11]

The Last of H. P. Lovecraft

J. B. Michel

> John Blythe Michel (1917–1969) was a science fiction fan and writer who published some stories under the pseudonym "Hugh Raymond." The following article, first published in the *Science Fiction Fan* 4, No. 4 (November 1939): 3–7, touchingly speaks of his visit, with Donald A. Wollheim, to HPL's last residence, 66 College Street in Providence. Michel's concluding remarks spurred a rebuttal by Autolycus (see below).

I never knew H. P. Lovecraft.

He died at a time when I had approached the point of writing to him in connection with some allusions of his to a story of mine which appeared in a certain issue of *The Californian* magazine.[12]

The total sum of knowledge concerning this remarkable man came then and comes now from Donald A. Wollheim who had something more than a nodding acquaintance with him. In all of his observations of the great writer I detected a note of colossal respect, an invisible, hidden obeisance to the mind (and later) to the memory of the man whom Robert W. Lowndes has called "the last great bourgeois philosopher."

Aside from these comments and sundry other observations, Lovecraft to me was always a great dark, legendary being, swathed in the folds of long-gone centuries, a man of whose actual existence in our times I was never too certain. When the round-table talk turned to him in the few months before his death this impression grew upon me. But when Wollheim proposed to a group of interested people his plan to save Lovecraft from being corresponded to death by the plethora of fans deluging him with mail, I suddenly became aware of him as a very much alive personality.

It is my ill luck never to have met him personally. But I am content with the few final impressions I have preserved of Lovecraft, the memory of two rooms in an ancient house in Providence, R. I., buried in the stately past that Lovecraft loved and to which he escaped from a world he never quite knew or understood, a harsh, cruel, cellophane-wrapped planet born too suddenly out of the soft hand-kissing ways of the eighteenth and nineteenth centuries.

Wollheim and I went to Providence for the purpose of visiting that house which even then had begun to be regarded as something of a shrine.

The city exuded an atmosphere so tangible that I felt it almost immediately we had left the train. From all sides about us low hills rose slantingly to the horizons. We stood in a sort of cup-shaped hollow and the town climbed about us in row on row of ancient, red-brick structures, with only the suggestion of a modern building or two in the business district.

It is a place of no especial rush and hurry. Except for the roaring railroad terminal it might very well have been just another country town lost somewhere in the hills. Civilization does not seem to have changed its soul. It is a town of tradition. We walked along "College" streets and "Pine" streets and "Market" streets, all lined with tall and stately trees. On our journey up the slope toward the great college in whose vicinity stands the Lovecraft home we met hardly another soul. On a sleepy Sunday, Providence is very still, very majestic and clean and white.

The house was a perfect frame for the life of the man who once lived in it. Shut off from direct view of the sloping street by a bend in a long, brick-walled alley, it hid from the large imposing library building beside it, the waving branches of trees surrounding it like upthrust arms warding off the threat of absorption into a busy, moving world. We stood before it at last and gazed down the hill through the quiet, still air.

To the eye, the house, the town, the trees and the sky was a frozen world of wax, and faded, imprisoned color. Steeples and gables of forgotten years filled the whole, circling horizon.

Lovecraft's aunt, Mrs. Gamwell, met us at the door. She was a very sweet lady, not long past middle age with an aura of crinoline and bouquets of violets and old lace about her. We walked up a flight of narrow stairs together. She took our hats, ushered us down a short corridor and into a large room.

Suddenly I realized why Lovecraft had withered outside it.

It was an artist's studio, minus the huge-slanting windows, but very reminiscent of the conventional, a low-ceilinged, broad and long sort of room with its walls and floor bathed in sunlight that poured in a flood of rich gold through quaintly curtained windows and half-hidden embrasures.

It was of another set of years, a dust collector of the traditions, tastes and substance of a particularly nostalgic section of the past when Poe wandered about the back streets and hill back alleys of this place.

A lot of oddly assorted moods and atmosphere seemed to have caught on its gingerbread character as it plowed through decades.

Plants and growing tendrils filled whole corners. Lovecraft's desk, set against the north west window, was untouched. His pencils, pens, blotting paper, instruments of writing and many scraps of note paper lay as though the author had left but for an instant.

Large squares of brilliant sunlight caught the desk-top in an interlocking web of light as the light came through the window, throwing the low-backed, angular chair behind it into polished relief. The window itself was wreathed in growths of vines and brightly colored flowers. It was the cheeriest spot in the room.

Outside it was mahogany gloom, scarred and heavy with shadows where the golden sunlight did not lay.

Mrs. Gamwell touched a photograph of Robert H. Barlow laying on a small, wicker-work table.

"He's a dear boy," she breathed.

We talked for many minutes. She told us of her nephew's last days, his dry humor and his indifference as death approached. He had gone out of the world in scorching agony, the victim of an obscure but malignant disturbance of the digestive organs. As she spoke it seemed as though he had died bereft of his friends but secure in the embrace of the past he clung to even in death.

We saw a new phase of Lovecraft through her words, an eager, boyish side, impulsive, even rash. Through her weaving it was easy to imagine him sitting wrapped in an old bathrobe on the spiderish chair before his desk, writing, a Voltaire *sans* smarting sarcasm and biting rhetoric.

There was another room, a small one, its door almost invisible amongst a wilderness of large chromos and hard-stacked bookcases. It was his bedroom, replete with countless tiny *objets d'art*, sculptures and paintings by Barlow, old prints and bits of glass. We lingered in it only a moment. It was repulsive, dingy, unrelieved by light.

Then for awhile we were alone.

Donald prowled, fingering the bindings of the books, that lay in the interminable rows of shelves by the hundreds. He glanced at them hungrily with the eye of the collector. I stalked about uneasily, ferreting out atmosphere, fingering gingerly smallish plaster sculptures by Clark Ashton Smith sneering somewhat at the air of faded primness and retreat that permeated the house. But as the afternoon wore on I felt a sympathy with the room, with its late occupant, growing. For a very little while I felt very close to Lovecraft. It didn't seem incongruous then, the identity in my mind of the austere, mature giant of literature and myself a very young and very immature man, callow, brash and filled with ignorant contempts.

The mood passed. I saw again, in a light of mixed sympathy and disinterest, the tumbled heaps of papers, the dirty, endless rows of books, ancient tomes and manuscripts, cracked with age, the dusty futile remnants of a life.

What a charming anachronism the house was! It does not belong in this world and it cannot long remain. It faded romantically into a twilighted distance as we left, lost in a horde of other houses wrapped in vines lit ruddy by the sun. I remember saying something then to Wollheim about his luck to have known Lovecraft. But I am not sure of my own desires upon that point. I am not too envious, even now that the distance of the years increases the stature of the author, of the group of people who knew him intimately, Barlow, Long, Campbell, Derleth, Loveman and others.

Lovecraft, for all his giant knowledge and piercing, calculating intellect, was the deadly enemy of all that to me is everything, an inflexible Jehovah-man, a gaunt, prophet-like high priest of dark rites and darker times, clad in funereal robes and funereal visage, gazing with suppressed hate upon a great new world which placed more value upon the sanitary condition of a bathroom fixture than all the greasy gold and jewels. The bones and dirt-crushed half knowledge of a thousand and a thousand-thousand kingdoms of the hoary past, whose faithful chronicle he was and in which he lived.

What of H. P. Lovecraft? or, A Commentary upon J. B. Michel

Autolycus

It is not known who is the fan hiding behind the pseudonym "Autolycus" (in Greek mythology, a son of Hermes and the grandfather of Odysseus). In this article, Autolycus takes exception to

J. B. Michel's criticism of Lovecraft's purported neglect of contemporary sociopolitical developments. The article first appeared in the *Science Fiction Fan* 4, No. 6 (January 1940): 11–15.

I, too, never knew Lovecraft. Though I have read his masterpieces of darkling fantasy, abhorrent evil and loathsome cults, though I have followed his gigantic strides toward the goal he finally reached—genius—, though I have been a humble admirer since his works first appeared in *Weird Tales* some fifteen years ago (I had already been through the First World War and three other campaigns when the first issue of *Weird* startled a realism weary world,—and that should date me as one of the oldest fans), yet I admired from afar and could not summon up courage even to write to one of the most amazing phenomena ever to enter American literary history.

Perhaps it was best that way. At times I deeply regret not having met Lovecraft face to face or to have had the honor of receiving one of his inestimable letters, yet perhaps it is best that I can view his writings dispassionately, as literature, without being dazzled by the aura of his personality. In this way, I can tilt a lance with J. B. Michel without a feeling of personal rancor. I am no sycophant, no Boswell.

To what does Michel object in his article on Lovecraft, appearing in the November FAN? Let me quote in part:—"Lovecraft was the deadly enemy of all that to me is everything—gazing with suppressed hate upon a great new world which placed more value upon the sanitary condition of a bathroom fixture than all the greasy gold and jewels, etc.—"

As I read it, Michel is disturbed and angered, not by Lovecraft the master of fantasy and horror, not by Lovecraft the alchemist who made words glow with a supernal light, but by a Lovecraft whose interest was in the past, in the imagination, rather than in the present or in the (we hope) glories of the future. In other words Michel condemns Lovecraft for not taking his place in the hurly-burly of today, and thus we are brought face to face with the most discussed, most troublesome problem of modern literature. Shall all writing be class conscious, or shall the occasional man of letters be permitted to remain in his ivory tower and send out to the world below words of beauty and glamor? Shall all feel toward the recluse as Auden does toward Housman in his famous (or infamous) poem beginning

> No one—not even Cambridge—was to blame.
> Or shall we permit the poet, the wizard of words,
> A leeway not granted other mortals?[13]

There are two answers. The first is obvious, that is, the man of genius will write what his inmost being generates and impel outward his deepest thoughts, without regard to the clamor or disdain of the crowd. Villon from a dunghill sang of purity and truth. (Of course he sang of other things too.) Poe from madness gave forth unsurpassed words of mystery and terror. Cervantes from prison sent forth his romance of the simple but lovable knight. Yes, the man of genius will write as he chooses; neither contempt nor fear will persuade him to be false to his urge.

The second answer, though not so obvious, seems to me to be equally true. I maintain that no reader should attempt to influence the course of a writer's thought or output. We can criticize a writer's ability, we can condemn his failure to preserve high artistic and aesthetic standards, but we cannot be permitted to dictate what he writes, his topic, his subject, his mode of treatment. We can depreciate his use of tools, but not the object he is trying to make. As well criticize grass for being green, the stars for twinkling. Those are in the nature of things, and so is a writer's creative urge. He must say certain things. If they are expressions of class consciousness, well and good. If they are imagery, illusion or hallucination, equally well and good. I emphasize, we can criticize how an author uses words, but not why he uses them.

As a matter of fact, if all writing were to become class conscious we would lose a universe of beauty, of grandeur, of exquisite aesthetic satisfaction. The same is true of music. Heaven knows Handel and Brahms, Palestrina and Bach (who were other-worldly conscious), Ravel and Stravinsky were not, in their music, class conscious. Suppose all writing were to become class conscious. We would, if differences of opinion were allowed (and this is hardly likely in a totalitarian State), have an unending quarrel, an everlasting polemic that would weary and bore to stupefaction the unlucky reader. God forbid that literature should ever be restricted to one subject. On the other hand, if (as is most likely in a totalitarian state) no differences were allowed, we would be driven insane by the iteration and reiteration of one topic. I like a clarinet, but I don't want to hear only one note on it ad infinitum and ad nauseam.

To repeat, writers of the highest skill will write exactly what they please (unless restrained by force and that, of course, would spell the end of genuine literature), and we, as readers should be grateful at the bounteous repast set before us—not a one dish diet, not a Barmecide feast, but a sumptuous banquet of divers dishes. Who would always dine on ice cream only—or tripe?

Lovecraft was a man of genius—I daresay no one will dispute that statement. He was also a solitary. In his ivory tower (though it was but a couple of rooms in a Providence house) he sat dreaming. His mind traversed immeasurable distances in time and space, he saw vistas of magnificence as well as of horror which are forever beyond the visions of most of us. We see reflected only in words—magic words though they be—what he saw in dazzling brilliance. Who would deny him the right to dream and to record his dreams in imperishable pages? Who would stultify his skill by diverting it into unwanted channels? Who would dare demand an earthly class consciousness of one who, in spirit, was not of this earth. Who would insist that Cthulhu speak the language of Karl Marx—or of the Union League Club?

I have no quarrel with Michel or with the class conscious writers. A Steinbeck, a Dos Passos, a Spender, they are invaluable in these days of travail and searching query when clouds darken the earth, and the future is bleak. We need writers to clang their hammers of words on the anvils of our minds, to drive home the dire necessity of setting our house in order so that civilization will not perish. Yes, we need such men to send out glowing, angry words to goad us to peace, security, and happiness for all and not only for the few.

But we need the others as well. We need a Robert Frost who sings quietly of a New England countryside as well as we need a Robinson Jeffers whose lightning illuminates—and cleanses—dark places. We need the gentle humor of a John Holmes, the historical aloofness of a Neil Swanson,[14] or the detachment of a Santayana, just as much as we need the biting, fiery language of the reformer or the radical. Balance sustains sanity. Variety means richness.

And we need Lovecraft just as he is (I refuse to think of him in the past tense, for his writings will always be alive). He lived in a world of his own, a world of past and future, a world of other dimensions, an alien, unreal world where unhuman entities prowled. He was set aside from the hustle of today, from our social and economic problems. He took no part in present struggles. Why not? Surely in this world of ours there are enough warriors to fight in the cause of justice and righteousness to permit an occasional faery mind to roam as it will in space and time. We need "bathroom fixtures in sanitary condition," yes, we need a thousand things to better the unhappy lot, the desperate plight of countless millions who are now downtrodden or outcasts. You and I, all of us, can strive to improve the world, to provide the "freedom" and "Equality" which our founding forefathers wrote into the most matchless social document ever produced. But I, for one—and I am confident the majority of fans are with me,—will not agree that the magic, the glamor, the fantastic genius of a man like Lovecraft should be distorted or diverted into strange channels. We have too few human beings who can penetrate the unknown realm of unreality and faery. Let us cherish and preserve them.

H. P. Lovecraft: Strange Weaver

J. Chapman Miske

Jack Chapman Miske (1920–2003) was a leading science fiction and fantasy fan of the 1940s. The following biographical article first appeared in *Scienti-Snaps* 3, No. 3 (Summer 1940): 9–12, a magazine of which he was associate editor. It must have been based upon information provided by one of HPL's colleagues, possibly R. H. Barlow. Miske later became involved in a hoax. He published a portion of a Lovecraft letter to Donald Wandrei (24 November 1927), with introductory and concluding paragraphs provided by himself, under the title "The Thing in the Moonlight" (*Bizarre*, January 1941). August Derleth, believing the item to be a genuine "fragment" by HPL, reprinted it in *Marginalia* (1944). Miske informed Derleth of the matter, but Derleth continued to print the item as a work by HPL.

Strange weaver and dark dreamer, H. P. Lovecraft wove his word-fabrics on looms not of this world. His scope ranged from ethereal dream tapestries to the more somber weave of the curtains that veil the door to Nightmare.

His fame could stand upon the basis of his ability as a supreme stylist alone; but when to that style is coupled his all-penetrating imagination, he rears indisputably as one of the titans of modern literature. Those are legion who think the greatest master of the macabre died on March 15, 1937, in the forty-seventh year of his life.

There is little about his life itself that is unusual. It is the man, Lovecraft, who makes the biographer's task a pleasure.

For Lovecraft was eccentric to the point of being born "out of his due time." Not freakish, simply different, by temperament, tastes, and, to certain degrees, actions.

Howard Phillips Lovecraft entered this world on August 20, 1890, in Providence, Rhode Island. He died within a mile of the same spot. However, during his life he travelled as much as his finances allowed, and he would very much have liked to do more journeying. As it was, he explored all of New England—a region of extreme fascination to his antiquarian tastes—his researches extending from Quebec to Key West and New Orleans. He valued these journeyings so highly that he often underwent comparative hardships in order to make them. He would ride for two days in buses, sleeping in them, so that hotel expenses could be saved.

He was an only child and early exhibited signs of the phenomenal mind which was to enable him to become a great scholar although ill health never permitted him to attend college. The scope of his erudition encompassed nearly every subject, for his constant illness made him an avid reader. He began reading fantasy at the age of four, and tried writing when only six or seven. Fantasy fascinated him from the first. He was nine when he first read Poe and immediately took him as his model.

His memory seemed without limitation, for anything he ever read he could always call forth at any time. His diction was as beautifully pure, yet wholly unstilted, as his writings. He lived a secluded life, and around him arose a very large circle of correspondents. His scholarship will be very clearly demonstrated when these correspondents' letters from Lovecraft are published as the third and last volume in the Lovecraft Memorial series. They will very probably establish him as a letter-writer to rank with the foremost. Better than anything else, they will show the many facets of his genius.

He was extremely allergic to cold, and for years before his death never ventured out if the temperature fell below twenty degrees above zero. Ninety-five degrees was the temperature at which he worked and felt best. He often remarked how he regretted the frigid climate of his beloved New England.

He disliked seafood intensely, and that aversion is reflected in many of his stories. He was an absolute teetotaler personally, but was not a prohibitionist.[15] He disliked typewriters, and wrote all of his letters and literary works in longhand, the latter being typed for him later. His chirography was incredibly minute, and he could probably have written hundreds of words on one side of a postal card.

In 1924, when his health was comparatively good, he moved to New York. During this period he married unsuccessfully and soon was divorced. In 1926 he returned to Providence, where he lived with his aunt till his death in 1937.

He was an antiquarian authority, his favorite city being Charlestown, about which he once wrote a brochure complete with maps.[16] This was mimeographed and distributed to a number of his friends. His home in Providence was an old Georgian structure from which could be seen (from his window) a cemetery to which Poe often came (a century before) to walk in meditation.[17] Lovecraft, Adolphe de Castro, prominent scholar and collaborator with Ambrose Bierce, and R. H. Barlow, a cousin of Lovecraft's, once visited this cemetery together and each wrote an acrostic sonnet on the name of Edgar Allan Poe. Lovecraft's and de Castro's were printed in *Weird Tales*.[18]

Some of Lovecraft's stories had their genesis in actual places. The novelette "The Shunned House" was inspired by a very old and deserted dwelling, not far from HPL's (as he was known to his friends and admirers) own home.[19] This story, incidentally, was twice rejected by *Weird Tales*, and was printed by the Recluse Press, operated by W. Paul Cook, of Athol, Mass., as a brochure; but the loose sheets were never assembled and bound. They are now in the possession of Mr. Barlow. However, the story was posthumously printed in *Weird Tales*. "The Horror at Red Hook" and "He" were full of New York local color, and expressed his detestation of that city.

Many of his tales were transcripts of dreams, especially his pure fantasy. "The Statement of Randolph Carter" is a complete nightmare, while "Celephais" is a number of mosaic dream fragments. He noted all fantastic dreams for possible future story use (see "The Very Old Folk" in this issue of *Scienti-Snaps*).[20]

His early stories he mostly destroyed when he was eighteen, devoting his time for the next nine years to writing poetry, criticism, and essays, no fiction being written during this period. Then he joined the United Amateur Press Association, and his first published story, "The Alchemist," appeared in *The United Amateur* in 1916. It had been written in 1908. His second was "The Beast in the Cave" in W. Paul Cook's *Vagrant* in 1917. This tale was written in 1905, when he was only fifteen.

Nineteen-seventeen also saw the writing of such tales as "The Tomb" and "Dagon." In 1918 was written "Polaris," and in 1919 "Beyond the Wall of Sleep," "The White Ship," "The Doom that Came to Sarnath," and "The Statement of Randolph Carter."

In 1922 HPL made his first professional appearance in *Home Brew*, a now discontinued publication. The story was "Herbert West–Reanimator." It appeared in six parts, each complete in itself. In later years HPL confided that the story was his "only attempt at hack writing." Later that year "The Lurking Fear," which later appeared in *Weird Tales*, was printed in *Home Brew* as a four-part serial. The story was illustrated by Clark Ashton Smith, who had met HPL through amateur journalism.

His first stories (the first written, not published) were almost completely pure fantasies, very similar to Lord Dunsany's works, although HPL had not then read any of the Dunsany tales.[21] Later, his unique tales of the Elder Gods began to appear. They introduced to weird literature the first new concept in years, and have since been widely imitated.

The Cthulhu Mythos is a fascinating product of an intense imagination. All the stories dealing with the Elder Gods, of whom Cthulhu was the most terrible, were written, HPL said, "on the fundamental lore or legend that this world was inhabited at one time by another race who, in practising black magic, lost their foothold and were expelled, yet live on the outside ever ready to take possession of this earth again."

Interesting too is his conception of Azathoth, the Idiot God, who sits at Chaos, the center of all things, attended by his unspeakable consorts, and guides the destiny of the worlds. HPL was an atheist.

Two other types into which his stories might be grouped roughly are the Randolph Carter stories, of which there are three;[22] and the New England stories, which dealt with certain of that section's decadent and sequestered towns. The locale of these is usually either Arkham or Kingsport (and, on one or two occasions, Innsmouth), made-over versions of the two ancient Massachusetts towns of Salem and Marblehead. The force with which these stories are told is perhaps best manifested by the fact that Arkham and Kingsport existed as real towns to most of his readers. Probably some one reading these words will learn for the first time they are imaginary.

Even more remarkable is how firmly he impressed upon his readers' minds the existence of "The Necronomicon," a wholly fictionally conceived volume purportedly written in the twelfth century by a mad Arab, Abdul Alhazred.[23] It would be interesting to know how many persons have vainly attempted to acquire that creation of HPL's mind from book dealers and libraries. To further the delusion, HPL wrote a "History of the Necronomicon," which was printed in a four-page folder in 1936 by the Rebel Press of Oakman, Alabama.[24]

The Necronomicon, incidentally, was supposedly a collection of the most terrible secrets of elder evil lore, including incantations for calling the fearful Elder Gods to Earth from the Outside.

Despite their "outside" qualities and the relatively small number of persons to whom such works appeal, HPL's stories received very considerable literary recognition.

"The Colour out of Space" in the September 1927 *Amazing Stories*, and "The Dunwich Horror" in *Weird Tales* in 1929, received Roll of Honor ranking in Edward O'Brien's annual yearbook of the short story. To the best of the writer's knowledge, virtually no other stories published in pulp magazines have ever been so honored. Truly a remarkable feat. O'Brien and the O. Henry Yearbook also gave mention to such of his stories as "The Rats in the Walls," "The Music of Erich Zann," "The Strange High House in the Mist," and many others. His stories were reprinted in such anthologies as "Creeps by Night," "Beware After Dark," "Not at Night," and others.

His own favorites among his stories were "The Colour out of Space," "The Music of Erich Zann," and "At the Mountains of Madness." The latter story was so badly mutilated when printed in *Astounding Stories* that HPL said he considered it unpublished. His stories in *Weird Tales* were sold with the provision that not one word was to be changed.

Among those of his works which he disliked were the aforementioned "Herbert West" and "The Tree." He also said "Celephais" was "not so hot," and characterized "The Quest of Iranon" as "mawkish." One is inclined to believe the latter two criticisms were inspired more by the nature of the stories (rather personal) than any faults they may possess.

He read all fantasy he could discover, and his favorites were Poe, Dunsany, Machen, Blackwood, M. R. James, and Walter de la Mare, among the book authors; A. Merritt, E. Hoffmann Price, C. L. Moore, Robert E. Howard, Clark Ashton Smith, and Frank Belknap Long, Jr., in the magazines.

Still unpublished are two novels, "Dream Quest of the Unknown Kadath" and "The Case of Charles Dexter Ward." It is surmised these will appear either in some magazine or the second Lovecraft Memorial volume, or both.

The first volume of the Lovecraft Memorial series is "The Outsider and Others," which went on sale recently in a private edition of 1200, 1000 of which are for sale, at $5.00 per copy from Arkham House, Sauk City, Wisconsin. It contains 550 plus pages (or almost all) of HPL's fiction, and his long, masterful essay "Supernatural Horror in Literature." It is beautifully printed and bound, and the strange book jacket is by Virgil Finlay.

The second volume in this series will contain all the rest of HPL's fiction, his non-fiction, and his poetry. It is tentatively scheduled for September 1941. The third will contain as many of his letters as can be included, and may appear in 1942. *Scienti-Snaps* recommends these volumes, and urges you to help this non-profit effort to perpetuate the works of the late master.

Lovecraft is dead, but the strange patterns he wove will always be appreciated by a small but intelligent group.

Lovecraft and Benefit Street

Dorothy Walter

> Dorothy C. Walter (1889–1967) became acquainted with HPL through her friend W. Paul Cook. Walter urged HPL to visit her in Vermont in early 1934; he did so, and she wrote of the visit in "Three Hours with H. P. Lovecraft" (1959). The following article first appeared in Cook's amateur journal the *Ghost* No. 1 (Spring 1943): 27–29, and was later printed as a booklet (North Montpelier, VT: Driftwind Press, 1943).

Benefit Street is one of the quaintly named older thoroughfares in Providence, Rhode Island, lying half way up College Hill between the campus of Brown University and the lower lying and parallel stretch of South and North Main Streets which used to form the business center in early days of the city.

In the fall and winter of 1942–3 this quiet street came in for a great deal of newspaper mention when David Cornel deJong, a young Hollander with several previous novels in English to his credit, used it as a setting for a new novel, and its name for the title of his book.[25]

Reviews both commendatory and otherwise brought "Benefit Street" to attention. Local sales mounted high and continued to be brisk for a long time, for the Rhode Island reading public enjoyed finding a novel set in scenes intimately known and ably described. However, the staid citizens of Providence found it disconcerting that many characters in the book were indecorous, and hastened to write letters in protest to the *Providence Journal* about how much they disliked the neighbors Mr. deJong had given them on Benefit Street, and how unfair they felt it to be to defame a whole street, and that an interesting and beautiful one, by giving its name to an account of the unpleasant goings-on of one boarding house full of fictional queer people. Others wrote in reminiscent vein, contrasting with Mr. deJong's characters those who had given the historical and literary flavor to the street—Washington, Abigail Adams, Poe, Mrs. Whitman and others who had graced the street with their presence in times past.

Just when the discussion of what kind of people one could expect to find there was quieting down, the Federal Bureau of Investigation gave it an added and ironic fillip by carrying the campaign against lawbreakers to Benefit Street, raiding a "vice palace" and bringing to justice its operators, who had been carrying on their bad business elegantly and quietly under the noses of the high percentage of reputable citizens whose minds were on more seemly affairs.

It being obvious that people of many sorts may be found even on rather short streets, it is not the purpose of these pages to discuss the truth or falsity of the characters assembled by Mr. deJong in Penny McGuire's boarding house on Benefit Street. Rather it is their purpose, with this preamble, to call attention to another Providence writer who made Benefit Street and its immediate neighborhood the setting for a number of short stories, peopling the region with denizens even more surprising than those created by Mr. deJong or unearthed by the F. B. I.

Howard Phillips Lovecraft, late of Providence, lived most of his not very long life in his native city, and the last few years of it in a house set a little back from College Street, almost under the eaves of the John Hay Library. He was a writer by profession, doing hack work for others and original work—essays, poems and tales. A life rather slowed down and shut in by ill health gave him time to read enormously, and as he seems never to have forgotten anything he read, he amassed a surprising fund of miscellaneous information on which he drew in his literary work. History and antiquarian lore attracted him, particularly the lore of witchcraft. Scientific concepts, evolution, relativity and the fourth dimension, and the long, long thoughts of astronomy interested him also and started his mind off on strange journeys of speculation in time and space. All this contributed to the realistically narrated but fantastically weird tales which it was his pleasure to write.

Mr. Lovecraft dearly loved "the ancient hill," as he called the neighborhood of his home, and in his night rambles, like Poe at an earlier day, he

> Prowled such sweet
> Ways as Benevolent
> And Benefit Street,*

alone or with friends, exploring every curve, highway or byway, learning by heart all the nooks and crannies, even to the graveyard back of St. John's

---

*The quotation is from "Irony," a poem in the volume *White Christmas* by Margaret Emerson Bailey.

Church, packing his mind with the details of graceful spires and interesting public buildings, but dwelling with peculiar pleasure on the Georgian architecture of the older homesteads. The eighteenth century was his favorite era, and so great was his love of old times in Rhode Island that he even liked to fancy himself an elderly gentleman of Providence, living back in the less populous, more leisurely days before the colonies had broken with the Mother Country.

Returning from such rambles in space and time to his desk in his sightly study from which he overlooked the treetops of Benefit Street, dark against the sky-glow of downtown Providence, he spent night after night, which was his working time, using the familiar localities, the characteristic family and Christian names of Rhode Island, and factual details of the present and past of the life and business of Providence to furnish a setting for tales of doings that were strange indeed. For the most part his plots deal with the struggles, not always victorious, of individuals and sometimes of whole families against the malign influences and ghoulish visitations of unnamed and horrible creatures from the sea, or monsters from ancient æons, or even inhabitants of other planets, remote and dim, beings visualized by him as entirely different from humankind in anatomy, abilities, and methods of communication, whose disturbing, mysterious, and baffling behaviour puzzled and bedeviled the characters in the stories.

He did not always make Providence his setting, for every excursion elsewhere gave him new landscapes to use as backgrounds, new local superstitions to weave into his plots. Thus a stay in a New England inland valley that was soon to be flooded for the reservoir of a city water supply gave him material both factual and imaginative for a particularly creepy story of the disintegration of a family and its farm ("The Colour out of Space"). Moreover, he often swung off into other worlds and other ages in his writing, sometimes very successfully. But mostly he wrote about the "Arkham region," an imaginary bit of New England coastline above Boston and near enough to Salem and the scenes of the witchcraft executions to lend support to the weirdness of his plots, or else about places closer at hand in Rhode Island.

In the making of imaginative tales of the sort that Mr. Lovecraft wrote there cannot help being a good deal of claptrap and mumbo-jumbo. His stories suffer, if too many are read in quick succession, from similarity in the method of producing a weird atmosphere. It is easy to tire of gothic effects in landscape and in weather when one knows that by such artifices one is being "softened up" to be bowled over at the appropriate moment by the horror of the narrative. One longs for a mystery to develop in a neat, ordinary house, or for a homicide committed in brilliant sunlight. Many of the stories are too long. Cutting would have improved them. And Mr. Lovecraft leaned too heavily on a few trick words that had come to have a heightened significance for him—*nameless* and *forbidden*, for example, to mention two. He also relied much too often on references to things distasteful to himself that he assumed would produce similar feelings of aversion or fear or disgust in others—fishy odors, for instance, which he couldn't endure and used again and again as a symbol of the evil and the malevolent; the strangeness of the foreigner; the unpleasantness of things squirmy and slimy; and chief of all, the sensation of cold. Things clammy and frigid are not very enjoyable for anybody, it is true, but few people could experience the gooseflesh and cold shivers that Mr. Lovecraft must have induced in himself from the chilling winds that blow through his stories and the dank caverns and cellars into which he so often conducted his readers, because few are as susceptible in their own persons to changes in heat and cold as he is known to have been. For him, as one of his friends reports, winter begins at seventy degrees! He would have agreed with Dante in making hell cold.

Also one misses humor in the stories. There is a sly humor there, to be sure, but it is not of a kind integral to the story, nor is it addressed to the readers, easing them kindly along, making the characters seem like folks and the horrific events all the more effective by contrast. Instead it is a private, tongue-in-the-cheek humor that mentions ancient (and imaginary!) books of magic by title and author in a manner so matter-of-fact that readers have been known to search the libraries in hopes of securing copies; a humor that wove the names of the author's close friends into some of the magic formulas muttered here and there in the tales, and that paid new friends who lived at a distance the odd compliment of adding their hometowns to the list of habitats in which the ghouls and monsters and queer creatures from other planets that swarm the tales are alleged to have appeared.

In spite of such defects, the fact remains that Mr. Lovecraft had an imagination of more than usual power and writing ability far beyond the ordinary to conceive such weird tales at all and to work them out so well. He was clever in originating his world of queer beings from "Outside"; and in building some of his stories around the camera, the submarine, the telephone, and other products of scientific wizardry, he interestingly links old necromancy and new. Back in the days before Hitler, when horror stories in real life did not appear daily in the headlines, and lovers of shivers had to satisfy their cravings by fiction, these tales of "illegitimate horror" sold readily to magazines devoted to weird narratives and had an eager reception from the readers of mystery stories. After Mr. Lovecraft's death two of his admirers from the mid-west, August Derleth and Donald Wandrei, brought out a giant volume of his tales, "The Outsider and Others," 553 large fine-print pages (Arkham House, 1939), and purpose to publish in 1943 a volume of his letters and at some future time one of his essays and poems. A pleasing and informing book, "In Memoriam Howard Phillips Lovecraft: Recollections, Appreciations, Estimates," was prepared by W. Paul Cook at the Driftwind Press (1941), and one issue of an amateur journal, *The Olympian*, published by Edward H. Cole, was devoted to tributes and recollections by a number of Mr. Lovecraft's friends. The residue of his manuscript material has been deposited in the John Hay Library.

But to get back to Benefit Street. The writer of this comment is not fond of weird tales; she does not easily fall under their spell, and when she does, experiences none of the peculiar pleasure that some people seem to derive from being scared out of their wits. But one below-zero night in northern Vermont, in search of a bedtime story, she opened the huge Lovecraft volume that a friend had loaned her. Her eye chanced on a familiar name in a story entitled "The Shunned House," and she read on just where she had opened the book, astonished to find herself in Providence, wandering along Benefit Street. It was pleasant to be transported so unexpectedly to a neighborhood well known since college days, interesting and amusing to find it figuring as a setting for the outrageous events of a weird tale when she had always considered it seemly and sedate. She read on, absorbed in the pleasures of recollection. And before she knew it, she was getting shivers and a crinkly spine out of the hair-raising particulars of an uncanny and not very believable yarn. Well, of course it was late, and a very cold night! But what more could a writer of weird fiction have asked for his efforts!

Benefit Street is a long street. It seems to be demonstrated that anything can happen on it. One can go to church there, for instance, or to art school, to the library or to court; the Historical Society now faces it, "The Players" perform upon it, the Handicrafters look out on it; little choir boys run along it on their way to school at St. Dunstan's; the Mounted Commands exercise upon it; a plaque upon one building announces that here a President of the United States was once entertained; the Brown Commencement procession cuts it and floods it with spectators; and somewhere in its length, so rumor says, old-time residents gather in a basement studio to interpret to their own satisfaction the plays of Shakespeare. One can savor early Providence under its elms, or the Yankee Providence of today, and one can also travel to foreign lands without leaving the street, if one has an open sesame to the pleasant hospitality of the Syrian, Portuguese, and Jewish homes that cluster around its opposite ends.

How comforting to reflect when strolling on Benefit Street that it is human beings who people it, both sides of the street, and not the ghastly monsters of Mr. Lovecraft's bizarre imaginings.

[Letters to the Editor]

Thomas Ollive Mabbott

> Thomas Ollive Mabbott (1898–1968), professor of English at Northwestern, Brown, and Hunter College, was a noted Poe scholar whose critical edition of Poe—*The Collected Works of Edgar Allan Poe* (1969–78; 3 vols. [1 volume of poems, 2 volumes of tales])—appeared posthumously. The following letters appeared in the *Acolyte* 2, No. 3 (Summer 1944): 25, and 3, No. 2 (Spring 1945): 32–33.

. . . I do not think that Lovecraft was much of a poet. He differed from Poe in that—for EAP was primarily a poet, and even the tales, grand as they are, were not, in my opinion, what his heart primarily desired. And after twenty years and more of study, there is the subject I know enough about to have an opinion. But the only poem of HPL that really gets me is the song in "The Tomb." It is the best imitation of the 18th century I have ever read, and the line "Better under the table than under the ground" is magnificent. But Lovecraft I think at bottom loved his prose work. And I feel with Leonardo da Vinci that only what one wishes to do can ever be one's finest work.

I think I was the first academic person to review HPL,[26] and I have no objection to telling you that it is one of the things I am proudest of. But there is a corollary to it—Lovecraft involves my greatest regret. I taught at Brown [Brown University, Providence, Rhode Island—eds.] in 1928-9, and was often no doubt within 50 feet of him.[27] And I had once had a hint that one might write to him without offence. But I did not know—and I never saw him with knowledge, and I never wrote him. He made one great contribution to pure scholarship—for he got the whole point of Poe's "House of Usher," which in print was not done to my knowledge before he wrote.[28] I mention it only in passing—but my respect for him includes respect for his criticism.

I have never quite been sure *how* great he was; though I do feel he was a great writer. But I know one thing; his fiction shares an honor with the works of Poe and Chatterton. They are the only authors of whom I can honestly say that I enjoyed every word of their fiction, and I have read all easily available of three. Now my honest philosophy about literature is this—in a world such as I have from boyhood perceived this one to be, the literature of escape is to my mind of the greatest value. As for morals—that is all right, and I'm all for it, but one can get all the pure moralising any man needs from the *Encheridion* of Epictetus, and maybe a bit of Walt Whitman. When people ask me what to read, I answer if they seek moral improvement I recommend those two authors. For the rest, what is harmless and makes this a more pleasant world is what I value.

Speaking of Lovecraft, as I often am, I was interested in what Leiber Jr. had to say of the mythology;[29] and believe I agree that his best work has only occasionally been picked as such by his admirers. I have myself some ideas on the Mythology, as at times embodying the "Truth as Lovecraft saw it." But I have always been very careful about it because I have always wondered what Lovecraft may have said plainly on the subject in letters or essays I may not have seen. However, I took one hint from the reminiscences of W. Paul Cook, who said that Lovecraft always asserted his "atheism" or "materialism" so strongly that Cook wondered if he had his doubts. I have met with nothing in Lovecraft that makes me suppose he was a very technical philosopher; and it is on record that no less a person than Shelley, after meeting Robert Southey, first learned he was not an atheist but a pantheist. (N.B. Only recently I got a bit of a surprise, for on telling a very learned minister I did not think even an omnipotent God could do ANYTHING, I learned the highly orthodox view was also that God could not make a square circle, and that what I thought my leading heresy was not so heretical after all; indeed apparently would not even get me in trouble with the pope!) Now what I think Lovecraft intellectually certainly rejected was what he supposed to be the idea of the supernatural. I wonder if he defined this correctly or not—indeed I wonder how he would have come out had he looked into real theology; assuming he was as little concerned with it as possible. (I do not mean Lovecraft believed what I do—that is beside the point, for I have some mystical tendencies—but I do mean that in rejecting the supernatural as commonly understood to mean events contrary to nature, I am not sure Lovecraft opposed himself so much to religionists as he may have supposed he did.) I think his mythology was primarily only for purposes of fiction; and that Lovecraft certainly did not believe in it. But (as Poe observed) a man cannot write a lot without giving away what he really thinks. Such a work as *The Dream-Quest of Unknown Kadath* is obviously extremely personal and self-revelatory. Here there is little talk of the elder gods, but constant mention of them. I think an antiquarian, such as Lovecraft, did think in the old days men had been more or less on the right track at times, and that the elder gods represent the fact, or maybe I should say the hope that men might ultimately come to their senses, and that Pope might be right, that back of apparently blind nature there might be "harmony thou canst not see."[30] I think Lovecraft's "mythological" characters represent extraordinary powers *within* natural laws. He seems to have speculated whether, even within natural law, considering the ideas of Einstein and others, extraordinary though not supernatural powers might be possessed by individuals, human or of other kinds. At least for fiction he accepted the possibility of such beings.

As for Nyarlathotep, he is often apparently evil and both deceptive and cynical, but he is a fairly decent person in the Kadath book. My friend Jack Birss once went with Lovecraft to the Metropolitan Museum, and tells me Lovecraft knew a lot about Egyptology.[31] The trouble is that Birss is no Egyptologist, and I cannot even guess what "a lot" means. Is it fair to say I think maybe Lovecraft knew what a person might easily pick up about Egypt—and assume he knew HOTEP means something? It means several things but "at peace" is the summary. The Nile at peace is my guess—that is, the universal fact of change is still productive of peace. Maybe Nyarla makes sense too and I may be off the track, but the little vocabulary in Budge's *First Steps in Egyptian* gives nothing suggestive, and I shall, until proof is offered, assume that is about as far as Lovecraft went in the matter—I suspect, however, he did know meanings of some common Egyptian words. I think, in the last analysis, Lovecraft regarded the world as at present in a mess (what thoughtful person will disagree with him?) and literature of escape for that reason of the highest possible value. But he also must have recognized there are some nice things about existence besides escape literature. I think he saw the universe as apparently purposeless, but including things (cats and men) that had some occasional apparent purpose. He personified terror and horror as powerful, but not all-powerful. Hence the Elder Gods.

A Plea for Lovecraft

W. Paul Cook

>The following article by W. Paul Cook (see p. 48) was first published in the *Ghost* No. 3 (May 1945): 55–56. It urges HPL fans to keep "one foot on the ground."

The best thing that can happen to the memory and the future reputation and real standing of Howard P. Lovecraft is to have his admirers, disciples, acolytes, devotees, get at least one foot on the ground. At present they are floating or suspended in some manner in the rarefied air of the empyrean with nothing substantial to get hold of, or have their noses so closely pressed to the ground in the attitude of worship that they are blinded to all real values. As one of the idolaters writes me: "Lovecraft is almost a god to me."

Irreparable harm is being done to Lovecraft by indiscriminate and even unintelligent praise, by lack of unbiased and intelligent criticism, and by a warped sense of what is due him in the way of publication of his works. In fact, I am afraid that what is due him has been entirely lost sight of, and that the only thing seen is the market for everything he wrote. So wide a circulation of even his worst stuff, and his worst was pretty bad, coupled with the assurance that it is the work of a master, is certain to have a definite reaction, and a very unfavorable one, as he comes to the notice of those whose knowledge of literary values is not blinded or stultified by personal friendship and unquestioning worship.

This awakening of the world outside of Lovecraft's comparatively small circle of admirers has already begun. In a review of *Creeps by Night* in the *New York Herald Tribune*, the writer calls "The Rats in the Walls" "pure clap-trap."[32] This is the plain truth. Of all Lovecraft's stories, that particular one is most open to the charge. Superb clap-trap, it may be, but clap-trap none the less. August Derleth, the editor of the volume, has a keen sense of literary values in classing, analyzing, and putting in their place his own writings and the work of most others, but when he comes to the work of Lovecraft he completely mislays his yardstick and is singularly obtuse, or pretends to be so. If he brought to the Lovecraft work the same critical acumen which he applies to his own work, it would be of more benefit to Lovecraft.

Arkham House can not be blamed for cashing in on the present Lovecraft furore. With great faith, courage, personal sacrifice and hard work they published the first omnibus volume, *The Outsider and Others*, and for several years held the bag before they got back their cash expenditure on it. Strange to say, it was the publication of the second omnibus (which should never have been published) that put Lovecraft over with a bang, and made the publishing of other weird books a lucrative business. This was due largely to the book being called to the attention of columnists like Vincent Starrett and others who were obliging and easy going rather than critical in giving it notices. Arkham House deserves the rewards when "The Ghosts Pay Off," as John Wilstach calls it in *Variety*. The game of course is to publish anything and everything of Lovecraft as long as Lovecraft fans are howling for more and more. So it will go on as long as there is a shred of paper remaining with a word scribbled by Lovecraft on it. This is all right for the Lovecraft fans. They should have what they want. But the fact remains that nothing worse could happen to the future standing of one of the masters in the weird field. Indeed, he may eventually come to be considered one of the supreme masters, but it will be in spite of all the present over-praise, and when his work is boiled down to one well-chosen volume of no great size.

I confess that I view with some misgivings the projected publication of a volume of Lovecraft's *Selected Letters*. It can be the very best of all his books—and should be. But it will be edited by a group who are much too "high" on the matter.

Of course there has been a conscious build-up for Lovecraft, and a build-up which has been eminently successful, in spite of the fact that it started with the distribution of the unfortunate second omnibus. The present boom in his name and works is loud enough so that he has even been heard about in Providence. Providence was the last city of any size to know about its native son, but even so, it was a triumph to make Providence hear at all.

Peculiarly typical of the Lovecraft criticism (or deliberate lack of it) is August Derleth's remarks on "The Outsider" in this issue of the GHOST.[33] In his very important thesis, *The Weird Story in English Since 1890*, Derleth in most of the article shows that same critical faculty which I have said he exhibits when dealing with his own work. But when he comes to deal with Lovecraft, suddenly his faculties are seemingly dormant. It may be said that since the writing of the thesis he has come to prefer "The Colour out of Space" to "The Outsider" as one of the very greatest of the Lovecraft stories; but at that time he thought the latter topped them all. In connection with "The Outsider" he says ". . . the revelation, which the author conceals to the very end." I am most certainly casting no reflection on Derleth's intellectual integrity, in which I thoroughly believe, when I say that he must know better than that.

When I first saw "The Outsider" it was in the typed manuscript, and at the bottom of a page were the words: "My fingers touched the rotting outstretched paw of the monster beneath the golden arch." There was the revelation; there was the story; and I thought that was the end of the story. I was struck with admiration at the artistic restraint of the work, and started a note of praise to Lovecraft when, lifting the sheet, I found there was more of it. Restraint disappeared and the author enjoyed himself throwing words around. All the rest was just verbiage, words, padding, anti-climax. I wrote him then that the story should have ended there. And I still think so.

Let's All Jump on H.P.L.

P. Schuyler Miller

> Peter Schuyler Miller (1912–1974) was a technical writer, book reviewer, and well-known science fiction fan. He also wrote a considerable amount of science fiction from the 1930s to the 1950s. In the following article, published in *Cepheid* 1, No. 1 (Winter 1945–46): 13–14, 19, he defends HPL from the attacks of Edmund Wilson and others.

It will be no news to fandom—thanks to the hard work of August Derleth and others of his good friends and literary heirs—that H. P. Lovecraft has at last been discovered by the public. Every new anthology of fantasia shouts to the world that it has discovered a new master, and the reprint houses are stumbling over each other in their hurry to get collections of his stories between some sort of covers. Undoubtedly H.P.L. is sitting on a gravestone somewhere in the Arkham Hills, enjoying the whole thing immensely.

Not to be outdone, the literary critics have also discovered Lovecraft, and with wholesome unanimity (it *is* nice to find so many people agreeing about something these days) are giving him a touch of their hobnails in the region of the short ribs. Everyone but Will Cuppy of the *New York Herald-Tribune*, who is lowbrow enough to like fantasy, has had a hand in the nasty work. The latest of the lot is the terrible-tempered, anthropophagistically inclined Edmund Wilson of the *New Yorker*, who last Winter disposed of the whole field of mystery-detective fiction from Sherlock

Holmes up with a series of short, hard belly-blows which brought howls of pain and rage from readers and fellow critics in every country of the world where the *New Yorker* hasn't been banned as a subversive influence.[34]

Mr. Wilson has apparently been persuaded by someone to read Lovecraft, just as some months ago he was persuaded to read a selection of the worst whodunits in a season which was remarkable for its poor tries. Later he did expose himself to a somewhat better selection of the works of the masters, but by that time his critical ulcers were badly disturbed and he stuck to his first verdict: mysteries are junk. This time he arrives at the same verdict on the literary cadavers of H.P.L.–and in passing of Machen and Dunsany. Oddly enough, he finds Lovecraft a good critic of a type of literature which (according to Wilson) he couldn't write for beans.

Now this man Wilson is a power in the world of literary criticism, if not in fandom, and it pays to look twice at what he has to say. That he's hot stuff, in the groove, hep, or whatever you prefer to call it, is proved by the fact that the two stories to which he gives grudging credit happen to be my own favorites: "The Colour out of Space" and "The Shadow out of Time." B'gosh, maybe the man's right!

I can claim, I think, to be a fan of pretty good and long standing compared with the braw, brash youngsters who turn out the host of fanzines today. I wasn't in on Lovecraft's first stories, by any means, but I did read most of the early, great yarns while they were early and great—and they carried more punch read under those circumstances than they do to an innocent novice stumbling into the midst of one of his collections today. If you want to take it that way, I'm going to jump on Lovecraft too....

It has often been said that the greatest weird tales of all time suggest more than they say. They leave it to the reader to fill in grim details from his own hereditary fears and imagination. They are simple. And they chill your marrow because they are just over the edge of everyday experience. They could happen.

We who share Western civilization also share a certain background of mythology and superstition—or we used to, before children were sent to the movies for their entertainment, instead of hearing venerable tales at their grandparents' knee. We can fill in details from this heritage of the macabre, and scare ourselves far worse than any poor writer could ever do it if he described a ghoul down to the last slimy hair on the critter's chin. The weird tales which the critics call great—which will grip almost anyone—are stories which have grown out of this common heritage. I have heard an Iroquois Indian speak off-handedly about manifestations which she considered the Indian equivalent of our ghosts, and got an inkling of the Indian point of view toward them, which I could never have had from reading the same words in print. I have no doubt that real Chinese or Hindu weird tales—the true native stock—would leave us cold, simply because we don't share the background—the culture, in the anthropological sense—of the people to whom those tales belong.

Lovecraft, and Dunsany before him, created a mythos which has no such roots in our culture, or has only feeble ones. Dunsany's was based, as much as anything, in the world of classical Greek Mythology—with Oriental trimmings. His images are not entirely beyond the average person's comprehension, and it is worth noting that the more he writes and the more popular he becomes, the closer his stories draw to our common heritage.

H. P. Lovecraft, on the other hand, fitted his tales into an artificial mythology or philosophy of the world and mankind which draws farther away from experience as it becomes more complete. At the beginning his stories where merely edging over the verge into nightmare. As he continued, two courses must have offered themselves to him: to hold to the elemental, so that each story would be self-contained and self-explanatory in terms of the average reader's heritage and imagination, or to build each on the ones that had gone before, adding to and rounding out the total structure.

He chose the latter course, and by doing so he automatically created a cult of readers who *could* fill in the gaps of suggestion because they had followed him through the earlier tales. Their minds were tuned to the same key; their imaginations had been trained to venture in the same directions. The details they filled in were at least close to those Lovecraft himself would have imagined had he chosen to be wholly explicit. They had made the Lovecraftian mythos a part of their heritage, their culture.

The outsider, the uninitiated, plunging into one of these later stories has no such background. The details he fills in will not be those of the Cthulhu Mythos; they will, as a matter of fact, be in many cases wholly irrelevant to it—and the story will leave him cold.

The same thing may be happening in science-fiction. Certainly John Campbell's readers form a kind of cult, for they take for granted vast generalities which once upon a time would have been explained in words of at most two syllables. There is no magazine today which corresponds to the old *Amazing Stories* of—say—the early *Skylark* days. There is danger of losing new blood by writing for the cult.

I know the same thing has happened to fandom. When I venture into the world of the fanzines and fan letters, I feel as much out of my depth as the innocent who first blunders into H.P.L. I don't know the lingo; I don't have the background; it consequently doesn't get across to me.

To my mind the task confronting Lovecraft's literary heirs is to tie his mythos into the common heritage wherever possible, at the same time that they amplify it in detail and concept. I envy Derleth, Wandrei, Smith, Bloch their ability to embroider the Lovecraft theme. I long to try it myself. But when I do, it will—I hope—be done without using the familiar terminology and formulae. Those who know nothing of the Cthulhu pattern will be able to fill in the gaps of suggestion from their own background, while Lovecraft's heirs will see a further significance, based on their own pattern of thinking.

If I am successful, the imaginations of both groups should trend in the same direction—for only when Lovecraft's heirs have woven his horrid pattern back into our common background, so that we can see new, grim, ghastly significance in simple things, will Lovecraft really come into his own.

Howard Phillips Lovecraft

Michael Harrison

Michael Harrison was the pseudonym of Maurice Desmond Rohan (1907–1991), a British novelist, biographer, and critic. He wrote about Sherlock Holmes in the treatise *In the Footsteps of Sherlock Holmes* (1958) and wrote pastiches of Edgar Allan Poe's detective stories in *The Exploits of the Chevalier Dupin* (1968). His article "Howard Phillips Lovecraft" first appeared in a British fanzine, *Prediction*, but this appearance has not been located. It then appeared in the amateur journal *Phoenix* 5, No. 5 (May 1946) and was reprinted in *Fantasy Advertiser* 2, No. 4 (November 1947): 21–23. An editor's note in the latter reprint states that the article in *Prediction* appeared as one of a series of articles on "The Occult in Literature."

Just over eight years ago, there died, in America, a man unknown to all but a few passionate admirers among his own people, and as little known in this country as though almost he had never been born. Nor did all those of the few who had heard of him agree on the matter of his merit, for while there were some who hold him to be a writer of the first class, by reason both of the quality of his style and that of his imagination, there were others who did not hesitate to assign his work to a place among the thrillers of the boys tuppenny libraries; of the genre of "Deadwood Dick," "Nick Carter," and "Jack, Sam and Pete."

It is eight years since Howard Phillips Lovecraft died at the relatively early age of forty-seven, after a life spent virtually as a recluse in the New England town of Providence, which bulks so largely in his collected tales. A man of strange whims—his misanthropy (and misogyny) were not the most remarkable of them—he yet had the God-sent gift of inspiring true affection as well as genuine admiration in certain others, notably young men of an intellectual turn of fancy.

There was, indeed, something Socratic in the life of this odd man;— wrapped up against the cold that he hated with a more than normal loathing; detesting the sea (and all marine life) with a sort of detestation,—of a pathological kind, which forces its victim to a morbid interest in the object of its loathing; loving the ancient, decaying culture of New England—with its sinister background of witchcraft and diabolism—with a fanatically jealous love, and contriving to communicate that perfervid adoration to his young disciples, many of whom were not of his boasted Anglo-Saxon descent, and had come from foreign stock, settled in the newer, more vigorous cultures of the West and the Middle West.

A man—or woman—may be a writer of the first class, but may yet fail to become an influence of account, even though he or she finds readers and admirers. Other writers seem to acquire an influence out of all proportions to their literary skill. H. P. Lovecraft was almost unique in that he is incontrovertibly the greatest master of the weird story since Edgar Allan Poe, and possibly the greatest literary influence since Richardson.

Why, then, you may ask, was Lovecraft so little known in his own country, and practically unknown in this? The answer is that Lovecraft was unlucky enough to fail to impress that small and group of 'the people that matter.' It is a sad reflection on the standards of our time that the approbation of this group is far more necessary to an aspiring writer or artist than the mastery of his technique. The 'people who matter' will make a success of a man who can neither write or paint, but Heaven help the man who wants success on merits alone! In Lovecraft's case he had to sell his short stories where he could; and that market bought them for what it considered their sensationalism, not regarding—or caring for—their exquisite style and faultless workmanship.

Yet, though the dime novel gave Lovecraft the only public notice that his works had in his own lifetime, he yet, by means of the friendships that I have mentioned, and by means of a truly enormous correspondence, carried on with all the volume possible only to a semi-invalid of restless energy and unflagging interest, contrived to exercise an influence on the younger of his contemporaries (especially those with literary ambitions) comparable only with the influence exercised by a Goethe, a Byron or a Wilde. It is to the regret felt by these 'disciples' of Lovecraft—and, of course, to the work that they will do in the fullness of time—that Lovecraft's memory will owe its salvation from oblivion. Let us be content to wait for that time and see what Lovecraft himself achieved.

His joint biographers, Mr. August Derleth and Mr. Donald Wandrei—themselves both noted writers of horror-tales—point out that it was Lovecraft who was responsible for the first orderly—and complex—presentation of a myth which had grown up through the works of several preceding writers, but which remained unsatisfactorily vague and ragged until Lovecraft, with his genius for giving form to the most inchoate of forms of nightmare, took it in hand and finished it off with the sure touch of a master, completing the rough sketch of an inspiring but necessarily inexperienced pupil.

This is what his biographers, in their masterly little memoir, published shortly after Lovecraft's death—have to say about the inception and development of this theme with which his fame will always be associated.[35]

After a time there became apparent in his tales a curious coherence, a myth-pattern so convincing that, after its early appearances, readers of Lovecraft's stories began to explore libraries and musæums for certain imaginary titles of Lovecraft's own creation, so powerful that many another author, with Lovecraft's permission, availed themselves of facets of the mythos for their own use. Bit by bit it grew, finally its outlines became distinct, and it was given a name: The Cthulhu Mythology because it was in "The Call of Cthulhu" that the myth-pattern first became apparent.

It is possible to trace the original inception of this mythology back through Robert W. Chambers' once popular but now little known, "The King in Yellow," to Bierce's "An Inhabitant of Carcosa" and Poe's "Narrative of A. Gordon Pym;" but in these stories only the barest hint of something "outside" had appeared, and it was Lovecraft who constructed the myth-pattern in its final form. In his stories he then merged fantasy with terror, and even his poems took on certain symbols of the mythos, so that presently he was writing: ". . . all my stories, unconnected as they may be, are based on the fundamental lore or legend that this world was inhabited by another race who, in practising black magic, lost their foothold and were expelled yet live on 'outside', ever ready to take possession of the earth again . . ." a formula notable for the fact that though it sprang from the mind of a professed religious unbeliever, is basically similar to the Christian Mythos, particularly in regard to the expulsion of Satan from Eden, and the power of evil. . . .

Now there is no place here in which to touch even lightly on the themes of Lovecraft's various stories, nor discuss the means by which he achieves his unique effects of all-pervading horror. But I should like to emphasize my own belief that revelation (I use the word in its relation to mystical philosophy) may come—and assuredly does come—through speech and writings that we may persuade ourselves spring from our 'imagination'; that we 'made them up.' Those who understand the origins of Man's impulses know how childish a perversion that is. It was not only St. Paul who spoke with the tongues of "men and angels"[36] . . . we all do; though not all of us are conscious of that fact. Years ago I wrote a novel in which (at the beginning of the tale) I described events which had happened using the same characters that I had known in real life. But only the beginning of the book was—as I thought—"factual." I believed the completion of the work to be 'imaginary.' Ten years after, I can read that book and see that all of it was taken from actual happenings.[37]

So with your writer of ghost stories that he believes spring only from his darkly brooding imagination. He believes, as well as any other author, that he had 'made the story up.' But his effects are secured not altogether by the excellence of his style, or the skillful unfolding of his plot; his effects are secured "because he tells the tale as though it had really happened." And . . . his readers are stirred to the inmost depths of their souls because they know in their inmost hearts "that it did really happen." It was not for nothing that the myth-pattern evolved from Lovecraft's 'imagination' astonished his biographers by its close resemblance to the tale told by the unknown writer of the book of Genesis, a piece of work that some people regard as no less fictional than Lovecraft's or any writer's story. But the truth is that Lovecraft—even though he professed no membership of any organized religion—came, by degrees, to the evolution of a strange tale similar to that which we may find in Genesis, because both he and the author of Genesis were telling the same story, either through some subtle stirring of memories from a time when Michael and Lucifer strove before the high battlements of Heaven, or—which seems more likely—that time, as we know it, exists only for us, and in our little world—and that the cosmic battle between what we call good and evil goes on eternally, so that the human being who sets out to be an artist (who gives himself or herself over to strange forces, in other words) invites Others to speak through his lips, though he or she may think it is other than this.

That is what is meant when it is said that the poets and the dreamers have garnered all the wisdom of the world; for it is only in dreams, as Lovecraft said so often, that we can make contact with the infinite reality which lies outside the trivial span of human existence and the infinitesimal space in which the human body has its pitifully limited adventures.

The Lovecraft Cult

Arthur F. Hillman

> Arthur F. Hillman was a British science fiction and fantasy fan about whom not much is known. The following article—a review-essay of four recent publications by or about HPL—appeared in *Fantasy Review* 1, No. 4 (August–September 1947): 2–4.

It is just ten years since Howard Phillips Lovecraft, American writer of weird tales, died at the age of 47, to be mourned by a few devoted friends and the comparatively limited circle of readers who knew and valued his writings. To those who regretted his demise it is some consolation that his fame and influence have grown, slowly but steadily, through the years. Despite the condescending attitude which some were pleased to adopt towards this self-confessed literary "amateur" and the humble origins of his work, its underlying brilliance is now widely recognised.

Of the score of anthologies of horror tales which have appeared in America of recent date, there are few that have not included at least one of Lovecraft's. Since August Derleth and Donald Wandrei, among his oldest and most ardent admirers, prepared those two magnificent collections of his stories, "The Outsider and Others" and "Beyond the Wall of Sleep," others have seized eagerly on his work, which is now familiar to a much larger public than he himself ever visualised.

These two fine books are not only out of print but such copies as do exist will never come your way except at prices that may surprise and even shock you. But if you have not read Lovecraft, or have only a dim memory of him from *Weird Tales* and want to read him again, you cannot do better than seek out a copy of the Tower Books collection of his "Best Supernatural Stories."

In this book are twelve of Lovecraft's most popular pieces which appeared in *Weird Tales* between 1924 and '39, including "The Haunter of the Dark," "The Call of Cthulhu" and "The Whisperer in Darkness," together with the memorable "Colour out of Space," which is said to have been published in *Amazing Stories* twenty years ago only because it was submitted there by accident. Also included are "The Dunwich Horror" and "The Thing on the Doorstep," which, with the remarkable *Astounding*

Stories serial, "The Shadow out of Time," were presented in a Bart House Mystery pocket-book at about the same time.[38] An earlier book in the same series, which you may still be able to procure, comprised "The Weird Shadow over Innsmouth," "The Whisperer in Darkness," and three short pieces including "The Outsider."[39]

"The Dunwich Horror" has seen print yet again, more recently, in the "Avon Ghost Reader." "The Haunter of the Dark" also makes another appearance, in the latest Avon pocket-book of supernatural stories titled "Terror at Night." The current hard-cover anthologies "Who Knocks?" and "The Night Side" both contain Lovecraft stories.[40] But if, in spite of all this, his work still eludes you, don't despair. Later in the year Avon will publish a new pocket-book collection of his tales titled "The Lurking Fear and Other Stories," and you can rely on it that the new *Fantasy Reader* will feature him fairly regularly.[41]

With this increasing recognition of Lovecraft's work over the past decade has emerged a growing interest in the man himself, amounting to a veritable cult. For this narrator of weird and horrific stories had facets to his character almost as strange as the bizarre channels into which his roving imagination delved. His secluded life and yet tremendous erudition; his absorption with things of the 18th century and his affectations of the Georgian period; his abnormal sensitivity to extremes of weather; the inherent reserve that made it practically impossible for him to cope with the realities of a cruel, workaday world—glimpses of all these peculiar features of his personality were always to be had from his stories. But of his charm of manner, his infinite patience and kindly humour, his gentleness, one could gather little apart from one testimony: the devotion that prompted his small circle of friends to ensure that his name and his work should become more than a fading memory.

August Derleth's biographical appreciation of "H.P.L." is of absorbing interest to those who have been caught up in the web of fascination that has been weaved about the recluse of Providence, Rhode Island. The profound effect on this sensitive writer of the Lovecraft influence is apparent throughout; yet, discounting the aura of semi-divinity that his earnest disciple has naturally fabricated around him, it enables us to penetrate further into the fascinating enigma of his personality.

We learn how, in the years of his childhood, he was shielded from the outside world by the solicitude of his aunts and the ancient tomes which were his companions. Later, his entry into the field of amateur journalism led to the gradual amassing of correspondents and interests that drew him partly out of his shell of reserve. Then followed the writing of his first stories, the opening of a market for them in *Weird Tales*, and the acquisition of a following of enthusiastic readers. There is an elaboration of the Cthulhu Mythos around which he framed some of his greatest tales, and a penetrating analysis of the reasons and motives for his work. To those who have read and admired his writings, and who have felt a burning curiosity concerning the half-legendary figure of their author, this little book will reveal much that is illuminating and conducive to a better understanding of his most bewildering creations.

"Marginalia," on the other hand, is essentially a book for the Lovecraft fan, already familiar with most if not all of his work and with at least a general knowledge of the literary circle which revolved around him. The casual reader, dipping into it, may be somewhat nonplussed by the peculiar variety of its contents and the narrowness of its subject-matter; for it is primarily a select excursion into the realm of H.P.L. and his satellites, and the inexpert traveller may well regret the absence of a guide-book.

Typifying the spirit that marked the initial launching of its publishers, it presents for the connoisseur a fascinating melange of lesser-known stories, essays and other pieces written by Lovecraft or re-written by him from the material of other writers he befriended, and covering the whole period of his writing life. The rest of the book consists of tributes in prose and verse by members of his circle, including such well-known fantasy writers as Henry Kuttner, Clark Ashton Smith and Frank Belknap Long; besides Wandrei and Derleth.

There are several photographs and drawings which are of equal fan-interest as the "Notes on the Writing of Weird Fiction" and "Some Notes on Interplanetary Fiction" must be to those who are concerned with these aspects of the fantasy field. And even if one is not a convert to the Lovecraft cult, the philosophical depth of the essays, the marked beauty of the language in which they are written, and the intriguing sidelights they throw on the whole Lovecraft tradition, render the book appealing. The initiate may not catch the enthusiasm displayed so vehemently by his followers, but at least he may glimpse the reasons for such veneration.

Of more general interest to the weird fiction reader, apart from those who cherish all his writings, is the Lovecraft essay, "Supernatural Horror in Literature," which has been reprinted from "The Outsider and Others" and which originally appeared twenty years ago in an amateur magazine called *The Recluse*. A comprehensive survey of the whole range of weird fiction, it traces its earliest beginnings from the ancient legends of folklore croaked at the hearthside by toothless beldames, up through the brooding Gothic romances of the 17th century, to the literary masterpieces of modern writers such as Algernon Blackwood, Arthur Machen, M. R. James and Dunsany.

But although one admires the diligent researches that went into the compilation of this now classic monograph, one sees definite signs of partiality in the criticisms it presents. For the Sage of Providence had emphatic views on the pattern of the perfect weird tale. He considered that it should take a series of steps towards a hideous denouement, each with its quota of cryptic allusions which slowly build up the cumulative force of the whole, and he gave perhaps an undue importance to those tales which fulfilled these mechanics. His thesis, while contributing immensely to the student's knowledge of supernatural fiction, thus artfully contrives also to propagandise the ideas which he upheld and turned to such notable account in his own writings.

The modern school of brisk, staccato writing has lately invaded the weird field, perhaps one of the last refuges of good English; and one is certain that Lovecraft would be pained to see how his beloved medium has been maltreated. On the other hand, several of the old Gothic tales over which he enthused have little now to recommend them apart from their style of writing, and are stilted [sic] by the prevailing artificialities of their age. But even if one does not share all the enthusiasms of such a rabid bibliophile as Lovecraft, his analysis of the field as it has been developed is fascinating reading; for much of the charm of the essay lies in the wonderful language he used so aptly and effortlessly.

The beginning and the ending, particularly, are clothed in words of rich beauty and lyrical effect such as are rarely encountered in this mechanistic age. To those who appreciate literary craftsmanship and who have a special interest in the emotional power of the supernatural story, we can doubly recommend this book.

Best Supernatural Stories of H. P. Lovecraft, edited with an introduction by August Derleth. World Pub. Co., New York, 60c.
H.P.L.: A Memoir, by August Derleth. Abramson, New York, $2.50.
Marginalia, by H. P. Lovecraft. Collected by August Derleth and Donald Wandrei. Arkham House, Sauk City, $3.00.
Supernatural Horror in Literature, by H. P. Lovecraft. Abramson, New York, $2.50.

Lovecraft Is 86

Francis T. Laney

> Francis Towner Laney (1914–1958) was a curious figure in Lovecraft scholarship. Initially fascinated with HPL, he founded and edited the *Acolyte* (1942–46), an early fanzine that contained much valuable writing about HPL and his colleagues. His "The Cthulhu Mythology: A Glossary" (*Acolyte*, Winter 1942) was reprinted in HPL's *Beyond the Wall of Sleep* (1943). But with the passing of years Laney grew disenchanted with both HPL and the entire fantasy fandom movement: he expressed his disdain in a pungent autobiography, *Ah! Sweet Idiocy!* (1948). The following article—first published in *Sky Hook* No. 8 (Autumn 1948): 6–8—exhibits Laney's revisionist views of HPL.

> "86."–Waitress slang for sold out, no more left, out of stock, finished, all done, passé.
> —McGivern, *Dictionary of Modern Slang*

Howard Phillips Lovecraft is dead. It would be a good idea to leave him that way, to call a halt to this shameless stirring amongst his bones which has gone far to raise him to the status of a modern myth among fantasites.

Let us try to observe Lovecraft objectively for a moment and see what basis there may be for this quasi-worship of him and his works which has built several fanzines and a small publishing house, and has enabled a number of nonentities to glean a certain amount of vicarious fame by riding on the mouldering coat-tails of a dead man.

Was Lovecraft a success as a commercial writer? The answer is definitely, no. He eked out a bare starvation existence doing rewrite work for other writers and through selling perhaps half of a very meager output of his own to one of the lower paying pulp magazines. Lovecraft himself would agree heartily that he was not a commercial success; in many instances in his letters he has stated emphatically that he wanted no part of commercial success anyway, that he considered it beneath his dignity to strive therefor.

Was Lovecraft a success as an artistic writer? Here again the answer seems to be no, although there is more room for doubt than in the previous instance. To determine Lovecraft's artistic stature, we would have first to decide what constitutes artistic success. If realism be any criterion, Lovecraft, a man who knew life only fourth or fifth hand, was a thundering failure. However, subjective horror need not necessarily be realistic, provided that it is presented in such manner as to convey to the reader the same sense of terror felt by the author. Did Lovecraft do this, other than imperfectly and partially? No. He has asserted that his technique was to maintain "a careful realism in every phase of the story except that touching on the one given marvel" (*Marginalia*, p. 138).[42] Here his utter maladjustment to society has made him incapable of visualizing or expressing an even remotely believable locale or action; his best effort is no more than a subjective caricature of reality. Other than through the temporary suspension of belief on the part of the reader, are the mundane settings of Lovecraft's tales even remotely plausible, particularly in the matter of logical motivation and characterization? Did Lovecraft play other than fumblingly on the strings of terror? No, indeed. He had a horror of the sea and of fish, a horror not shared by most of his readers. It made no difference to Lovecraft—a fish-being was the quintessence of horror, so he'd say "fish" in a hollow sepulchral voice and wonder why the readers didn't all faint. And he had a most annoying trick of applying totally subjective definitions to different words—especially ones dealing with age, time, cold, horror—and he would then pour these words on. The net effect was less one of horrific atmosphere than of overdone hamminess.

And there is of course his worst writing fault, his almost consistent telegraphing of the punch line. Writing up to a twist ending, he would usually give himself away by the time he was halfway through his story. There was none of the skill manifested by James, for example, or Bierce, or Chambers. These men would write up to the very denouement and then, BAM, they would hit the reader in the teeth with a punch line that would rock him on his heels. But they didn't achieve this spectacular result by tipping their hand halfway through the story. It is not entirely possible to determine if Lovecraft considered himself an artistic success, but the weight of evidence seems to be to the contrary. Certainly it is a well-established fact (viz., W. Paul Cook's appreciation of Lovecraft in *Beyond the Wall of Sleep*)[43] that HPL was forever dissatisfied with his work and constantly wished to disavow all his stories but the most recent ones. While of course much of this was perhaps modesty, it scarcely points to any strong feeling of satisfaction with his achievements in his chosen profession.

Was Lovecraft a success as a man? Here we tread on shaky ground. But Dr. David H. Keller's recent psychoanalysis of Lovecraft in *Fantasy Commentator* (Summer, 1948)[44] at least casts a modicum of doubt on Lovecraft's integration and psychological stability. From all accounts, even his own, Lovecraft seems to have been a profoundly maladjusted person, out of step with the world on nearly every phase of life.

There is of course no sense in being worshippers of success. But on the other hand, does it make sense to deify a man who was so completely unsuccessful? Is there any valid reason to use him as the basis on which to establish a cult?

Certainly Lovecraft was a likable fellow, a staunch and loyal friend who gave far too generously of himself to his associates. There can be no question but that his selfless help and encouragement made it possible for several members of the Lovecraft circle to become moderately successful writers. They indubitably felt keen grief at his passing, and most certainly are to be commended for feeling gratitude towards him for his help and encouragement.

But is there any valid reason why a man such as August Derleth, a first class writer in his own right, should attempt to keep the torch burning for Lovecraft when he could take the time and energy and intelligence which has made Arkham House such a successful publishing venture, and write material of his own which is likely to be of far greater importance than anything Lovecraft ever produced?

Is there any valid reason why a character like Francis T. Laney, who never even heard of Lovecraft until three years after his death, should be enabled to build *The Acolyte* into fame and success in its own little microcosmos, simply by loading the early issues with mouldy scrapings out of HPL's literary breadbox? Certainly it was easier than to build up a top fanzine with genuinely amateur efforts.

Why should any fanzine ever again publish anything by Lovecraft, or even about him? If fanzines more or less drop HPL from consideration, and if Derleth and one or two other pros stop beating the drums for Lovecraft for even as little as one year, HPL will drop back to his proper status in American literature—almost completely unknown and forgotten.

Of course, Derleth can do as he will, and he will no doubt continue to publish vastly of Lovecraftiana. A man of his prodigious energy and endless contacts can keep the Lovecraft myth alive for many years to come by what might be called artificial respiration. But there is certainly no valid reason for fan publishers to help furnish the iron lung for Lovecraft. Not only is the subject of Lovecraft written out and passé, but the available store of unpublished Lovecraft writings is almost nil. From time to time Derleth may graciously permit some fanzine to publish something by Lovecraft—he has been more than generous in the past—but why should fanzines bother with it? If it isn't good enough for Arkham House, is it worth the trouble of stencilling for a fanzine?

It is harder to write original material of merit than to fill a magazine with the refuse from professional authors' wastebaskets. And it is difficult for any amateur editor to forego the egoboo of publishing something by Lovecraft. But why not build up your own stable of writers? Maybe one of them may be a big name in his own right some day. Wouldn't it be better to publish the early stuff by a future great, than the castoffs of a dead questionable?

Rusty Chains

John Brunner

> John Brunner (1934–1995) was a prolific science fiction writer; his novel *Stand on Zanzibar* (1968) won the Hugo Award. Early in his career he wrote the following discussion of HPL as a contribution to his column, "Rusty Chains," *Inside and Science Fiction Advertiser* No. 14 (March 1956): 17–21. The article appears to reflect the views of many science fiction writers of the 1950s and 1960s in regard to HPL. The September 1956 issue of the fanzine included rebuttals by various supporters of HPL, with a reply by Brunner (see below).

When I was fifteen or so, I discovered jazz. In the atmosphere of an English public school, it isn't easy to foster an interest like that (though I and some friends changed that eventually). Moreover, what with shortage of spending money and other such problems, I was quite unable to hear for myself enough by the greats of jazz to be able to form my own opinions. The result was that I went around basking in other people's criticisms of various so-called titans of the music and retaining them in ill-digested second-hand shape.

I shudder nowadays to think of some of the vague notions I entertained of what was and wasn't good.

But I don't think that can be so uncommon. For a year or two later I also discovered—no, not s. f.; I'd been reading as much of that as I could lay hands on since I was seven—but means of access to American magazines and books, and the all-important fact that there really was a body of serious critical opinion on the subject. Leafing through the letter section of *Startling*,[45] for example, I'd find people harking back with nostalgic delight to the classic Kuttner yarns, to Brackett's Martian pirate stories, and to Merritt.

Naturally, I yearned to read these magnificent epics, which doubtless surpassed what was currently being published as Shakespeare surpasses Addison.

I almost cried when I finally got hold of these so-splendid works, for I found that they had been by-passed in the intervening years by people who had done things which might be similar but which were nonetheless vastly better. One by one they tumbled: Weinbaum's "Martian Odyssey"; the Kuttner stories; Brackett; John W. Campbell as a novelist; Clark Ashton Smith's "The Singing Flame"—even Heinlein himself (for a sample of the disappointing stuff see his collection *Assignment in Eternity*).[46]

Yet they all had one thing in common. It was abundantly plain that when they were first published they deserved to stir up a commotion—they had in many cases set a new fashion which had subsequently been superseded. That they were not as smooth and accomplished as more recent stories in the field—less thoughtful and less thought-provoking—could hardly in honesty be laid against them.

But the biggest disappointment was still to come.

Left, right and center, people were talking with enthusiasm of one Howard Phillips Lovecraft. Bloch and Derleth were still writing stories based on his themes; they were lousy, but since they were derivative and admitted it, that was hardly surprising. Eagerly, I borrowed a copy of one of the Derleth anthologies (*The Other Side of the Moon*, if I remember rightly) of which about a hundred pages were taken up by Lovecraft's "At the Mountains of Madness," and settled down to read it.[47]

After fifty pages I was going so slowly, and so little had happened, that I gave up in disgust. I chalked up the first writer with a big reputation that I had yet run across who had *nothing whatever* to recommend him for it. In defence of my opinion, I mark here that I was currently studying for Advanced Level General Certificate of Education in—among other things—English Literature, which I later got with distinction, and that my literary background is pretty varied; I am writing this facing a shelf full of pocket books, including Anderson, Balchin, Cloete, Colette, Faulkner, Flecker, Shaw and Thurber.[48]

I've been mentioning this fact in a slightly puzzled voice at intervals ever since, and have found that few of my fan friends can read Lovecraft—or have even done more than attempt to! Recently I was moved to express my feelings in a letter to Mike Rosenblum, which commented on a rave article about HPL published in his *New Futurian*.[49] A short while later, I received a note from Graham Stone[50] in Australia, referring to my letter in *New Futurian,* and lending me additional ammunition in a number of confirmatory and well-chosen phrases which appear later on in this article

Please let it be understood, however, that I am not attacking Lovecraft from personal distaste for his ideas. My claim is merely that he is an overrated and generally bad writer. I can't read Milton, but I wouldn't deny his claim to fame on those grounds. Perhaps more to the point, I'm a great fan of Edgar Allan Poe; for reasons which follow, I claim that the similarity in some respects between him and Lovecraft is not enough to excuse the latter.

I was asked to make this article as detailed an possible. Herein I'm handicapped; I so dislike the man that I haven't a single work of his in my collection of around 900 science fiction and fantasy magazines and books, aside from a few bad poems reprinted in *Weird Tales* shortly before it went bust. I did, however, hunt pretty hard for this so-magnificent writer a few years ago, and borrowed and tried to read many of his stories. I have a fair memory—not eidetic, but verbally retentive, at least. Moreover, the quarrel I have with HPL is so fundamental that detail is unimportant.

First and foremost, Lovecraft was supposedly a master of horror. His fantastic mythos, built up with great care and not a little ingenuity, deals with forces of evil, personified or localised into presences haunting certain places, against which his human characters fight a generally losing battle through some basic inadequacy. A diffuse pessimism regarding the fitness of the human race to survive is one of the first impressions to be garnered from reading Lovecraft. It is implied that probably the only reason we are still on Earth today is that in the dark past certain "priests" were opportunist enough to enlist the aid of these powers of darkness. Good! A fascinating concept in outline . . .

Spoiled by a manner of treating it which gives the impression that Lovecraft ate a Roget thesaurus before spewing it over the paper and calling it a story.

Horror is a dangerous and difficult medium in which to work—perhaps the most difficult of all forms of fantasy except humor. In our Western Society, until very recently—less than a hundred years ago and probably nearer seventy-five—our concept of evil in the absolute as distinct from evil manifested in human behavior was dominated by the battle between Christianity and the fertility religions whose magical ceremonies are still with us: we dance widdershins the wrong way of the sun in the ball room because that is the way witches dance at a coven meeting. The struggle was long and fierce, and colored Christian ideas of evil from James I's treatise on witchcraft through the Salem trials and the Hell-Fire Club to that last affected cult of deliberate evil, the Baudelaire-Wilde school of decadence and its obsession with scarlet-lipped women dying of TB under an enormous pale moon.

In the days of Edgar Allan Poe, therefore—probably the first writer to treat horror in a manner to be respected as literarily valuable†—the comparatively rational world of intelligent people which gave rise to the mechanistic physics of Kelvin and other such incredibly assured and quite false views of the universe, when the double standard of conscience, which was a standard possession of the reading public and which prevented them from seeing wrong in anything they themselves did, the necessary appurtenances of horror were cabalistic and pagan. Poe's Dupin might have been a model for some of Wilde's wilder (no pun intended) flights, with his refusal to venture forth by day, his horror of fresh air, and his preference for "ghastly tapers" as illumination. M. P. Shiel, motivated by a driving admiration for Poe, carried this to its illogical extreme in his Prince Zaleski stories.

That was horror; *that* was evil—to an age which could see nothing bad in confining servants to dank cellars whose walls shone with water and were spotted with fungi. Such things only became redolent of evil when people like themselves were confined there—and that, of course, could only happen in fiction, or in one of those dens of vice kept by the decadents whose works were to be kept from the daughters of the house and read over with furtive pleasure in privacy. Most important of all, this was an age when standard treatment for the insane was incarceration and restraint. Their impression of madness, therefore, was third-hand and highly colored; they might order out the carriage and go play Lady Bountiful at the workhouse at Christmas, but to a lunatic asylum—never! If it became necessary, they would provide their own, and forget to outward appearances about their "unfortunate" relation.

Poe was inevitably the last, as he was the first, to tap this vein with real success, for it was narrow, unrewarding and repetitive. Nowadays it provides thriller material for Dennis Wheatley and turgid tracts for C. S. Lewis. Even the originals like Sheridan Lefanu give us a quiet chuckle more often them they give us a frisson of terror.

A mixture of influences spelt its ruin. One was the rapid awakening of a social conscience, the lowering of ideals and the raising of morals which

---

†Interested readers should study Dorothy L. Sayers on the developing technique of the fantasy story in the second volume of her *Detection, Mystery and Horror* series—a corollary to her famous essay on the detective story in the first volume.

resulted in a total betterment of society (see Cyril Pearl's *The Girl with the Swansdown Seat* on Victorian morality in general).[51] Another was the rapid spread of education, which expanded the reading public unbelievably. Christianity, too, suddenly finding its supremacy no longer quite complete, invented a new weapon in its fight against paganism—it didn't beat it, it joined it. Nowadays the local parson will cheerfully join in a fertility rite thinly disguised as a traditional country dance.

Instead of it being said that human beings were all right, which made fiction the only suitable place for licensed evil, it become abundantly clear that human beings were largely all wrong. The development of psychology opened undreamed-of vistas for exploration—and achievement—and fiction grew up with one enormous bang. It is my firm contention that in the past hundred years fiction has become objectively about five hundred per cent better.

The first truly capable horror story I have been able to trace is Wells' "The Red Room."[52] Told in an efficient, almost matter-of-fact style, it bears the timeless stamp of subtlety. In essence, Wells, with his usual gift for being half a century ahead of the crowd, realised that the only common denominator in everyone's reaction to terror is the fact of fear itself. The aura of smug self-satisfaction was mercifully dead. That which is truly horrible is not the evil which is forced to hide away in the Mountains of Madness or the high plateau of Leng, or even in the graveyard at night—it is that which is not afraid to come forth by day, which walks with us on the city streets and lies in wait around the next corner. . . .

Lovecraft was a throwback, an atavism, deliberately cultivating the modes and manners of an earlier and vanished day. He turned back to the appurtenances of the "House of Usher"; he populated decaying, Charles Addams-ish granges with the fauna of the local charnel-house. He seemed obsessed with things which created disgust, rather than horror, and this obsession crept into his writing. He was fond of inventing nameless horrors—but there was no subtlety in his presentation of them, for he went on and on *saying* that such-and-such was too horrible for words. Yet he spent literally thousands and thousands of those words which he claimed were useless (rare honesty!) in setting the stage for their appearance. Stasis is his hallmark; the most insignificant details of a situation (as distinct from episode—he was very short on action) are sprawled on his pages in resounding terms—borrowed from the most recondite corners of the Oxford English Dictionary, serving no purpose save to bemuse and confuse the reader.

Nowhere, incidentally, is this more acutely obvious than in Lovecraft's so-called poetry—those halting, clumsily constructed and baldly factual pseudo-ballads in which his inadequacy as a craftsmen, partially concealed in his prose by the battering-ram of his exotic terminology, is as apparent as in the works of William McGonigal (of immortal and howlingly funny memory).[53] Whether one quarrels or not with the subject matter of these verses, one surely must agree that his poetic ear was at fault. One could borrow almost wholesale from Aldous Huxley's essay in On the Margin[54] regarding those early English poets who had forgotten about Chaucer; they had learnt from Petrarch and the other Italians that a line should have a set number of syllables, but nothing more—whence they composed with their fingers more than with their minds, counting as they went along.

A parallel criticism may be levelled at Lovecraft; he knew what form he was trying to produce, but lacked the talent to utilise it intelligently.

Graham Stone puts it neatly—I quote his recent letter to me: "His preoccupation with nameless horrors may have clinical interest, but as fiction it fails. The whole idea of fiction is to tell a story; the whole idea of language is communication; and long-winded ramblings about something which is never defined or described do not communicate much. Derleth and others say it can 'evoke' (favorite word of the cult, but what does it mean?) an 'atmosphere' (ditto) of horror, dread, etc., by suggesting things too uggy for words." (In passing: That "uggy" is strictly sic—one of the most perfectly apt typographical errors I've ever run across!) This is supposed to be good. The truth to that if you pinned the man down the horrors would be either pretty tame, or indescribable for the excellent reason that he didn't have anything special in mind. Lovecraft used so much space in build-up that he spoiled the effect."

Lovecraft shared his fascination with madness with certain German poets of the end of the last century; according to Jethro Bithell,[55] some of them were proud of the time they spent in asylums. Yet despite the fact that more had been learned about madness in the twenty years before he began to write than in the previous two thousand, Lovecraft made no attempt to use that knowledge. His madmen go insane in the grandiloquent manner of Poe—and equally phonily.

By the 1940's, even a professional pulp writer without contentions of genius like Ron Hubbard could utilise the available knowledge (as distinct from overblown fantasies) of psychosis to create a master-work like "Fear"; Kuttner turned up with "The Devil You [sic] Know."[56] Both of these are epitomes of subtlety and convincing depictions of the evil to which day and night are indifferent. Crossing a graveyard at night one is troubled by instinctual, fundamentally emotional fears at which reason laughs; once one is safely back on the highway one forgets the momentary qualm. But the danger which is eminently reasonable, which one's intellect accepts—*that* is horrible.

Surely, if by the forties more professionals writing for bread and butter could capitalise thus on available knowledge, a genius, such as his fans claim Lovecraft was, could have had his imagination sparked in the twenties to produce arresting, original, enduring work?

But no, apparently; he had to go hunting his black fane of horror in outlandish regions with neither shape nor substance. Drunk on the splendor of words and feverishly seeking to capture the unreal weirdness of an opium dream, he was harried by black demons of his own invention to wander among imagined realms of evil whose only existence lay in the bewildering wood of dislocation produced by his use of obsolete terms without meaning to his readers, when on his and every one's doorstop the true terrors waited patiently for someone to notice them. They could afford to wait; they were too strong to have to hide at cock-crow.

We ourselves live in a world which bears no relation to Lovecraft's. We talk in present-day English. We *do* things—we do not spend, as Lovecraft did, hours in haunted burrowing through the recesses of our minds. We live on the conscious level, and so do the true terrors.

Each age renews the wellsprings of evil. The ancient ghouls are, mercifully, dead; they had not long to live in any case, for they were sick and cankered. For a while Lovecraft gave them artificial respiration, and made them into gangling puppets without the power to terrify or convince.

But now the demons walk in sunlight.

Some Notes on HPL

Sam Moskowitz, Fritz Leiber, Edward Wood, and John Brunner

> John Brunner's article inspired several rebuttals, published in *Inside and Science Fiction Advertiser* Nos. 16/50 (September 1956): 32–35, 57. The rebuttals are by Sam Moskowitz (1920–1997), leading science fiction fan and historian; Fritz Leiber (1910–1992), celebrated science fiction and fantasy writer and correspondent of HPL; Edward Wood, a longtime science fiction fan. Brunner adds a response.

1.

Everything that John Brunner says against Lovecraft in "Rusty Chains" is true, at least to the extent that his criticism can be buttressed by many examples from Lovecraft's fiction. Yet his entire argument becomes meaningless when by his own admission we find that he has read very little of Lovecraft. ("I twice tried to get through At the Mountains of Madness and twice came to a crashing halt about one-third of the way through. First, when it originally appeared in Astounding in 1936 and I was sixteen. The second time when it was reprinted in Strange Ports of Call in 1948 and I was more mature.")[57] This limitation has resulted in his making two serious blunders. First, judging Lovecraft by his worst instead of his best material. Second, entirely misinterpreting Lovecraft's contribution to the field.

"The Dunwich Horror" was no failure. It has weaknesses, but taken in its entirety, it is, relative to other tales of its type, a literary masterpiece. That it is a narrative with real story interest is testified by the fact that it was successfully adapted to a major radio dramatization and the leading role enacted by Ronald Coleman.[58]

"The Dunwich Horror" also epitomizes Lovecraft's major contribution to the literary fantasy scene—the adaptation of science fiction material to the weird and supernatural tale. In this story, and in many of his more successful stories, such as "The Shadow out of Time," "The Whisperer in the Darkness," "The Call of Cthulhu," "The Temple," etc., he attempted to write tales of horror with a background of plausible science.

To this end Lovecraft was peculiarly well fitted, since he had an overwhelming interest in science from his youngest days, his first amateur publication being an astronomical journal. His notebooks with scientific calculations in this regard are owned by Dr. David H. Keller.[59]

Lovecraft's library had probably more scientific texts than any other single category of books.

Probably the best essay on Lovecraft's mingling of scientific with horrific themes was written by Fritz Leiber, Jr., in his fine article "The Works of H.P. Lovecraft: Suggestions for a Critical Appraisal" and appeared in the Fall 1944 issue of The Acolyte.

Lovecraft was far from alone in this school of writing. He was joined by such able compatriots as Clark Ashton Smith, Nictzin Dyhalis, C. L. Moore and others. This school of writers was greatly encouraged by Farnsworth Wright, late editor of the also late Weird Tales, who was faced with a constant war between readers of his magazine who desired stories either more weird or more scientific. He welcomed the Lovecraft approach as a solution that satisfied both.

I completely and utterly disagree with Mr. Brunner that Weinbaum's "The Martian Odyssey" has suffered at all from the effects of time. I have reread it on the average of once every three years, sometimes aloud, and this, like a good portion of his other works, still has the polish of a jewel. You may weep for some of the others, but not for Weinbaum.

The other examples given, such as Campbell's and Heinlein's, suffer from the same fault as Lovecraft's. You are judging those men from some of their worst examples, not their best.

While I consider Lovecraft's mingling of science and horror to be particularly fine in "The Dunwich Horror" and "The Temple," sometimes he was superb in pure fantasy.

I refer to stories like "The Strange High House in the Mist" and "The Quest of Iranon." The realism engendered by "The Shadow over Innsmouth" in the remarkable description or the decadent New England countryside, industry, social life and philosophy was truly memorable.

Like Mr. Brunner, I have never been able to finish "At the Mountains of Madness." I think "Dream Quest of Unknown Kadath" is absurd, that many of Lovecraft's minor prose pastels are not exceptional, but again, a man does not pin his reputation upon his worst work but upon his best. Ernest Hemingway was roundly panned for *Across the River and into the Trees* which appeared in 1950. In 1953, however, he received the Pulitzer Prize for *The Old Man and the Sea*. In the history of literature he will be judged by the latter.

Lovecraft was not an important poet, but he definitely was an eminently readable and entertaining one in the weird vein.

—Sam Moskowitz

2.

People being given a big build-up about Lovecraft and then finding themselves sharply disappointed by his writings is an old story, and an understandable one, and one that gets itself told about other big names in fantasy and science fiction. Take Stapledon, for instance:

A newcomer to the field hears that *Last and First Men* is the great work of modern science fiction, the seminal epic. He is led to expect something along the lines of *Brave New World, 1984, Men Like Gods*,[60] a kind of science fiction *War and Peace*. Finally he gets his hands on the book and what does he find? Something halfway between an encyclopedia entry and an article in *The New Republic*. A large and cumbersome book without dialogue, deep psychology, meaty characters, or more than three or four vivid metaphors or pictures. And with a lot of banal stuff such as (ye gods!) giant brains and gelatinous Martians. No wonder he is disillusioned. It will be some time (if ever) before he grasps the importance, in its own right, and to science fiction, of that "essay in myth creation."

Same thing goes for such a gorgeous and measured melodrama as Eddison's *The Worm Ouroboros* or such a crabbedly endearing legend as Tolkien's *The Lord of the Rings*.[61] Great expectations rudely let down. Rather childish imaginary countries and rather pompous wars that are old-fashioned both in technique and spirit. Poems by John Donne and phrases from *The Duchess of Malfi*.[62] A lot of nonsense in High Elvish and Low Dwarvish. Black-and-white moral values. And the books are even (worst of crimes today!) "very slow reading."

And the same goes double for Lovecraft. Stirred by phrases such as "modern master of the macabre" and "inventor of the Cthulhu mythos," the neophyte comes to expect a super-Poe, a profound John Collier, a William Hope Hodgson with style and sophistication, a Charles Williams without the religious trappings, a writer who has gone many steps further than Arthur Machen in naming nameless horrors. Finally he tackles the real Lovecraft and has a rough awakening. He finds masses of long paragraphs without dialogue or titillating modern tricks; a style half-way between that of a gloomy, florid poet and an unworldly scholar painstakingly writing up an experience; a man in love with several periods of the past, who rejects modern sophistication because it is tawdry and unmannerly, and sentimentality because it is contrary to scientific materialism; a writer who claims little for his stories and persistently thinks of himself as an amateur.

The disappointment is understandable; it may even go so far, as in the case of John Brunner, to make the reader decide, in a burst of irritation, that here is a writer with "*nothing whatever* to recommend him." But it renders the reader at least temporarily blind to Lovecraft's genuine artistic creations, his wide and deep education, his devising of a legend of the supernatural suitable to scientific materialism. Above all, it is an expression of the rather pampered modern distaste for any writing that is slow or difficult, that has not been carefully pruned and speeded up by clever, up-to-the-minute editing.

I am thoroughly in sympathy with modern psychiatry and humanist ethics, but I do not believe, as Brunner seems to, that they have banished the irrational from life or caused us and our terrors to live wholly on the conscious level. The horrors evoked by Poe and Lovecraft had elements of class attitude, but these are not their chief explanation. Freud has complicated but in no way solved the writer's problems. "Haunted burrowing through the recesses of our minds" is still inevitable and more necessary than ever. There are demons that still walk in darkness.

—Fritz Leiber

3.

While a critic has a right to his opinion about the merits of anyone's particular story, I should think that before dismissing the entire output of an author, the critic so doing should read more than a smattering of that author.

It seems to add up to:

1. John Brunner has read some of Lovecraft's poems and part of "At the Mountains of Madness."
2. John Brunner does not like Lovecraft.
3. Lovecraft is over-rated.

Regardless of Mr. Brunner's education, certificates and all, I cannot see the above as being a syllogism. He is at liberty to like or not like anyone he wishes. We are all at liberty to do the same.

There are some Lovecraft stories I don't like. There are many that I do like. Anyone who has a reasonable critique of Lovecraft's works will find a willing and eager reader in this person.

Almost everyone who has a reputation is over-rated at times. This is more often the fault of the over-rater than of the over-ratee. Also too many people seem to forget that science fiction and fantasy are read for extra literary values. Thought, logic, concept, etc., play a major part in the Cthulhu Mythos. This is more than I am able to say for 99% of the material that saturated the field in the last five to six years.

Lovecraft was content to live his life as he wanted to, writing those things he wanted to write, indulging in certain harmless eccentricities as do most of us, harming no one.

If all the so-called writers, authors, what-have-you, that have debased, commercialized, corrupted science fiction and fantasy over the last three decades were to be eliminated from our midst, there would be the names of a few that have honored our field. They did it for love, not for money. Among that small but glorious group would be the name of Howard Phillips Lovecraft.

—Edward Wood

4.

As to the letters you were kind enough to pass on, I don't think I ought to waste your valuable space by attempting a point-by-point counter attack; I'll just say a few things.

Moskowitz's letter I think is excellent, but does not call for reply particularly; he's made new statements rather than countering mine. (I'm interested by his reaction to "A Martian Odyssey"; I've never got beyond page three of it, though I used my standard break-in trick of looking for a situation in the middle which would whet my appetite and make me want to see how the author got to it. *The Black Flame* is the only Weinbaum I've really enjoyed.)[63]

I remember when I was at school and getting the Derleth anthologies through a postal s.f. library, I always used to turn up the Leiber stories first; I knew they would lead the pack. It seems odd to be standing up against a past master of s.f., whom I've admired so long and consider one of the top half-dozen in the field, when I'm a neophyte at the same trade. But I must.

Last and First Men I have read—twice, and with enjoyment—and I've reread excerpts more than that. Since I also like Donne, and think *The Duchess of Malfi* a greater work than several of Shakespeare's plays, I can't quite appreciate some of the comparisons he uses to illustrate coming to HPL for the first time. The best parallel, I think, would be David Lindsay's *Voyage to Arcturus*,[64] which I read on a personal tip from C. S. Lewis; a compulsively brilliant but thoroughly poisonous work, by a man with no status as a writer—only a commandingly powerful imagination. Imagination, however, does not redeem either the style or the theme.

I'll just say to Wood in passing that his "sillygism" (bless Lewis Carroll for that one!) isn't acceptable to me, either; the statement that I had tried to read many of Lovecraft's stories is literal. Out of the twenty or thirty I have attempted to enjoy, surely only a malign fate could have prevented me from finding something great if it was there?

Mr. Leiber, though: he has done me the great service of accepting that I am aware of and appreciate Hodgson, Collier, Charles Williams and the rest; it wasn't, however, in a "burst of irritation" that I made my sweeping statement—it was after prolonged disappointment that I referred to it. Now I am not, I swear, addicted to impatience because of lack of up-to-the-minute editing. On the contrary, I firmly believe that the English language is the finest tool of communication ever developed by man. It has twice the resources, literally, of the nearest competitor. Therefore, it behooves a writer to make the fullest possible use of it.

But as an instrument of communication.

There is probably only one work in English which can afford to stand up and just be beautiful—*Kubla Khan*—because its function disappeared with the remainder of it on the arrival of the Person from Porlock. I know of only one novelist currently who has achieved the perfect fusion of beautiful prose and a maximum level of communication, and that's George R. Stewart,[65] a man who seems to be so much in love with English that his most casual statements achieve the functional beauty of good engineering, while his passages of description produce an interplay of image and event without the slightest veil of verbal confusion to mask the effect.

(While I think of it: perhaps someone would oblige me by explaining why the arrant rationalist HPL was so fascinated by the horror story.)

Alan Paton[66] and Stuart Cloete, at his best, run in Stewart's company. Their use of language is so efficient, if you like—because they are never preoccupied by confusing word with image or concept.

However, I have a feeling that this argument will in the end wind up where all critical arguments seem to among personal prejudices. I do suspect that since the most ardent Lovecraftians belong to the generation before me, they may have produced a reaction by over-rating him; I admit, too, that I'm just naturally against euphuistic English. Frank Arnold (*Wings across Time*—remember the guy?)[67] has promised to look me up some HPL I haven't read, which he recommends, and those kind people who took up the cudgels in defense of him can know I do try and see their point of view.

—John Brunner

V. Notices from the Literary Community

Mystery and Adventure

Will Cuppy

Will Cuppy (1884–1949) was a widely published humorist and literary critic. His best-known work is *The Decline and Fall of Practically Everybody* (1950). Cuppy was, however, a devoted reader of mystery and detective stories. He assembled three anthologies of mystery stories and, more significantly, reviewed more than 4000 titles in his long-running column "Mystery and Adventure" in the *New York Herald Tribune* (1926–49). The following review appeared in *New York Herald Tribune Books* (17 December 1939): 14.

THE OUTSIDER AND OTHERS. By H. P. Lovecraft . . . 553 pp. . . . Sauk City, Wis.: Arkham House . . . $5.

Lovers of horror in fiction are offered in this package enough to keep them blissful for quite a spell. Thirty-six stories by the late Howard Phillips Lovecraft (1890-1937), collected by August Derleth and Donald Wandrei, are included in this giant omnibus or young library of 553 large and closely packed pages totaling by rough count about 330,000 words, the equivalent in verbiage of four or five novels. Mystery fans might do worse than dig into the devil-haunted depths of this book for strange thrills and a general review of dreams, drugs, demons, magic, nameless crimes, the unspeakable Shub-Niggurath, the Hooded Thing that bleats, and why it is that in Ulthar, which lies beyond the river Skai, no man may kill a cat. You'll never be quite the same again, we promise you, if you attempt to swallow all these heady compositions at one sitting. Might be a good plan to read first Mr. Lovecraft's long and scholarly essay on "Supernatural Horror in Literature," in which he traces the subject from the dim beginnings up to date.

As for the stories, some customers may prefer such short takes as "Dagon" and other wholly hellish pieces, or perhaps those where reality plays a larger part, as "The Strange House [sic] in the Mist" or "The Thing on the Doorstep," an impressive novelette compounded of madness and the black art. Another starter could be "The Call of Cthulhu," a piece in which, according to the editors, the author's myth pattern first became apparent—it's known as the Cthulhu Mythology. Still, Mr. Derleth and Mr. Wandrei provide enough expert guidance in their preface, where they go into the matter of favorite themes and so forth. They state: "His closest successors to his unofficial title of master of the macabre were among his best friends: Clark Ashton Smith and the late Henry S. Whitehead. His only potential equals—Edith Wharton, Gertrude Atherton, Irvin S. Cobb, Dubose Heyward and some few others have done too little work in the field for all the excellence of what they did write." Of his own work Mr. Lovecraft wrote in 1931: "It is excessively extravagant and melodramatic and lacks depth and subtlety. . . . My style is bad, too—full of obvious rhetorical devices and hackneyed word and rhythm patterns. It comes a long way from the stark, objective simplicity which is my goal."[1] He seems to have been a modest genius as well as eccentric.

Horror Story Author Published by Fellow Writers

> The following unsigned review-article—published in *Publishers' Weekly* 137, No. 8 (24 February 1940): 890–91—was an important token of HPL's ascending posthumous celebrity, appearing as it did in the leading publishers' organ in the United States.

Booksellers with customers who like horror stories and who have a hard time finding good ones to satisfy them will be particularly interested in an unusual publishing venture which was first called to our attention by Bill Sloane, of Holt.[2] During December arrived, among the books sent for entry in the *Weekly Record*, a volume called "The Outsider and Others," by H. P. Lovecraft. It carried the imprint of Arkham House, of Sauk City, Wisconsin. We had never heard of either author or publisher; but the book was edited by August Derleth, author of numerous books and novels, the most recent being "Restless Is the River" and "Narracong Riddle" (to be published in March),[3] and Donald Wandrei, writer of weird tales and plays. From Mr. Derleth and Mr. Wandrei we've got the complete story of Arkham House and "The Outsider."

These two authors had been close friends and admirers of H. P. Lovecraft, a writer of horror tales who died in March, 1937. During his lifetime, Lovecraft had won a considerable following, almost a cult of worshippers, for his horror tales, which appeared in magazines like *Weird Tales* and *Astounding Stories* and in anthologies like "Beware After Dark"; "Creeps by Night"; and the "Not at Night" series issued in England. Lovecraft's work, it seems, became sufficiently well known to attract the attention of book publishers, eight of whom wrote to him at different times asking to see a selection of stories.[4] Nothing ever came of it, Derleth and Wandrei tell us, partially because Lovecraft had so little faith in the chances of book publication that he sent in, in reply to these requests, half-legible carbons or tattered tear-sheets from old magazines.

After his death the two authors decided to take on themselves the responsibility of seeing his tales collected and published in book form. They tell us that they had little idea of how formidable the task would prove to be. Fortunately, Lovecraft had left a list of his stories, and with notations of the dates of publication. The two authors already owned practically complete files of the magazines and anthologies containing his stories. After securing the authorization of Lovecraft's heir and literary executor, they hired a couple of typists and went to work.

When the majority of the stories were finally collected, they made a typescript of 1350 pages. For good measure it was decided to put in as an appendix Lovecraft's long historical survey, "Supernatural Horror in Literature," which added 150 more pages. What happened then is described to us by Mr. Derleth and Mr. Wandrei as follows:

"We took the giant around to three different publishers, and rather to our surprise one of them nearly published it. It was passed and recommended by the editor-in-chief, but rejected by the editorial director four months later. Rather than delay for months or years longer trying other publishers, while Lovecraft's name receded with time, we decided the only sure way to see the book come out was to publish it ourselves.

"That decision brought on a whole new crop of headaches. We had to face the old dilemma of whether to use a large type and run up such staggering paper costs that the book couldn't be got out for less than $7 or $8, or whether to use a small type that nobody could read without developing acute myopia and astigmatism. We compromised, like all publishers since the year one, and used a 9-point on 10 which, while smaller than desirable, is satisfactory if the thirty-six stories are read one at a time. Then came proof-reading, another arduous job that required a solid three weeks' time. We more or less arbitrarily set the edition at 1200 copies, since horror stories have a limited market, and since we were told by everybody with any publishing experience that collections of short stories just don't sell. We picked the name 'Arkham House' because a kind of myth-pattern is developed in many of Lovecraft's tales, in which a New England town called Arkham is mentioned most often. The costs finally worked out to a retail price of $5, which couldn't be helped."

Among other headaches, the question of copyright requirements had to be straightened out. But the publication of "The Outsider and Others" is only part of the story. The authors-editors-publishers decided that since they had begun publishing Lovecraft, they might as well make a complete job of it, so, with more fortitude than caution they started collecting his poems, informal essays and his letters.

The letters proved to be astounding. Lovecraft was a recluse and apparently for him letters had become a substitute for the personal contacts of ordinary social life. He corresponded regularly with some 200 people all over the country and had hundreds more occasional correspondents. He wrote to many of these people over a period of 20 years, with letters seldom spaced more than a week or two apart, and often on successive days. He wrote a number of letters that were each the equivalent of a full-length novel: letters of 50, 60 and 70 sheets, typewriter size, minutely covered on both sides with Lovecraft's fine penmanship.[5] These would run to 50,000 to 100,000 words to a letter. Furthermore, all Lovecraft's correspondents had preserved all his letters.[6] When Mr. Derleth and Mr. Wandrei called for letters they got them—by hundreds and thousands. Another typist was added to the two already at work. Training a typist to read Lovecraft's handwriting and understand his scholarly, erudite style was a job in itself. Already the collection has run to 27 volumes of extracts alone, 100 single-spaced typewriter sheets to each volume. The end is nowhere in sight for the publishers expect to have 50 typewritten volumes before they're through.[7]

Arkham House will publish two more books to complete the job. The second volume will consist of Lovecraft's two long, unpublished novelettes, a few stories that he wrote in collaboration, his complete poems and a selection of letters.[8] The third volume will contain letters alone.

Mr. Derleth and Mr. Wandrei tell us that their shirts are still on their backs but since "The Outsider and Others" was issued, "We now have perfect hindsight in understanding why such a volume of short stories, next to poetry, elicits about as much enthusiasm from the average publisher as would a stray cobra." Yet sales have been good, though not spectacular, and orders continue to come in.

[Review of *The Outsider and Others*]

T. O. Mabbott

T. O. Mabbott (see p. 145), a leading Poe scholar, was the first academician to review HPL. The following review appeared in the leading scholarly journal devoted to American writing, *American Literature* 12, No. 1 (March 1940): 136.

THE OUTSIDER AND OTHERS. By H. P. Lovecraft. Collected by August Derleth and Donald Wandrei. Sauk City, Wis.: Arkham House. 1939. 553 pp. $5.00.

This is a large volume, the first of a promised three-volume collection of the writings of an author known for striking and original stories of horror, for which he invented a mythology of his own. He was a typical New Englander, though in some senses a follower of Poe and Dunsany. Time will tell if his place be very high in our literary history; that he has a place seems certain. For if the popular magazines, as he felt, forced him to be melodramatic, his style was unhampered, and has a fine quality. The present volume consists chiefly of stories. Among them his own favorite seems to have been "The Color out of Space" or "The Music of Erich Zann," to which, however, the reviewer would prefer the Poesque "Tomb" and a characteristic fantasy from which the volume is named "The Outsider."

At the end of the volume is included the hitherto not accessible essay "Supernatural Horror in Literature." This is all too brief, and leaves untouched the work of several authors one would expect to find, and tends to underrate Stevenson, and overrate Dunsany. But it contains discussions of Poe, Hawthorne, and Bierce, so penetrating, sympathetic, and imaginatively keen that scholars will not want to miss them. Lovecraft understood the "House of Usher," and in a story called *At the Mountains of Madness*, makes a brief allusion to the identity of Yaanek in Ulalume and Mt. Erebus in the Antarctic, which is probably correct. Messrs. Derleth and Wandrei have done a service in collecting Lovecraft's works.

Such Pulp as Dreams Are Made On

Robert Allerton Parker

> Robert Allerton Parker (1888–1970) was an American journalist, editor, critic, and biographer. The following article, examining the pulp writings of HPL and Clark Ashton Smith from a sociological perspective, was first published in *VVV* Nos. 2/3 (March 1943): 62–66.

Forests are decimated and the dismembered corpses of trees are tossed into a hell-broth concocted by industrial chemurgy, and so reduced to cellulose. This wood-pulp is converted into paper of various types. Nine hundred and sixty-nine mills are engaged in the primary pulp and paper industry in the United States; more than a million persons are supported by this process. These figures do not include those masses engaged, in one way or another, in the various skills of spreading ink upon paper.

All this multifarious activity has grown up in response to one basic human craving—that insatiable appetite to escape from the "low dark prison" of segmented existence. Some might define this unconscious drive as a passion for participation; others as the revolt against the boredom of life imposed by the dictatorship of the Machine. The "news" purveyed on paper may intensify and temporarily nourish, in vicarious fashion, the hunger for communal participation, and provide a temporary release from the rigors of everyday monotony.

To some thirty millions of Americans, pulp-paper publications open avenues of release; yet, in the hierarchy of contemporary literature, the "pulps" are relegated to the lowly caste of the untouchable. Disdained by the literary experts, they are preserved in few libraries; they have never been diagnosed by sociologists and psychologists, who remain blandly indifferent to the significance of their widespread and enduring appeal. The "literature" of the subject is sparse and well-nigh inaccessible.

Nevertheless, from the point of view of communication by the printed word, the "pulps" function efficiently. They engage the loyalty of millions of faithful and habitual readers, who vociferously express their approval with reader-response letters, organize themselves into "fan" clubs, even hold annual conventions and trade their cherished fantasies with each other—even to the extent of printing bibliographies of their preferences and masterpieces of "futurian" literature.

Successful communication may be likened to an electric current. Writer and reader, in such a communal experience, are lifted out of their individual isolation and fused into a single, all-enveloping identity. The *I* is transfigured by the *We*. The reader-response published by the editors of the pulps, if authentic, is adequate testimony of this communal participation.

This caste of untouchables populates the newsstands with impudent density. The pulps thrive with the hardihood of weeds—or the ambiguous hemp-plant. They bring to mind the words of Hamlet: ". . . an unweeded garden that grows to seed; things rank and gross in nature possess it merely."[9] The life of the individual pulp is brief, evanescent, ephemeral; but the species spawns and pullulates. Some of them answer the subconscious craving for purely physical derring-do: "action" stories, "westerns," aviation adventures. Others purvey *ersatz* opiates designed to assuage thwarted sexual impulses. Still others indulge in masked orgies of murder, torture, violence, sadism, sterilized and rendered morally innocuous by the automatic triumph of the forces of law and order.

Most fascinating, perhaps, are those pulps devoted to super-realistic "wonder,"—to the weird, the horrendous, the pseudo-scientific, the resurrection of ancient myths and folklore. In these we discover a wild, undisciplined jail-break from the concentration camp of the mundane, a carefree defiance of all the physical laws of the universe, a flight from the penury of life in three or four dimensions. Here is explosive volatilization of repressed imaginations, wrenching off the manacles of Time and Space!

These "scienti-fictions" catapult the reader (by "spaceship") to the remotest reaches of the solar system. With Thomas Traherne the pulpeteer cries out: "'Tis mean ambition to define a single world; to many I aspire, the one upon another hurl'd."[10] Some of these "interplanetaries" (the technical name for such tales) transport you in the twinkling of an eye to any one or another of the 1380 (or is it 1381?) planets, asteroids, or planetoids, of our own solar system. You find yourself, perhaps, in some "hot spot" in Io City, megalopolis of the planet Jupiter. There (in surreptitious defiance of the interplanetary Gestapo) "spacefarers" and "space-rats" carouse and plot. You, reader, are really the hero—a *right guy*, a *regular fellow*, a prince among your comrade star-rovers. You pick up bits of startling information from "slender snake-like Venusians," lepidopterous Mercurians, or good-natured Brobdingnagian Jovians. You plot the downfall of the Hitlerian dictator of the solar system; and from the sidereal double-talk of five planets you inadvertently learn of a colossal snatch-racket: a gangster-star from the other side of infinity is plotting to kidnap our Brother the Sun! Or you may speed through space-lanes regulated by interplanetary traffic cops to the rescue of some translunar princess. As they thrust out their revolting serpentine feelers toward the princess in distress, you lasso giant man-eating pitcher plants. Or else, you discover the populace of two alien and irreconcilable dimensions battling for the supremacy of our little world. In all these variegated adventures, the naïve reader experiences a dilation of consciousness, the expansion of belief beyond the boundaries of the credible, release from that disagreeable little patch of experience men know as the plausible. *Credo quia absurdum!*[11]

The exhilaration experienced by hardened addicts is suggestive of the ecstatic elevation induced by hashish or marihuana: the soaring into a Paradise of Mahomet, the distorted awareness, then weightless, effortless flight, followed by a sudden, chilling drop to reality, the addict feels himself larger, stronger, far freer, the dominant feeling "one of immense joy and liberation." His experience recalls De Quincey's with laudanum: "The sense of space, and in the end the sense of time, were both powerfully affected. Buildings, landscapes, etc., were exhibited in proportions so vast as the bodily eye is not fitted to receive. Space swelled, and was amplified to an extent of unutterable and self-repeating infinity. This disturbed me very much less than the vast expansion of time. Sometimes I seemed to have lived for seventy or a hundred years in one night; nay, sometimes had feelings representative of a duration far beyond the limits of any human experience."[12]

August Derleth and Donald Wandrei have salvaged the work of two extraordinary "stars" of the pulpwood fiction-factories—H. P. Lovecraft and Clark Ashton Smith. Convinced that Lovecraft (this name is slightly incredible, but it is no *nom de plume*) was of more than passing significance, Derleth and Wandrei collected thirty-six of his tales (Lovecraft had died in 1937), and submitted the huge manuscript to leading publishers. Most of them promptly rejected the project as a "poor commercial risk." Undismayed, these two young *littérateurs* set up their own publishing house, the Arkham Press, in Sauk City, Wisconsin. Lovecraft's work was printed in a bulky volume of 553 closely-printed pages, including an introduction and Lovecraft's own exhaustive essay on "Supernatural Horror Literature."

Whipped on by some inner compulsion to write, Howard Lovecraft passed most of the forty-seven years of his life in an old Georgian house in Providence, Rhode Island, timorously shunning all rough-and-ready contacts with the workaday world. At an early age, through the medium of his own microscopic calligraphy, he began to create his own subjective universe. This imagined cosmos was peopled with ghouls and demons, primordial creatures of Manichean evil surviving from prehistory, or supercosmic Titans ready to take possession of the human race at some unguarded moment. Lovecraft spun his own endless filature of ink as an armour against the external. He communicated with other sympathetic minds through the medium of letters. With more than two hundred unseen friends he corresponded regularly—letters of fifty, sixty, or seventy sheets of standard typewriter size, covered on both sides with spidery penmanship. Some of these letters grew longer than a full-length novel, bulking from fifty to one hundred thousand words.

Precocious wonder-children create their own imaginary kingdoms, complete with custom, currency and costume. Like them this recluse mapped and charted his own subjective archaeology and fantastic prehistory. The recluse was oppressed by the presence of *"Old Ones,"* who might return to take possession of the human mind and unleash the powers of darkness. "All my stories," Lovecraft confessed, "are based on the fundament lore or legend that this world was inhabited at one time by another race, who, in practising black magic, lost their foothold and were expelled, yet live on outside, ever ready to take possession of this earth again." With Arthur Machen he agreed that "it is possible that man may sometimes return on the track of evolution."[13] He found support for his own neurotic sense of doom in Algernon Blackwood's disturbing warning of "a survival of a hugely remote period when consciousness was manifested in shapes and forms long since withdrawn before the tide of advancing humanity—forms of which poetry and legend alone have caught a flying memory, and called them gods, monsters, mythical beings of all sorts and kinds. . . ."[14]

Lovecraft's tales eventually found publication in such pulpwood publications as *Weird Tales, Astounding Stories,* and others devoted to the supernatural. His financial rewards were infinitesimal, averaging less than a cent a word. Lovecraft recalls Dunsany, Algernon Blackwood, Arthur Machen and Poe. He overstrains his efforts to strike terror. Like all verbomaniacs, he fails to master his obsessions: he is too wordy, too explanatory, too rhetorical. He is at his best when he retreats into the universe of his own creation, or indulges in flights of pseudo-archeology, and leads his readers in grim expeditions to hunt down traces of the prehistoric malevolence, as embodied in the "Old Ones." Most impressive, in my opinion at least, are "The Call of Cthulhu" and *At the Mountains of Madness.* Here he frees himself from the conventions of fiction in its standardized forms, and presents an uncensored testimony of his inner adventures.

"The Call of Cthulhu" is a long narrative in search of "the Great Old Ones who lived before there were any men, and who came to the young world out of the sky. These Old Ones were gone now, inside the earth and under the sea; but their dead bodies had told their secrets in dreams to the first man, who formed a cult which had never died." The story ends with the imagined narrator testifying:

> "Cthulhu still lives . . . again in that chasm of stone which has shielded him since the sun was young. His accursed city is sunken once more, . . . but his ministers on earth still bellow and prance and slay around idol-capped monoliths in lonely places. . . . Who knows the end? What has risen may sink, and what has sunk may rise. Loathsomeness waits and dreams in the deep, and decay spreads over the tottering cities of men."

In *At the Mountains of Madness*, Lovecraft transports us, by plane of course, to the ruins of a lost primordial, super-cosmic super-city founded by Titans who were both animal and vegetable, a city that formed the primary nucleus and center of some archaic chapter of earth's history.

> "Here sprawled a Paleogaean megalopolis compared with which the fabled Atlantis and Lemuria, Commoriom and Uzuldaroum, and Olathoë in the land of Lomar are recent things of today—not even of yesterday; a megalopolis ranking with such whispered pre-human blasphemies as Valusia, R'lyeh, Ib in the land of Mnar, and the Nameless City of Arabia Deserta. As we flew above that tangle of stark Titan towers my imagination sometimes escaped all bounds and roved aimlessly in realms of fantastic associations—even weaving links betwixt this lost world and some of my own wildest dreams concerning the mad horror at the camp.
>
> "The things once rearing and dwelling in this frightful masonry in the age of dinosaurs were not indeed dinosaurs, but far worse. Mere dinosaurs were new and almost brainless objects—but the builders of the city were wise and old, and had left certain traces in rocks even then laid down well nigh a thousand million years—rocks laid down before the true life of earth had advanced beyond plastic groups of cells—rocks laid down before the true life of earth had existed at all. They were the makers and enslavers of that life, and above all doubt the originals of the fiendish elder myths which things like the Pnakotic Manuscripts and the *Necronomicon* affrightedly hint about. They were the great 'Old Ones' that had filtered down from the stars when earth was young—the beings whose substance an alien evolution had shaped, and whose powers were such as this planet had never bred."

The expedition to the "Mountains of Madness" ends with the allegorical and semi-prophetic admonition: "It is absolutely necessary, for the peace and safety of mankind, that some of earth's dark, dead corners and unplumbed depths be let alone; lest sleeping abnormalities wake to resurgent life, and blasphemously surviving nightmares squirm and splash out of their black lairs to newer and wider conquests."

More arresting, from the point of view of unconscious revelation, is the Californian Clark Ashton Smith, a collection of whose tales has just been published by Messrs. Derleth and Wandrei.*[15] As an explorer of the grotesque, the interplanetary and the trans-dimensional in pseudo-scientific fiction, Smith has for many years enjoyed widespread popularity among pulpwood "fans."

Born in Long Valley, California, Clark Ashton Smith began to write at the age of eleven. Almost wholly self-educated, at seventeen he was selling stories to The Black Cat. Before he was twenty, his first collection of verse was published. This boy-poet of the Sierras soon discovered that juvenile and provincial fame is fickle. He could not live on the acclamation of his admirers. In his twenties, Smith became a journalist, a fruit-picker and packer, a woodchopper, a typist, a cement-mixer, a gardener, a hard-rock miner, mucker, and windlasser. He was past thirty-five when he resumed the writing of short stories as a profession. Then, with publication in Weird Tales of "The End of the Story,"[16] he came into his own in prose. The success of this story inspired others, all weird, macabre, fantastic, all flights from "the real."

Smith has tried his hand at all types of pseudo-scientific fiction. Throughout his tales, as now collected, the reader is haunted by a sense of gloominess, of isolation. They are, perhaps unconsciously, autobiographical.

In "The Uncharted Isle,"[17] for instance, a shipwrecked sailor is beached upon a strange island of the Pacific and finds himself in a jungle that might have been painted by Rousseau le Douanier.[18] The plant-forms are not the palm-ferns, grasses and shrubs native to South Sea islands: leaves, stems, frondage, are of archaic types, such as might have existed in former eons, on the sea-lost littorals of Mu. The sailor is overwhelmed with intimations of a dark and prehistoric antiquity. "And the silence around me seemed to become the silence of dead ages and of things that have gone down beneath oblivion's tide. From that moment, I felt that there was something wrong about the island."

The sailor discovers the main town of the strange island, where the inhabitants move about in perplexing and perplexed fashion:

> "None of them appeared to notice me; and I went up to a group of three who were studying one of the long scrolls I have mentioned, and addressed them. For all answer, they bent closer above the scroll; and even when I plucked one of them by the sleeve, it was evident that he did not observe me. Much amazed, I peered into their faces, and was struck by the mingling of supreme perplexity and monomaniacal intentness which their expression dis-

---

*Clark Ashton Smith: Out of Time and Space. [sic] Arkham Press: Sauk City, Wisconsin. $3.00.

played. There was much of the madman, and more of the scientist absorbed in some irresolvable problem. Their eyes were fixed and fiery, their lips moved and mumbled in a fever of perpetual disquiet; and, following their gaze, I saw that the thing they were studying was a sort of chart or map, whose yellowing paper and faded inks were manifestly of past ages. . . . These beings were so palpably astray and bewildered; it was so obvious that they knew as well as I that there was something wrong with the geography, and perhaps with the chronology, of their island."

The poet wanders here in isolation in a silent, alien universe, striving vainly to communicate with his fellow-humans. They live in another age, another dimension, wrapped in their own perplexity. In other tales the Pariah wreaks unspeakable revenge upon the Tyrant. In one story the magician calls forth a cavalcade of giant stallions. "Like a many-turreted storm they came, and it seemed that the world sank gulfward, tilting beneath the weight. Still as a man enchanted into marble, Zotulla stood and beheld the ruining that was wrought on his empire. . . . Closer drew the gigantic stallions . . . and louder was the thundering of their footfalls, that now began to blot the green fields and fruited orchards lying for many miles to the west of Ummaos. And the shadow of the stallions climbed like an evil gloom of eclipse, till it covered Ummaos; and looking up, the emperor saw their eyes halfway between earth and zenith, like baleful suns that glare down from soaring cumuli."

"The City of the Singing Flame,"[19] a tale of transdimensional adventure, is weighted with allegorical and mystical implications. After venturing into alien dimensions, following the faraway alluring music of the "singing flame," the narrator wonders why he came back again to the human world.

"Words are futile to express what I have beheld and experienced, and the change that has come upon me, beneath the play of incalculable forces in a world of which no other mortal is even cognisant. Literature is nothing more than a shadow. Life, with its drawn-out length of monotonous, reiterative days, is unreal and without meaning, now, in comparison with the splendid death which I might have had—the glorious doom which is still in store."

He ventures into the Inner Sphere, in which ". . . a whole range of new senses had been opened up in me, together with corresponding thought-symbols for which there are no words in human speech . . ."

He becomes "a larger, stronger and freer entity, differing as much from my former self as the personality developed beneath the influence of hashish or kava would differ." His dominant feeling is "of immense joy and liberation, coupled with a sense of imperative haste, of the need to escape into other realms where the joy would endure eternal and unthreatened." This trans-dimensional explorer discovers possibilities of "boundless, unforeseeable realms, planet on planet, universe on universe, to which we might attain, and among whose prodigies and marvels we could dwell or wander indefinitely. In these worlds, our brains would be attuned to the comprehension of vaster and higher scientific laws, and states of entity beyond those of our present dimensional milieu."

In our search for the typical, we are ineluctably led to the un-typical. Even in the naïvest of pulp fiction, we detect the unending conflict between the conscious craft and the unconscious drives—the controlled versus the uncontrollable. Were we adepts in academic research, we might trace the mongrel ancestry of this pseudo-scientific and fantastic allegorizing back through Lord Dunsany and Algernon Blackwood, H. G. Wells, Samuel Butler and Jules Verne, the satirical "futurists" like the Russian Eugene Zamiatin (author of *We*), the Voltaire of *Micromegas* and the Swift of *Gulliver*. On and on, to ever more remote sources, we arrive finally at the Islamic, oral storytellers of the *souks*, or the anonymous compilers of *The Book of a Thousand Nights and a Night*.

The origin of all modem expression is always far more ancient than we suppose—even of the talking motion pictures. So the ephemeral pulps of the newsstands bear a striking analogy to the *Arabian Nights*. With its subjective universe dominated by Ifrits and *djinn* (with their magical powers of transforming themselves into beasts, plants or insects), its malicious negation of external morality, its sly fusion of magic and reality, and especially its bold suspension of distressingly insistent physical laws, that endless involuted Persian (or Indian) labyrinth of narrative survives as the most audacious and most captivating revolt from the objective world ever depicted. It entices the reader into a never-never land in which individual responsibility is swept aside, a realm of surcease from iron laws of the dismal sciences, where Euclid and Newton never ventured.

W. B. Yeats once wrote: "Children play at being great and wonderful people, at the ambitions they will put away for one reason or another before they grow into ordinary men and women. Mankind as a whole had a like dream once; everybody and nobody built up the dream bit by bit, and the ancient storytellers are there to make us remember what mankind would have been like, had not fear and the falling will and the laws of nature tripped up its heels . . ."[20] But right here and now, under our very eyes, between the lurid covers of the pulps, we find storytellers carrying on the same rôle—transforming the concepts of micro-physics and astrophysics into horrendous imps, Ifrits and *djinn* endowed with the magical powers for enslaving or liberating mankind. Thirty millions or more addicts, through these vicarious adventures, still play, as in the childhood of mankind, at being "great and wonderful people," still seek release from the world outside themselves, a holiday from the "reality" of that external realm, despite the grandeur of all its miracles and the nobility of all its myths.

The significance of all this is not limited to mere "literature." Large-scale communication has tended more and more to restrict and thwart the individual, be he writer or reader. The voice of the individual is lost in the whirr of the well-lubricated machinery of mass-production—even in the mass-production of fantasy. Individual can no longer commune with individual, but only with the "masses"—glib symbol of a non-existent entity! Driven to wholesale production of standardized merchandise, the pulp-fictioneer strives with all conscious craft to meet the demands and schedules of his publishers. Yet unconscious impulses and compulsions, suppressed and thwarted in seeking their natural outlet, take their revenge in unconscious ways. As in all fields of art and literature, this clash between conscious endeavour and unconscious revolt generates the reader's interest and focusses his attention. Knowingly or unknowingly, the isolated reader, in being reduced to means instead of being respected as an end in himself, shares the suppressed struggle of the writer toward emancipation. This must be one basic reason for the appeal of such writers as Clark Ashton Smith or H. P. Lovecraft, and for the phenomenal prosperity of the pulps.

The pulps are engaged in the mass-production of mass-dreams. They are frankly and without shame completely escapist in nature. They mock at the piddling, puny, hypocritical plausibility and credibility of the commercial product of the more honored castes of contemporary letters. Here among the ridiculed and rejected, impartial assay may discover craftsmen who are carrying on the ancient and cryptical tradition of the storytellers of the Orient.

The pseudo-scientific tale is developing a new school of illustration. The draughtsman is challenged to use all the resources of his imagination—with the most direct and most economical of means. The illustrations (presented herewith) from the various pulp periodicals offer encouraging evidence of this super-realistic school. Especially noteworthy are the drawings of Hannes Bok, a young, artist who was born near Seattle.[21]

Macabre, Lyrical and Weird

Peter De Vries

> Peter De Vries (1910–1993) was a critically acclaimed satirical novelist. He contributed for many years to the *New Yorker* (1944–87), often working on conjunction with James Thurber. The following review appeared in the *Chicago Sun Book Week* (26 December 1943): 4.

Beyond the Wall of Sleep. By H. P. Lovecraft. Arkham House. 458 pp. $5.

All I can say of H. P. Lovecraft is that the man is not quite on my wavelength, by no means thereby barring the possibility that he may be on yours. Lovecraft's writing is a curiosity, a kind of literary exercise in an archaic tradition—a Poe-like romantic-macabre vein full of rotund cadences and baroque locutions. There are youths wandering about town with myrrh in their hair, old men who know where cats go on St. John's Eve, peasants moved by weird and lyric dreams, unmentionable deeds in the vilest quarter of town, and bats clustering on corpses from which amulets have been taken.

"Beyond the Wall of Sleep" is a collection of Lovecraft's dreams and visions, tales and allegories, and occasional gelatinous prose poems, case histories and horror fantasies which form the second volume in a projected "Lovecraft Trilogy." There are moments when he strikes fire, achieving exquisite eerie details, but on the whole his somewhat dated content, his languid and pearly style, adds up at best to a competently wrought anachronism rather than the creative individuality his publishers claim for him—a knick-knack on the whatnot of Neo-Romanticism.

"St. John and I followed enthusiastically every aesthetic and intellectual movement which promised respite from our devastating ennui. . . . Baudelaire and Huysmans were soon exhausted of thrills, till finally there remained for us only the more direct stimuli of . . ."[22]

Reading passages like that is a good deal like seeing a couple of reels of "The Perils of Pauline" run over. At least, to say that it is difficult to read without a smile is putting it mildly. Frequently one cannot help admiring the perfection of his fabrications, turgidly literary as they are; but a little of it goes a long way in ushering at least one reader toward that mystic realm specified in the title, and, however exotically and variedly it is prepared, it is still corn.

Mystery and Adventure

Will Cuppy

The following review appeared in *New York Herald Tribune Weekly Book Review* (2 January 1944): 10.

BEYOND THE WALL OF SLEEP. By H. P. Lovecraft . . . Collected by August Derleth and Donald Wandrei . . . 458 pp. . . . Sauk City, Wis.: Arkham House . . . $5.

Since the literature of horror and macabre fantasy belongs traditionally with mystery in its broader sense, we herewith recommend to fandom this outsized volume, stuffed and crammed with some of the weirdest material on record. Following up "The Outsider and Others," issued in 1939, "Beyond the Wall of Sleep" contains another huge helping of the works of the late Howard Phillips Lovecraft, who died in 1937 after what seems to have been an amazing career in writing fields largely unknown or overlooked by the average reader of published books. We confess that we are knocked silly by the mass of mania, nightmare and such in these Lovecraft collections, both of which should be possessed, or at least perused, by any citizen who goes for hideous dream states, demons from the vast abyss, humans doomed and damned, things unnamable and so forth in truly astonishing variety.

Main part of this non-stop thriller starts with several prose poems, and goes on to pieces ranging from a few pages to novel length. One of the long ones, "The Case of Charles Dexter Ward," kept us awake until dawn with its early New England atrocities of the sort you seldom get in America. This has detectives in it, too, and all manner of hideosities—hellish rites, charnel terrors, superhuman sins and all that. Among the shorts there's "The Other Gods," the story of Barzai the Wise, who dwelt in Ulthar, beyond the river Skai, and unwisely climbed to the summit of Hatheg-Kla, and "The Quest of Iranon," how a youth fared in the granite city of Teloth and elsewhere, very impressive. Included in the volume are an informative short introduction, a brief autobiographical sketch, selected poems, an appreciation of Lovecraft by W. Paul Cook and other paraphernalia of interest to weird fans As a whole, it's scarier than an armful of conventional fiction. Heartily recommended to all that way inclined.

Nightmare in Cthulu

William Poster

Little is known about William Poster. The following review appeared in the *New York Times Book Review* (16 January 1944): 19.

BEYOND THE WALL OF SLEEP. By H. P. Lovecraft. 458 pp. Sauk City, Wis.: Arkham House. $5.

Howard Phillips Lovecraft died five years ago at the age of 47, leaving behind an imposing mound of manuscript, either wholly unpublished or confined within the coarse covers of the pulp magazines. His tales of supernatural horror, black magic, prehistoric demons and spirits that inhabit the outer rim of the universe never achieved, within his lifetime, the dignity of a book. But before he died Lovecraft had succeeded in constructing a complete and detailed imaginary cosmos and mythology, the realm of "Cthulu," the sticky, green, winged water-god, "Nyarlothep," forever howling in the outer darkness, and hordes of greater and lesser demons and deities, complete with genealogy, habitat and spheres of influence.

Lovecraft was one of those rare individuals who seem to have been perfectly fitted by nature to do one thing surpassingly well. Poor health prevented him from participating fully in the normal life of children and at an early age he took refuge in his imagination. Most of his mature life he spent as a recluse in an old Georgian house in Providence, charting his private cosmos and populating it in successive narratives, with fantastically horrible survivals of untamed antiquity and projections of the more fearsome elements of the unknown present.

He was a voluminous writer. His stories grew longer with the years and made publication increasingly difficult. But Lovecraft, spurred on by internal compulsion rather than profit, never made the slightest effort to alter them for a market. He also helped many fellow-contributors to "Weird Tales" and "Astounding Stories" and carried on an incredible correspondence with some two hundred persons. Purveyors of the supernatural still lean heavily upon the Lovecraft pantheon. His fabulous bible of evil, the "Necronomicon of the mad Arab, Abdul-Alhazred," is constantly referred to by his successors and still frequently requested from bewildered librarians.

Whatever the ultimate status of their master of "weird writing" August Derleth and Clark Wandrei have made a commendable plunge into the neglected ocean of pulp-writing, salvaging a large quantity of entertaining reading. "Beyond the Wall of Sleep," the second volume in a projected trilogy, contains Lovecraft's lesser writings, two short novels, poems, prose poems, short stories and collaborations. For zealous Lovecraftians there are a few choice tidbits—a short autobiography, his commonplace book, and his "History and Chronology of the Necronomicon."

Lovecraft's poems and prose poems tend to reveal his weaknesses rather than raise his stature. Without the coloring excitement of narrative suspense and climax his language seems thin and obvious, getting most of its effects by the hypnotic repetition or judicious timing of adjectives like "slimy," "nameless," or "loathsome." But one of the novels, "The Case of Charles Dexter Ward," is a good story in the New England witchcraft tradition, well seasoned with alchemy, vampirism, ancient documents and mummy-stealing.

The two stories which did the most for my insomnia were "Herbert T. West, Reanimator," who performed reanimations on dead bodies with remarkable results; and the tale of an unfortunate couple who get into trouble with Yig the snake-god.[23]

Though nothing in it equals the best in the first volume, this second installment does contain a sufficient quantity of first-rate "weird writing" in its 450-odd pages of microscopic print to keep a responsive reader's hair standing on end for days.

Books Alive

Vincent Starrett

> Vincent Starrett (1886–1974) was a celebrated American critic, journalist, and bookman. He did much work on Ambrose Bierce and Arthur Machen, compiling a bibliography of Bierce (1929) and two volumes of miscellany by Machen. His book *Buried Caesars* (1923) discussed many obscure writers, some of them weird. He also did much work on Sir Arthur Conan Doyle and Sherlock Holmes; his most celebrated book is *The Private Life of Sherlock Holmes* (1933). He corresponded briefly with HPL in 1927–28. Starrett wrote the "Books Alive" column for the *Chicago Tribune* from 1942 to 1967, and he took note of HPL's works on several occasions. The following article appeared in the *Chicago Sunday Tribune* (2 January 1944): Sec. 6, p. 12. It was reprinted in part in Starrett's *Books and Bipeds* (1947).

V. Notices from the Literary Community

He died in Providence, R. I., on March 15, 1937, one of the strangest figures in American literature. If there were any mystery about the facts in the life of Howard Phillips Lovecraft, which there is not, a plausible solution might relate him in some queer way to Edgar Allan Poe, whose pupil he was, altho he was born 40 years after Poe's death. It is simpler to say that temperamentally he was endowed to carry on the Poe tradition and did so, with single minded devotion and artistic integrity, for a quarter of a century; then he died, aged 47, and became a legend and a cult. He may end—who knows?—as a solar myth.

Lovecraft, a semi-invalid, a recluse and an antiquarian, was until his death America's premier fantasist the field of the macabre. Thousands of readers of "Weird Tales" and similar occult fiction magazines know his work and believe it to be a work of genius. No book by him was published in his lifetime, but since his death two have appeared, edited and produced by his friends, August Derleth and Donald Wandrei, under the imprint of Arkham House—a private publishing venture inaugurated, in the first instance, solely to publish the complete writings of H. P. Lovecraft. A trilogy was planned, the second volume of which has just appeared—"Beyond the Wall of Steep." An earlier volume of tales, "The Outsider and Others," is still available, I believe, and a third volume of Lovecraft's letters to his friends is now preparing. When the task is completed, the three handsome books will mark as notable a tribute to friendship as the history of our letters can offer. Arkham House is situated at Sauk City, Wis., under the broad Balzacian brow of August Derleth.

In his introductions, Derleth speaks of Lovecraft as "the late great master of horror stories," and nobody is likely to dispute the characterization. Readers who revel in Poe and Lord Dunsany, Arthur Machen, and Algernon Blackwood are pretty certain to like the charnel fairy tales of Howard Lovecraft. But to me Lovecraft himself is even more interesting than his stories; he was his own most fantastic creation—a Roderick Usher or C. August Dupin born a century too late. Like his heroes in Poe's gigantic nightmare, he fancied himself as a cadaverous, mysterious figure of the night—a pallid, scholarly necrologist—and cultivated a natural resemblance until it was almost the real thing, altho he was first and last a "literary cove." Like Dupin he created the illusion of darkness, when day appeared, by drawing down his shades and turning on the electric lights, and he ended up looking rather like the sepulchral hero of "The Fall of the House of Usher."

But if Lovecraft was a self-conscious *poseur*, a macabre *precieuse*, he was genuine too: his poses never had any relation to commercial success, which he didn't achieve, and there is no question about the sincerity of his artistry. In his field he was important. He pretended to be modest and deprecatory about his work, and perhaps he was; but I have no doubt he was a considerable egotist in reverse. He wrote himself—as Poe did—into many of his tales, describing himself carefully and accurately in the haggard, romantic portraits he drew of his central figures.

His major premise is best described in his own words: "All my stories . . . are based on the fundamental lore or legend that this world was inhabited at one time by other races who, in practicing black magic, lost their foothold and were expelled, yet live on outside, ever ready to take possession of this earth again." Did he believe that? I don't know—he claimed to be a mechanistic materialist—and probably the question is beside the point. I am reminded, tho, of a remark once made by Arthur Machen. We had been discussing Blackwood's work and his own, and at length I asked: "Well, what *do* you believe?"

"Tennyson," Machen replied, "says 'the cedars sigh for Lebanon,'[24] and that is grand poetry. But Blackwood believes the cedars really do sigh for Lebanon—and that, Starrett, is damned nonsense!"

It is supposed to be unfair to relate a fiction writer's product too intimately to his life; but I have little doubt that most fiction is autobiography of a sort.

It is the misfortune of most "weird writers" that in large part they must gain their effects by rhetoric—Poe was no exception—and that significant words and private symbols and allusions lose their effectiveness when they are too often used. Lovecraft was not the equal of his masters, and I think he would have benefited immeasurably by a little more humor in his makeup; but that is carping. He was a born eccentric, a dilettante, and a *poseur par excellence*; but he was also a born writer, equipped with a delicate feeling for the beauty and mystery of words. The best of his stories are among the best of their time, in the field he chose to make his own.

Bookman's Holiday

Charles Collins

> Charles Collins was a book and theatre critic for the *Chicago Tribune* in the 1930s and 1940s. The following segments from his column "Bookman's Holiday" appeared in the *Chicago Sunday Tribune* (11 June 1944): Sec. 6, p. 12, and (18 June 1944): Sec. 6, p. 13.

In "Great Tales of Terror and the Supernatural" [Random House],[25] an omnibus volume ambitiously planned to end all such omnibuses, an obscure figure in modern American literature named H. P. Lovecraft comes into his own. Two of his tales are reprinted in this collection of 52 certified masterpieces, and thus Lovecraft, heretofore rated as a bush leaguer, is batting as strongly as Edgar Allan Poe in the big league. His ascension may be credited, aside from his genuine merit as a story teller, to August Derleth and Donald Wandrei, who form the publishing partnership called Arkham House, which operates in the small town of Sauk City, Wis.

Lovecraft died about five years ago, leaving nothing between book covers. He had been, however, a voluminous contributor of weird tales to the pulp paper magazines, and was recognized among a small group of freelance writers as a unique talent in the field of the "grotesque and arabesque," as Poe called it. He had invented a rich genealogy of supernatural beings, known as the Cthulhu mythology, and some of his disciples borrowed from it in tales of their own imagining, with his consent and approval.

August Derleth, whose fertile literary talent thrives in his Wisconsin birthplace without need of the dubious inspirations of New York and Hollywood, has been an addict of tales of terror ever since "Dracula" scared him out of a year of high school growth. He became a Lovecraft reader and entered into a correspondence with the wizard of Cthulhu, who lurked in Providence, R. I., which eventually taxed the capacity of his filing cabinets. The twain never met, but after Lovecraft's death Derleth resolved to give him library recognition.

Several years ago Arkham House of Sauk City, Wis., published a Lovecraft collection called "The Outsider and Others." Last fall it issued a second volume, called "Beyond the Wall of Sleep," containing lesser tales, poems, and a miscellany of Lovecraftana, including a long biographical study. A third volume, which will be delayed because Wandrei is in military service and paper is scarce, is ready for the printers. It will consist largely of Lovecraft's letters.

Until Derleth turned part of his enormous energy toward the memorialization of Lovecraft in this manner, the man was as unknown to literary scholars as any newspaper reporter. His name does not appear in "Who's Who," "Twentieth Century Authors," or "American Authors and Books."[26] The two latter volumes, by the way, are comprehensive, and contain records of numerous sandflies of the writing trade who happened to live on the right side of the tracks or know the right people. Lovecraft was a recluse, a strange neurotic, who fainted in cold weather, and a midnight delver into quaint and curious volumes of forgotten lore. As a personality he was a modern Poe, without the spectacular color of the whisky bottle.

The Lovecraft tales in "Great Tales of Terror and the Supernatural" are entitled "The Rats in the Wall" [sic] and "The Dunwich Horror." They are causing specialists in American literature to ask questions about the author, and to all such, eager for footnotes to their dissertations for the doctorate, we point the way toward Arkham House. On arriving at Sauk City they should head toward the Place of Hawks, the manor house where Derleth spreads his wings. If the pilgrimage is made by motor, passing traffic should be scanned carefully, for Derleth occasionally commutes between his habitat and Chicago in the cab of an egg truck.

To supplement this column's remarks of last Sunday on H. P. Lovecraft's expanding vogue, after years of obscurity, August Derleth, his discoverer as a fascinating figure in American literature, submits this new evidence:

"The Outsider and Others," published 1939, out of print December, 1943, is commanding as much as $25 the copy; "Beyond the Wall of Sleep," published December, 1943, is almost out of print also; about 150 copies left.

A little paper bound, selling at a quarter, titled, "The Weird Shadow over Innsmouth and Other Supernatural Stories," by H. P. Lovecraft, has just been published by Bartholomew House for newsstand sale.

Philip Van Doren Stern of Armed Services Editions, Inc., is currently examining the first Lovecraft omnibus for 15 stories or so to make an Armed Services Selection.[27]

"The Rats in the Walls" will appear again in Derleth's own horror anthology, "Sleep No More!" [Farrar & Rinehart, Sept. 21].

Arkham House will publish late this autumn a third and extra Lovecraft volume, entitled "Marginalia," containing various essays, "revisions" [Lovecraft practically rewrote stories he was paid to revise], a ghostwritten piece by Houdini, fragments, photographs—in short, everything which would have no place in the two volume "Selected Letters," which will come out after the war.

Derleth has just signed a contract with World Publishing company for a Tower edition of "The Best Supernatural Tales of H. P. Lovecraft," to come out in the spring or summer of 1945.[28]

[. . .]

We missed the bull's-eye when we remarked recently that H. P. Lovecraft's tales were not between book covers when he died. E. W. Fitz of Oak Park corrects us gently, thus:

"A book of Lovecraft's was published in April, 1936, nearly a year before his death. Its title was 'Shadow over Innsmouth'; its publisher [probably as fugitive as the name would imply] was the Visionary Publishing company, Everett, Pa. It sold, I believe, for a dollar. This story is included in the first Arkham House volume of Lovecraft's work, 'The Outsider and Others.'"

Arkham House of Sauk City, Wis., specializing in the weird, has just issued a prospectus covering its plans for the next year or two: four collections of tales by its special group of authors. This neat brochure also says: "Arkham House conceives it the obligation of the firm to point out allied books from other publishers which will certainly interest our readers." It mentions 12 titles, which include C. S. Lewis' "Out of the Silent Planet" and "Perelandra," and "Sweet Chariot," by Frank Baker.[29] The latter was cited in this column nearly two years ago.

[On Lovecraft]

Algernon Blackwood

> Algernon Blackwood (1869–1951) was one of the weird writers HPL himself most revered; he considered "The Willows" the greatest story in the entire range of weird fiction. Blackwood, however, did not fully return the favour. Having been given some HPL stories by an American correspondent, Allen McElfresh, and by August Derleth, Blackwood wrote the following in a letter to McElfresh (5 February 1945). The letter is cited in Mike Ashley's article, "Lovecraft and Blackwood: A Surveillance," *Crypt of Cthulhu* No. 51 (Hallowmas 1987): 7.

I have read Lovecraft with keen enjoyment but, while appreciating to the full his gorgeous imagination and feeling for atmosphere, the thrill of Fear I demand in such stories did not come. He has the material in plenty, in more than plenty, but I am oppressed rather than thrilled by what I feel to be overloading. There is a piling up and up of detail that, for me, defeats its own end. From a comment in your own letter about this I feel you partly agree with me that he is never wholly what we call "master of his material" and that the cumulative effect is a bit bludgeoning on the mind. I long for *something* to be left to the imagination, suggested, insinuated, instead of forced upon me with an adjectival wealth that tends to weary. I also do not react sympathetically to his preoccupation with corpses and decay; indeed, it was all I could do to finish reading his "Rats in the Wall," a tale that stirred repulsion rather than woke horror. What we call "spiritual horror" stirs fear in me while physical horror leaves me unresponsive, even antagonistic. For instance, I find a climax of sheer spiritual horror in the "Turn of the Screw," the ghastly menace to the souls of the two children, though this hideous tale, I notice, is not among your favourites. I am interested that we should disagree here. I can't read the "Screw" even in daylight without a genuine shiver down my spine, whereas no one of Lovecraft's stories really held me at any point. For that matter, neither Monty James nor Bierce have ever frightened me, tho' Machen once or twice nearly achieved this and your letter mentions other stories that have also managed really to scare me!

Mystery and Adventure

Will Cuppy

> The following review appeared in the *New York Herald Tribune Weekly Book Review* (11 February 1945): 16.

MARGINALIA. By H. P. Lovecraft. Collected by August Derleth and Donald Wandrei. 377 pp. . . . Sauk City, Wis.: Arkham House. . . . $3.

This volume contains a variety of matter by and about H. P. Lovecraft, prolific writer of weird stories who died in 1937. Lovecraft items include a sample of his ghost writing (for the late Harry Houdini), certain revisions of pieces by other hands, essays on several subjects, juvenilia and fragments from his maturer years. There are also fifteen articles about Mr. Lovecraft by his admirers and numerous illustrations. "Marginalia" should find its best audience among those who have read and liked the previously work of an author whose output has been called almost everything from sheer genius to rubbish. Messrs. Derleth and Wandrei pay tribute in a foreword to "the late great master of the macabre who is slowly but surely assuming his rightful place among the great writers of the genre in English."

Poesque Doodles

Marjorie Farber

Marjorie Farber (1910–2005) was a literary critic and journalist who wrote for the *New York Times Book Review*, the *New Republic*, and other periodicals. The following review appeared in the *New York Times Book Review* (25 February 1945): 16. She would later discuss HPL briefly in the article "Subjectivity in Modern Fiction" (*Kenyon Review*, Autumn 1945).

MARGINALIA. By H. P. Lovecraft. 377 pp. Sauk City, Wis.: Arkham House. $3.

The present dividend from Arkham House should cause intense satisfaction among disciples of the late great Master of Necrology, on whom the mantle of Poe is said to have descended. Sandwiched between three volumes of weird stories and the projected "volume or two" of correspondence, this one contains the Master's essays, revisions, juvenilia, marginalia, photographs—of his house, his study, his manuscripts, doodlings, drawings, friends, publishers—and two rare shots of Lovecraft himself. There are prose tributes from fifteen of his closest admirers and a very pretty musical composition, rather Griffes-like, entitled "Lament for H. P. L."[30]

Lovecraft, similar in temperament to Poe, was most unlike him professionally; in fact, he remained a determined amateur. For thirty of his forty-six years he was so oppressively coddled by his mother that he apparently never knew just where his oppression lay; he rebelled all his life against "the prison of natural laws" and the dictates of time itself. After her death he tried a brief and disastrous marriage with an older woman. Then he settled down with an elderly aunt, referring to himself as "The Old Man" and living on cheese, ice cream and incredible quantities of sugar, which he kept in the dark-curtained study where he worked by night and slept by day. His loathing for fish was even stronger than his aversion to sex; and his conservatism was particularly marked in architecture. While detesting Joyce, Lawrence and other literary rebels, he liked Hart Crane, cats and the New Deal, which he conceived as "a gentleman's government headed by the Squire of Hyde Park and administered by an intellectual aristocracy."[31]

Thus closeted, cosseted and protected, Lovecraft achieved a kind of "famous obscurity" as an amateur and later as a pulp writer. Since he never put his genius to any stringent professional test, he was able to use the horror story as a presumable means of gaining personal mastery over nightmares and delicate health. And through his vast correspondence he could inspire his countless admirers, all impressed by his personality ("he was his own most fantastic creation") and by his erudition. Self-taught, he had indeed acquired an encyclopedic knowledge of certain portions of astronomy, ethnology, the more demonic aspects of history and other sciences which led "outside" (i.e., outside nature). A professed naturalist, scholar and littérateur, his whole career seems an effective protest against "natural laws," against genuine scholarship and against literary craftsmanship. Only as an *undiscovered* genius can a writer really protect himself from failure.

Books Alive

Vincent Starrett

> The following column was published in the *Chicago Sunday Tribune* (4 March 1945): Sec. 6, p. 8. It was reprinted in part in Starrett's *Books and Bipeds* (1947).

The task of documenting the legend of late Howard Phillips Lovecraft, master of "weird" stories, goes forward without appreciable pause and is itself an interesting phenomenon. Two collections of his macabre tales, "The Outsider" [1939] and "Beyond the Wall of Sleep" [1943], went out of print with the celerity of a conjuring trick, and now bring astonishing prices in the rare book mart. The third title of a projected trilogy, his "Letters," must be delayed until after the war; it is announced by Arkham House, his publishers; but an interim volume of "Marginalia" has been assembled to meet the demands of avid readers. For those who, with Dr. Johnson, prefer the biographical side of literature, it yields nothing in interest to the earlier books.

Edited by August Derleth and Donald Wandrei, as were the other volumes, "Marginalia" brings together a selection of Lovecraft's minor pieces, including a famous article ghost-written for Harry Houdini, and a sheaf of quite remarkable tributes from friends and colleagues. These tributes are the best things in the book, I think—perhaps because they seem to me to confirm my own notion that Lovecraft the man is more interesting than his work. Poe might have invented him. Indeed, Poe did invent him a number of times; reading about Lovecraft it is difficult to realize that he ever had an existence outside the pages of "Usher" and the Dupin stories.

He did exist, however; and here in the reminiscences of his friends he comes alive, an appealing and fascinating figure forever lost in one of his own somber tales.

I will confess that my blood has never been properly curdled by the studious graveyard horrors of H. P. L.—which at their best seem to me only superior experiments in pastiche—but the man's own story is profoundly moving, in many ways a work of genius. Lovecraft lived it admirably, courageously, artistically, sometimes ludicrously—partly from pose, I think, partly from necessity. He had a flavor that was unique in this century. He should become one of our most colorful legends.

Nothing in these remarks is intended to disparage Lovecraft's sheer writing ability, which was considerable, and which I admire—altho this side idolatry. He was an excellent artist. His talent was not small, but special and derivative. In the case of a writer of negligible talents, oblivion sets in about three days after death. That is not the case here. Lovecraft, dead since 1937, enjoyed a "famous obscurity"—in the fine phrase of Winfield Townley Scott—during much of his writing career, very much as did Ambrose Bierce, one of his masters. Now he is emerging from that penumbra; and I wish he might have waited in person for his triumph. It would have pleased him.

The Phoenix Nest

William Rose Benét

> William Rose Benét (1886–1950) was an American poet, critic, and editor, and the brother of Stephen Vincent Benét. He helped to found the *Saturday Review of Literature* (1924f.) and wrote the column "The Phoenix Nest" in it for many years. The following column appeared in the *Saturday Review of Literature* 28, No. 1 (17 March 1945): 32.

Those who are familiars of the weird and fantastic in literature have no doubt followed the publications of Arkham House in Sauk City, Wisconsin, run by August Derleth and Donald Wandrei, and know also that strange book "The Outsider and Others," by the late Howard P. Lovecraft; the horror stories of a modern Poe. This volume was collected back in 1939. Lovecraft died in 1937. "Beyond the Wall of Sleep" was the second Lovecraft omnibus, and one or two volumes of selected letters of the Providence genius-in-his-own-field are contemplated. Now comes a smaller book, "Marginalia," a most interesting miscellany designed as a stop-gap for those readers whose thirst for Lovecraft's brand of horror is not easily quenched. It contains an example of his ghost-writing for Harry Houdini, several of his revisions of work by other hands, his essays on the writing of weird fiction and cognate matters, several examples of his juvenilia, some fragments, and a number of appreciations of him both in prose and verse.

To the former, in prose, the Providence poet, Winfield Townley Scott (a new volume of whose poems, by the way, is about to be published by T. Y. Crowell),[32] and Thomas Ollive Mabbott, the Poe expert, both contribute. There are many valuable illustrations to the book, showing Lovecraft and his various friends and disciples, his home, his study, some drawings by him, and so on. He abhorred fish, both to see and eat; hated the ocean as their abode; could consume fabulous quantities of ice-cream of all flavors; loved cats; and would never allow himself to get sunburned, cultivating a pallor of countenance set off by dark clothes. He stayed up all night and slept all day, and was during his youth completely under the domestic sway of his mother. Vincent Starrett has called him "his own most fantastic creation," but his tales have a singularly weird quality. In a sense he remained a gifted amateur, but he did the sort of thing for which I myself have a great fancy. I hope that, later on, a new edition of his best tales, gleaned from "The Outsider," "Beyond the Wall," etc., will be given presentation in larger type than they can at present claim, with illustrations perhaps by Virgil Finlay who has done such phenomenal work for *Famous Fantastic Mysteries*, a periodical to which I am now addicted.

In their March, 1944 number, as well as reprinting Chesterton's "The Man Who Was Thursday," F.F.M. did the same by "The Ghost Pirates" of William Hope Hodgson (1875–1918); and I have now received a mimeographed publication called *The Reader and Collector*, which is issued occasionally by H. C. Koenig, 2 East End Avenue, this city, the June (last) number being dedicated especially to Hodgson, and containing appreciations of him by Koenig himself, Lovecraft (exempted [sic] from his long "Supernatural Horror in Literature" in "The Outsider"), Clark Ashton Smith (whose work I first knew as poet on the Pacific Coast when he was hailed by the late George Sterling, and whose latest weird tales from Arkham House are "Out of Space and Time" and "Lost Worlds"), August Derleth, Ellery Queen, and so on. Years ago I remember delighting in the stories in "Carnacki, the Ghost Finder," recommended to me by Elinor Wylie, though I see that Howard P. Lovecraft rates this book below Hodgson's others. "The Night Land" was Hodgson's longest story and, says Koenig, "one at the longest fantastic romances ever written, running close to six hundred pages. It is a story of the world in the future when the sun has died and the 'Last Millions' are living in a large redoubt, a huge pyramid of gray metal nearly eight miles high and five miles around the base." I like the gentle title of one of his chapters, "The Swine Things."

[Review of *Supernatural Horror in Literature*]

Fred Lewis Pattee

> Fred Lewis Pattee (1863–1950) was an American literary historian, novelist, and critic. He was author of *A History of American Literature Since 1870* (1915). HPL owned a copy of his semi-weird novel *The House of the Black Ring* (1905). The following review appeared in *American Literature* 18, No. 2 (May 1946): 175–77.

SUPERNATURAL HORROR IN LITERATURE. By Howard Phillips Lovecraft. With an Introduction by August Derleth. New York: Ben Abramson. 1945. 106 pp. $2.50.

To trace the element of supernatural horror through the literature of the world from the time of the "Book of Enoch" and "The Claviculae of Solomon" would seem to be a task requiring volumes, but the author of this study has packed it into a monograph containing less than one hundred pages. And he has omitted nothing important. According to his index he has recorded and criticized some 250 horror books and tales. One's first impression is that it is a remarkable piece of literary compression. The fact that it was first published as a serial in the little magazine *Fantasy Fan*[33] kept it perhaps within restricted limits.

The writer of the introduction, August Derleth, himself a leading writer of horror literature, mentions the author of the book, H. P. Lovecraft, as the late "recluse of Providence," author of a single volume, a weird collection, *The Outsiders and Others*, 1938, a work unnoticed save by a small coterie. The present study, written in 1933, was a part of that collection.

That the article was again deemed worthy of republication, this time as a critical monograph, shows good judgment on the part of its editor. It is a brilliant piece of criticism. The author starts with a limiting definition and holds to it to the end:

> The true weird tale has something more than secret murder, bloody bones, or a sheeted form clanking chains according to rule. A certain atmosphere of

breathless and unexplainable dread of the outer, unknown forces must be present; and there must be a hint, expressed with seriousness and portentousness becoming its subject, of that most terrible conception of the human brain—a malign and particular suspension or defeat of those fixed laws of Nature which are our only safeguard against the assaults of chaos and the daemons of unplumbed space.

The study, which is in eight parts, concerns itself with the evolution of supernatural horror in literature from the era of jungle horror and superstition to the science-minded present. Always can an age be classified by the elements in its terror tales. For instance, the eighteenth century, especially in its English ideals and atmospheres, lives embalmed in a few shuddery tales. Out of no other century could have come the Gothic romance. Here are its elements:

> This novel dramatic paraphernalia consisted first of all of the Gothic castle, with its awesome antiquity, vast distances and ramblings, deserted or ruined wings, damp corridors, unwholesome hidden catacombs, and galaxy of ghosts and appalling legends, as a nucleus of suspense and daemoniac fright. In addition, it included the tyrannical and malevolent nobleman as villain; the saintly, long-persecuted, and generally insipid heroine who undergoes the major terrors and serves as a point of view and focus for the reader's sympathies; the valorous and immaculate hero, always of high birth but often of humble disguise; the convention of high-sounding foreign names, mostly Italian, for the characters; and the infinite array of stage properties which includes strange lights, damp trap-doors, extinguished lamps, mouldy hidden manuscripts, creaking hinges, shaking arras, and the like.

From "The Early Gothic Novel," the "Apex of Gothic Romance," "The Aftermath of Gothic Fiction," and a review of "Spectral Literature on the Continent," the author makes his way to America, lingering longest with Hawthorne and Poe. Both worked with materials from "The Weird Tradition in America," prominent in its Puritanism transported into the wilderness and allowed to run wild.

> In Hawthorne we have none of the violence, the daring, the high colouring, the intense dramatic sense, the cosmic malignity, and the undivided and impersonal artistry of Poe. Here instead is a gentle soul cramped by the Puritanism of early New England; shadowed and wistful, and grieved at an unmoral universe which everywhere transcends the conventional patterns thought by our forefathers to represent divine and immutable law.

To Poe he gives more space than to any other writer. Thus he sums him up: "Whatever his limitations, Poe did that which no one else ever did or could have done; and to him we owe the modern horror story in its final and perfected state."

After Poe more and more brilliant artistry was required to hold a reader to the end of a supernatural horror tale. In his final chapter Lovecraft's "Modern Masters" are all skilled technicians. Heading the group he places Arthur Machen:

> Of living creators of cosmic fear raised to its most artistic pitch, few if any can hope to equal the versatile Arthur Machen, author of some dozen tales long and short, in which the elements of hidden horror and brooding fright attain an almost incomparable substance and realistic acuteness.

As to the future of the genre the critic ventures no prophecy.

Pilgrims through Space and Time

J. O. Bailey

> James Osler Bailey (1903–1979) was an American critic and professor. He taught chiefly at the University of North Carolina at Chapel Hill. In 1930 he briefly corresponded with HPL while working on his treatise *Pilgrims through Space and Time* (New York: Argus Books, 1947), which became the first academic study of science fiction. In the following extract from his book, appearing on pp. 178–81, Bailey discusses HPL's contribution to science fiction.

The tale of terror thrives today with new rationalizations from science. The Elder Things of ancient myth are explained to be, perhaps, life-forms from an alien planet, and the "ectoplasm" of spirit mediums is likely to show up with a molecular formula.

Howard Phillips Lovecraft's "At the Mountains of Madness" (1936) combines material from the "dreaded *Necronomicon* of the mad Arab Abdul Alhazred," the closing chapters of Poe's *Arthur Gordon Pym* (along with a suggestion from "Ulalume"), and geology and the theory of evolution; the result is a tale of terror with every effect of the supernatural. The story is told to discourage any further scientific expeditions to the South Pole, by a scientist who took part in the ill-fated Miskatonic University Expedition.

In this expedition, two whaling-boat loads of scientists, graduate students, and their assistants go to the region of the South Pole. When they reach Ross Island, a student named Danforth identifies Mount Erebus as Poe's Mount Yaanek. But these literary identifications (even when birds like those of *Pym* are seen) do not interest the scientists. The party separates into two groups. The group headed by Lake, the biologist, ponders markings found in the slate that indicate Cambrian or pre-Cambrian life there, something more than five hundred million years old. Lake goes forward to a range of mountains' higher than the Himalayas. Boring beneath the ice-crust, he breaks into a hollow space, a tunnel filled with well-preserved animals of a kind never seen before: eight feet long, and barrel-shaped with star-shaped heads. The hide is tough; the blood is greenish like the sap of vegetables. Lake dissects one of them; the dogs are furious. Then a windstorm cuts off communication between groups.

The main party looks for Lake. The dissected bodies of the strange creatures are found and carefully buried. Then Lake and the others are found dead; one man is missing; another man has been curiously dissected. The narrator and Danforth take airplanes to cross the lofty mountains. They come to a city of towered stone buildings stretching for a hundred miles in geometric patterns. Exploring in the city, they find carvings that enable them to read its incredibly ancient history. When earth was young and the South Pole was warm, the Elder Things—no doubt those spoken of in the Pnakotic Manuscripts and the *Necronomicon*—came to earth, filtered down from the stars. The city was built nearly a thousand million years ago. These Old Ones, shaped by an alien evolution and possessing powers that man does not have, created the life of earth; they manufactured "multicellular protoplasmic masses capable of molding their tissues into all sorts of temporary organs under hypnotic influence" to serve them as slaves. (The amorphous masses must be the Shoggoths of the *Necronomicon*.) The land-masses of the South Pole broke up into continents; alien creatures from yet other planets came to do battle for earth; the Old Ones fought with atomic weapons and throve till the great cold came. Then they retreated first into the sea, and then into a sea in the interior of the earth.

Finding a tunnel, the explorers venture downward. They come upon the body of the man missing from Lake's camp, frozen and preserved; acrid odors rise. They come upon headless bodies of the star-headed creatures, the bodies sucked dry of blood. Then a mist rises and a formless thing advances, coming down the tunnel like a piston in a cylinder. The narrator and Danforth barely escape alive; their plane takes them over the mountains as strange birds cry, as in *Arthur Gordon Pym*, "Tekeli-li!" Perhaps the formless thing is simply Shoggoth, shapeless, living protoplasm, from fragments of which all life on earth evolved through the millenniums.

A similar quasi-scientific mythology underlies a great many stories from

Lovecraft's pen, especially "The Shadow out of Time" (1936).† This time, the discovery of the weirdly awful past that is none the less rationally explained, and the bringing of this past and the present into juxtaposition, are accomplished by (1) The metempsychic transfer of the mind of the narrator into the body of a member of an eldritch race that dominated the earth before the forms that produced man appeared, and then (2) the narrator's discovery of ruins from this ancient time and his recognition of their familiar symbols.

The story is presented as a manuscript written by Professor Nathaniel Wingate Peaslee of Miskatonic University and presented to his son, a professor of psychology. Following experiences so strange his mind can hardly credit them, Peaslee must formulate them for his son, above all to warn mankind to abandon the explorations of the strange stones in Australia.

The background is known to the general public: in 1908, while lecturing to a class in political economy, Peaslee slumped into a stupor; he awakened a victim of amnesia, able to speak only a stilted English; his behavior estranged his wife; he insisted on pursuing researches into ancient, forbidden documents in out-of-the-way corners of the world; after some years, he awakened from the amnesia to complete the sentence he had been speaking to his class in political economy.

Peaslee's conscious mind remembers nothing of the lapse of years. But in repeated, consecutive, horrible dreams, his lost years come back to him. Dreaming, he is in the grip of a nonhuman entity, dwelling in a civilization of vast stone cities, one of a Great Race that lived "somewhat less than 150,000,000 years ago." This Great Race had come "from that obscure, transgalactic world known in the disturbing and debatable Eltdown Shards as Yith," to inhabit strange bodies and to conquer an elder, half-material, "horrible elder race of half polypous, utterly alien entities which had come through space from immeasurably distant universes," drive it underground, and seal it there. Members of the Great Race, including Peaslee, are "immense rugose cones ten feet high, with head and other organs attached to foot-thick distensible limbs spreading from the apexes.

---

†Howard Phillips Lovecraft (1890–1937) was one of the most sensitive and powerful writers of our generation in the field of the quasi-scientific tale of terror. Both the stories described here were originally published in *Astounding Stories*. Similar pieces appeared in *Amazing Stories* and *Weird Tales*. Lovecraft built up a following of readers who regard him as a twentieth-century Poe. His work seems worth wide literary recognition, delayed perhaps because he published in magazines. Since his death, Arkham House, Sauk City, Wisconsin, has collected his stories and published them as *The Outsider and Others* and *Beyond the Wall of Sleep*. August Derleth has a biography and critical commentary, *H. P. L.: A Memoir*, published by Ben Abramson, New York.

They spoke by the clicking or scraping of huge paws ... and walked by the expansion and contraction of a viscous layer attached to their vast, ten-foot bases." They rove "all over the habitable world in titan airships or on the huge boat-like, atomic-engined vehicles which traversed the great roads" and delve curiously "into the libraries containing the records of the planet's past and future." They are masters of the secret of time-travel; with mechanical aids, "a mind would project itself forward in time, feeling its dim, extra-sensory way till it approached a desired period." Then it would seize a victim, as one had seized Peaslee. The victim would be compelled to inhabit the body of the creature, to submit to questions, and to write out a descriptive history of his own time; while the alien creature would inhabit his victim's body and explore the new world. The exploration completed, the process is reversed; all memory of the experience is blotted from the conscious mind of the victim.

In his dreams, Peasilee becomes acquainted with the other victims: a mind from Venus of the incalculable future; one from a moon of Jupiter six million years in the past; minds from the "winged, star-headed, half-vegetable race of paleogean Antarctica; one from the wholly abominable Tcho-Tchos; two from the Arachnid denizens of earth's last age," and so on. He learns from the Great Race that it will live its vast span, and then in the face of deadly peril, perhaps rebellion by the imprisoned horrors underground, the "cream of the Great Race" will skip over man's brief age and enter suitable bodies of "the mighty beetle civilization" that is to follow.

Supposing that all these dreams are sheer dreams, Peaslee writes an article describing his visions for the *Journal of the American Psychological Society*. Then a letter from Australia reports that stones with carvings such as he describes are to be found in a desert there. Miskatonic University organizes an expedition; miles of the stones are found, half uncovered by the shifting sands. The fragment of a memory draws Peaslee to a particular spot, where he finds an entry into a cavern—a gallery familiar to him in all its details. He proceeds across tumbled masonry, down tunnels, and into a room; he searches in a cabinet opened by a combination he "remembers"; he finds the astounding article he seeks. Then something damnable, something not material, that whistles like a sighing wind, seems coming through the darkness, up out of the dreaded doors that had been scaled. Peaslee flees, stumbles, crawls, and scrambles, till somehow he finds himself in the desert. He has dropped the priceless record he had sought and he dares not return for it; but he had seen it under his flashlight for a moment, the story of his own time, written in his own handwriting on sheets of perdurable metal.

These stories by Lovecraft meditate a combination of the measureless past of geology and astronomy, some grotesque suggestions from the theory of evolution, and ideas from various mythologies. They are splendid examples of scientific fiction turned to the uses of the tale of terror.

Imagination Runs Wild

Richard B. Gehman

Richard Boyd Gehman (1921–1972) was an American journalist and editor. He edited the *Oak Ridge Journal* (1943–48), the official weekly of the atomic bomb project. In the following article, first published in the *New Republic* 120, No. 3 (17 January 1949): 15–18, Gehman assesses HPL's importance in the contemporary popularity of "science-and-fantasy."

> The United States is studying the possibility of creating a military outpost hanging like a tiny "moon" far up in the skies . . . it was disclosed today by Secretary of Defense John Forrestal. *Associated Press, December 29, 1948.*

Recently, in New York, a man walked into the Argus Book Shop and asked for *The Outsider and Others*, published in 1939 at five dollars. When it was produced he glanced at the price and, without blinking, sat down and wrote a check for sixty dollars. He considered this a bargain—the book often had brought a hundred.

The Outsider is a collection of stories by the late H. P. Lovecraft, a writer esteemed by readers of science-and-fantasy fiction. That it sells today at twelve times its published price, and more, is informative.

It is also informative that another New York bookseller has a standing order from a Pittsburgh minister for every science-and-fantasy item that comes in; that a Pasadena manufacturer keeps his collection, which numbers about two thousand volumes, in a concrete vault with four-foot walls; and that a drugstore in Oak Ridge, Tennessee, sells out 150 copies of *Astounding Science Fiction*, the leading magazine in this field, within three days of its publication each month.

The fact is that science-fantasy has come into its own, has been a rapidly expanding literary fad, perhaps even a trend, since shortly before the end of World War II. A foreigner, making a cursory survey of our magazines and bookstores and deducing that the country has gone mad for the subject, might well be correct. Here is some evidence.

¶ During the past three years, trade publishers have brought out more than fifty anthologies and novels of science-and-fantasy.

¶ Five new publishing houses devoted exclusively to the *genre* have sprung into existence.

¶ Twenty-odd magazines in the field are enjoying unprecedented circulation booms.

¶ Such relatively cautious publications as the *Saturday Evening Post* and *Harper's* have run stories about vampires and interplanetary intrigue. The *American Scholar*, with an article by Harrison Smith, has made note of "The Rise of Fantasy in Literature."[34]

¶ Scores of forgotten books are selling at inflationary prices. Some of the Mars novels of Edgar Rice Burroughs, published at two dollars, are going for ten.

Despite this popular frenzy, it is difficult to say exactly what science-and-fantasy is. Seasoned fans contend that it is best to split it into two general headings, "Science Fiction" and "Fantasy Fiction," and to discuss them separately.

"Fantasy," in itself, usually deals with beings, creatures or forces outside man's empirical knowledge, such as spirits, ghosts, elves, werewolves, elementals, demons and the like.

"Science" employs facts now within knowledge or experience, carried to probable (or improbable, depending upon how you look at it) extensions of the imagination: time-travel, interstellar commerce or wars, utopias, mutations, and so on.

Yet the two fields overlap. Often, a story based on a valid scientific concept will take off into fantasy; sometimes a basic scientific proposition will be employed in a fantasy. It seems, then, that "science-and-fantasy" is the only broad phrase that is accurate.

Readers of science-and-fantasy, like readers of detective fiction, come from all classes and occupations. But unlike the whodunit fans, they seem to be infected with a virus. They read, reread and analyze stories with the zeal of scholars tracking down the key word in a Shakespearean play. They correspond with other sufferers, sometimes in letters running to twelve pages. They snip favorite stories out of magazines and bind them into their own private anthologies.

They also publish magazines—*fanzines,* as someone (someone who reads *Time,* no doubt) has called them. One bibliography of fan magazines recently listed more than a hundred titles, adding apologetically that several more may since have come into being.

Some of the magazines are *Satyric, En-Garde, Wudgy Tales,* the *Nucleus,* the *Science Fiction Savant, Fan-Dang, Walt's Wramblings, Fandomania, We Just Had to Do It* and *Have at Thee, Knaves!*

Their contents run from unblushing adoration to minute critical analysis, and their editorial tone falls somewhere between *Partisan Review* and *Modern Screen*. The articles may contain such sentences as "Love that Lovecraft!" or "Bradbury's creations illustrate the phenomenon of a childlike perception projected through the sensibility of an agile, adult imagination."

Fantasy Commentator, perhaps the best of the fanzines, once ran a history of fan magazines, written by Sam Moskowitz. It was published in eight instalments, each more than 3,000 words long.[35]

A substantial body of peripheral and complementary work, more or less scholarly, has grown up. A history of science fiction, *Pilgrims through Space and Time*, by J. O. Bailey, is selling steadily; so is H. P. Lovecraft's survey, *Supernatural Horror in Literature* (both published by Ben Abramson, New York). *The Checklist of Fantastic Literature*, edited by Everett F. Bleiler (Shasta Publishers, Chicago), lists some 6,000 titles and is the result of seven years' research by several men.[36]

Most of the famous writers in history have had a crack at either science or fantasy at one time or another. A partial list would include the names of Nathaniel Hawthorne, Henry James, William Dean Howells, Kipling, Gautier, Aldous Huxley, Shelley, Dickens, Galsworthy, Dreiser, Fielding, Anatole France, Thomas Mann, Jack London, Maugham, Conrad, Defoe, Charlotte Brontë and Samuel Butler. The *Checklist* also reveals an imposing number of writers whose output consisted of almost nothing but science-and-fantasy.

Predecessors of today's super-imaginative fiction were being written as early as the middle of the seventeenth century. In 1641, a founder of the Royal Society, Bishop John Wilkin, described a telegraph, a phonograph, and a flying machine. In 1785, two years after the Montgolfier brothers began experimenting with their famous balloon, the anonymous *Aerostatic Spy* predicted the development of a guided balloon. This predecessor of the dirigible was constructed of animal skins and powered by a stove. The locales, characters and subjects have changed as man has advanced his knowledge.

J. O. Bailey has divided the travel journals into these general categories: wonderful machines (usually flying machines, but often telegraphic or television devices); voyages to unexplored lands of the earth; voyages to the center of the earth (presumed to be hollow, and inhabited); and voyages to other planets, usually the moon.

Other early tales were concerned with the creation of life (*Frankenstein*, by Mary Shelley, is an example), longevity potions, mesmerism, alchemy, strange beings from dimensions beyond the third ("What Was It?" by Fitz-James O'Brien) and scientific principles applied in the detection of crime.

As communication and industry became more highly developed, the idea of a world catastrophe began to appear. Mary Shelley was one of the first to write of "The Last Man" alive in the world. Her story takes place in the twenty-first century, after a great plague has virtually destroyed civilization.

Edgar Allan Poe was also interested in this idea. In "The Conversation of Eiros and Charmion," two souls discuss the end of the world as caused by a collision with a comet. This was the first known use of a subject which later became familiar fare.

Poe and Jules Verne, his disciple, were perhaps the most important of the nineteenth-century writers. Poe's work was not confined, as many believe, to stories of horror and the supernatural. He was also fascinated by aeronautics, the transmutation of metals, robots, and travel to the center of the earth.

Not all his stories were seriously motivated. One, dealing with a robot chess player, revealed that the machine was so constructed that a human being could hide inside. Poe presumably wrote this story to attack a similar robot which was attracting great attention at a contemporary exposition.

Verne based many of his tales on inventions and theories which already were being speculated upon seriously by scientists. His reputation as a prophet thus was not as firmly grounded as many believe. *Twenty Thousand Leagues Under the Sea* dealt with the submarine in remarkably accurate terms, and *Journey to the Center of the Earth* presented much information about evolution and geology in a popular form. He was preoccupied with the potentialities of electricity. His submariners shot fish with electric guns, and his *Underground City* (written in 1877) was illuminated by incandescent lamps. Edison perfected the electric lamp in 1879.

The Industrial Revolution had a profound effect upon science fiction, and to some extent upon fantasy. Each invention, as it cut off an avenue for prophetic stories, also suggested new possibilities to the writers.

With the advent of H. G. Wells, writers began to branch out considerably. Utopian fiction had always been popular, but Wells gave it a currency never before attained. Of all the writers in the field, he had perhaps the best scientific training.

Wells was greatly interested in the world of the future, both as utopia and as chaos, and also in interplanetary travel (*The War of the Worlds*). As early as 1914, he was writing of atomic bombs (*The World Set Free*).

In 1905, he described a utopia that would be completely equipped with fast trains and airplanes, enclosed cities, air-conditioning and plastics. The state would own all land, utilities and resources, and would be governed by a group of people who would excel mentally and physically. Individuals would be free to follow their own pursuits.

In the early years of this century, new themes began to replace the old. Writers became absorbed with evolution, in machines to defy gravitation, photo-synthesis, relativity, telepathy and, of course, atomic energy.

The last was so common in science fiction before the war that when the National Censorship Board asked all publications to cease using the words "atom" and "nuclear physics," the science-fiction magazines escaped the silencer. It was felt that their readers might become suspicious if the terms suddenly disappeared.

Today, science fiction still deals in subjects which were popular in Wells's time. Not many new subjects have come along, although A. E. Van Vogt has written two books in which the action is based on non-Aristotelian logic.[37] And a story by William Tenn has suggested the existence of a sort of futuristic "Erector" set for children: The Bild-A-Man Kit.[38]

After the announcement of the atomic bomb, the stories took an ominous, gloomy turn. They now incline to presuppose a Third or Fourth World War in which all civilization will be destroyed. They deal with mutants created by radioactivity, and sometimes with supermen whose full powers have been attained with the help of atomic energy.

Fantasy fiction, on the other hand, has remained pretty much the same as it always was; it is limited not by knowledge but by free play of the imagination. If anything, it has become more horrible and unbelievable.

Although science-and-fantasy was always popular in England and in France, it didn't get a foothold in this country until about twenty-five years ago, despite the occasional appearance of popular writers like Poe, H. Rider Haggard, Verne, Wells, A. Merritt or Lord Dunsany.

The old *Harper's*, *Munsey's* and *Argosy* would now and again print a story of this type, but it wasn't until 1923, with the founding of *Weird Tales*, that writers began to find a real outlet in America. *Weird Tales*, by the way, is still going strong.

Weird Tales printed fantasy, for the most part. It was followed, in 1926, by *Amazing Stories*, edited by Hugo Gernsback. This was a reprint magazine at first, but it gradually began using original material as the audience grew. (*Amazing*, too, is still being published.)

Howard Phelps [sic] Lovecraft was the first notable modern practitioner of science-and-fantasy in this country. A shy, sensitive recluse who lived alone in an old dark house in Providence, Rhode Island, he was something of a prodigy. He wrote his first story at fifteen, and at sixteen he was contributing an astronomy column to a local newspaper.

Lovecraft was influenced, to some extent, by such eighteenth-century "Gothic" novels as Horace Walpole's *The Castle of Otranto*, and by Poe and Lord Dunsany. As fantasy writers go, his output was not large. He published only one small book in his lifetime, and most of his stories never reached an audience larger than that of *Weird Tales*. He died in 1937.

Lovecraft is notable, however, for the tremendous influence he exerted over other writers. In creating the *Cthulhu Mythos*, a series of legends concerned with cosmology and prehistoric races, he provided himself and other writers with material to draw upon for years to come. The *Mythos* was taken up, expanded and enlarged by Clark Ashton Smith, Frank Belknap Long, Robert Bloch, Henry Kuttner, August Derleth and others.

Derleth might be called the man most responsible for the current craze. He and Lovecraft had been correspondence-friends for about twelve years. Shortly after Lovecraft's death, Derleth and Donald Wandrei, another science-and-fantasy writer, submitted his *The Outsider* to two trade publishers.

When both turned the collection down, Wandrei and Derleth indignantly decided to publish it themselves. They thereupon founded Arkham House, named for the Massachusetts town of Arkham, another Lovecraft creation.

That was in 1939. Today, the most recent Arkham House catalogue lists about thirty-five titles. Ten others, out of print, are selling for unbelievable prices. (Lovecraft is not the only Arkham House author: others include M. P. Shiel, Algernon Blackwood, Ray Bradbury, A. E. Van Vogt and Cynthia Asquith.)

Not content with publishing books, the apparently indefatigable Derleth (who as writer and editor now has some fifty volumes to his credit, not all of which are science and fantasy) collected several anthologies for other publishers.

The titles include *Sleep No More*, *The Night Side* and *Who Knocks?* (all Rinehart and Company, New York), and *The Sleeping and the Dead*, *Strange Ports of Call* and *The Other Side of the Moon* (all Pellegrini and Cudahy, New York). The newcomer to science-and-fantasy who wants to find out what it's all about, might well begin with one of these.

The reader who wants to dip into Lovecraft need not spend sixty dollars. He can get a respectable collection of fourteen tales for about sixty cents: *Best Supernatural Stories of H. P. Lovecraft* (World Publishing Company, Cleveland).

V. Notices from the Literary Community 219

A number of anthologies published in the past two years might interest the casual reader. Doubleday (New York) offers two: *Man into Beast,* strange tales of transformation, edited by A. C. Spectorsky, which includes John Collier's "Green Thoughts" (man into plant) and Franz Kafka's famous "Metamorphosis" (man into cockroach); and *Travelers in Time,* edited by Philip Van Doren Stern, which includes H. G. Wells's "The Time Machine."

Groff Conklin his edited two excellent collections: *The Best in Science Fiction* and *A Treasury of Science Fiction* (both Crown, New York). The two biggest fantasy collections are *Great Tales of Terror and the Supernatural,* edited by H. A. Wise and P. M. Frazer (Random House); and *Pause to Wonder,* edited by Marjorie Fischer and Rolfe Humphries (Julian Messner).

There are several possible explanations for this new interest in science-and-fantasy.

Since the war and the dropping of the atomic bomb, the intimations of biological warfare and of supersonic flight, the radar beams bounced off the moon, the improbable inventions upon which German scientists were working, people suddenly have realized that the fantasies of the past are rapidly becoming realities.

These developments have removed much of the skepticism about science fiction. A New York editor recently said, "It occurs to me that atomic fission has lowered the threshold of improbability. If you can believe in the transformation of matter into energy, it follows that there is damned little else you can't believe in."

Harrison Smith has written, ". . . The age of invention rapidly became the age of anxiety . . . and certainly the age of fear. . . . The scientific fantasy story may, indeed, be explained as a necessary device . . . as a buffer against known and more conceivable terrors."

But if readers use fantasy as a buffer, it may also be that they are fascinated by it, like a frog by the rays of a flashlight. It may be that there is something hypnotic about tales of terror to come, and stories of beings outside natural law.

Another possibility lies in the unrest of the times. The citizen today feels confused and impotent, and many science-and-fantasy stories present a hero who operates outside of organized society, cutting across all barriers, untouched by laws by virtue of his very existence. Certainly this must be a subconsciously attractive idea to the millions who feel that the complexities of the modern world are stifling them and their activities.

But what is by all odds the most likely reason is also the most frightening. Much of the current science-and-fantasy is concerned with utopian societies of the future. It may be that people today, disturbed by the threat of war, by domestic insecurity and discontentment, feel a kind of nostalgia for the safety the future may represent. It may be that they are eager to embrace a world where wars, high prices and racial inequalities do not exist—a world that exists only in fiction—as a kind of substitute for wrestling with the intractable realities the inflexible times.

If this is the case, there can be no doubt that the prophets among the science-and-fantasy writers—the new prophets of doom—will not only continue to enjoy their popularity, but live to see their prophecies come true.

Books Alive

Vincent Starrett

> The following column appeared in the *Chicago Sunday Tribune* (18 December 1949): 4.

Fortunate, indeed, in his collaborators has been Dr. Adolphe de Castro, two of whose short stories are included in Arkham House's new collection of the miscellaneous writings of H. P. Lovecraft—"Something about Cats and Other Pieces," edited by August Derleth. It is well known that Lovecraft, a fascinating figure in our literature, eked out a precarious existence by revising and in part rewriting the tales of less expert craftsmen. One of his clients, it now appears, was de Castro, and the Lovecraft touch is clearly evident in the stories preserved by Mr. Derleth in this perhaps final volume of Lovecraftiana.

At the beginning of his writing career de Castro, then a San Francisco dentist, I believe, had the luck to bring Ambrose Bierce to his assistance. Their collaboration, "The Monk and the Hangman's Daughter," is a masterpiece of the macabre that is probably a classic. Originally a translation by de Castro from the German of Richard Voss, under the hands of Bierce the tale became one of the great short stories of literature; it was published in Chicago, in 1892, by F. J. Schulte & Co. The stories now preserved against oblivion by Howard Lovecraft are not in the same class, but they are readable yarns and, in the circumstances, they were worth saving.

Collectors and bibliografers will note that de Castro was originally Gustav Adolph Danziger, which is the name that appears on all early editions of the "Monk." Later editions carry the new name.

Other examples of Lovecraft's excellent revision are included in "Something about Cats," together with several critical and biografical articles by men who knew him. For specialists there are his extensive "notes" for a number of his best known stories. The reminiscent pieces by Rheinhart Kleiner, Samuel Loveman, Sonia H. Davis [for five years Lovecraft's wife], and E. Hoffmann Price, and the critical pieces by Fritz Leiber Jr. and August Derleth are of the highest interest; indeed they are the best things in the book.

A Bookman's Notebook

Joseph Henry Jackson

> Joseph Henry Jackson (1894–1955) was a longtime book reviewer for the *San Francisco Chronicle* (1931–55). He also wrote and edited several books about California literature and culture. The following column appeared in the *San Francisco Chronicle* (6 January 1950): 14.

Twelve years ago there died in Providence, Rhode, Island, one of the most interesting minor figures in American literature, Howard Phillips Lovecraft.

For something like 20 years (he was 47 when he died), he had written stories in the fields of fantasy and horror which placed him in the tradition of Bierce and Poe. Though his fiction, when it was written, appeared for the most part in such magazines as *Weird Stories* [sic], *Astounding Stories,* and the like, Lovecraft was far better than most who contributed to that group of periodicals. More important, he exercised a strong influence on others who were writing this type of story.

Since his death his fame has grown among those who specialize in horror fiction, stimulated greatly by the devoted persistence of August Derleth, whose Arkham House has made a business of "rescuing" Lovecraft. Now comes what Mr. Derleth calls the penultimate volume of Lovecraftiana, "Something about Cats and Other Pieces" (Arkham House; $3.00). There will be one more collection, Mr. Derleth notes, a volume of "Selected Letters."

In this present volume the work done wholly by Lovecraft himself is confined to essays such as the title piece, fragments of editorial comment and the like chosen from Lovecraft's many contributions to amateur journalism, some poems, notes, and a whimsical burlesque done for pure amusement.

For the rest, the book contains several stories on which Lovecraft helped, either by collaboration or by detailed criticism and rewriting, and some short biographical pieces by those who knew and worked with him, including Sonia H. Davis who was his wife for some years. For the Lovecraft enthusiast, these last will constitute the book's chief interest; many of them provide revealing glimpses of the withdrawn, often difficult personality of the man.

Here Mrs. Davis' notes should have been the best, but unfortunately they are not. From the standpoint of plain biographical information, Mr. Derleth himself is the most useful. From the standpoint of transmitting Lovecraft's personality to the reader, the memoir by Reinhart [sic] Kleiner does the job best. And the notes by Fritz Leiber, Jr. on Lovecraft's approach to the horror story, including comment on his method and techniques, come the closest to interpretation of the man's work. Vincent Starrett contributes some graceful verses on Lovecraft's death, and Mr. Derleth a fancied dialogue between the shades of Poe and Lovecraft as they meet at midnight on the streets of Providence.

The Lovecraft cult is a rather special affair, to be sure, but general interest in horror stories seems to be well on the upgrade, and there are undoubtedly many more potential readers for even this barrel-scraping collection than there would have been half a dozen years ago. True fans, however, will take this book in stride and reserve their full enthusiasm for the collection of Lovecraft letters which Mr. Derleth is preparing. Meantime, it may serve to introduce new readers who like a literary chill now and then to such representative Lovecraft works as "The Outsider and Others" and "Beyond the Wall of Sleep," in which they will find something quite special in the line of shudders.

Sabbat-Night Reading

E. O. D. Keown

> Eric O. D. Keown was a British writer and critic. His weird story "Sir Tristram Goes West" (1932) was adapted into the film *The Ghost Goes West* (1935). The following review appeared in *Punch* No. 5755 (28 February 1951): 285.

The Haunter of the Dark[39] is not a book to explore alone in a benighted cottage; at high noon on top of a bus in Oxford Street it would be sufficiently disturbing. H. P. Lovecraft was an American who died before the war, when his remarkable gift for the eerie was not yet widely known; this collection of his uncomfortable ghoulish short stories is the first to be published here. At his best, as in "The Outsider" and "The Thing on the Doorstep," his power to give overwhelming conviction to the wildly abnormal brings him close to Poe. His lesser pieces lack economy and suffer from an excessive use of grisly adjectives, but in nearly all of them is the same rare ability to convey terror in the fourth dimension. Most of the stories, set in the remote American countryside, have to do with dark creatures of the immemorial past, summoned from farthest space by hick devotees of black magic. Lovecraft was undoubtedly a minor master of cosmic horror.

Of Good and Evil

[Anthony Powell]

> The following review appeared in the [London] *Times Literary Supplement* No. 2612 (22 February 1952): 137, the most prestigious review journal in England. The review was published anonymously, but it has now been identified to be the work of the celebrated British novelist Anthony Powell (1905–2000), chiefly noted for his twelve-novel cycle collectively titled *A Dance to the Music of Time* (1951–75).

The Case of Charles Dexter Ward[40] brings us back again to the occult, in the manner of works deriving from Poe. Such books must remain peculiarly a matter of taste. Perhaps Mr. H. P. Lovecraft has written at too great length. Short stories such as those of M. R. James attain an extraordinary degree of horror, but they depend on relatively limited suspense. Mr. Lovecraft supplies a wealth of eighteenth-century pastiche in building up his chronicle of reincarnation and unspeakable wickednesses. In fact he rather overloads the canvas. There are, however, undeniably some eerie moments among the corpses.

The Genius Who Lived Backwards

Vincent H. Gaddis

> Vincent H. Gaddis (1913–1997) was an American writer most noted for coining the term "Bermuda Triangle." He wrote numerous books about weird phenomena on land and sea, in the manner of Charles

Fort. The following article was published in *Writers Forum* (Kansas City) 1, No. 2 (February 1954): 5–7, 9, 59–60.

Howard Phillips Lovecraft was a strange man. While other men slept, he worked and roamed the night-shrouded streets and cemeteries of his native Province, Rhode Island. Within his own consciousness he recreated the thought, speech and literary forms of the eighteenth century. He fought against the shackles of time and space and natural law, hiding his genius in a curious anonymity that is only beginning to live now that he is dead.

And he dreamed strange dreams—of cyclopean archaic cities buried beneath the sea and inhabited by the sleeping Old Ones, of multi-dimensions beyond the known where dwelled alien monstrosities, of nightmare visitors from the far dark stars. From the black gulfs of night his visions invoked scenes of long-vanished eons and whispers from forgotten gods. For Lovecraft is the Edgar Allan Poe of our time—a master of the macabre whose fantasies of cosmic terror are being hailed as masterpieces by noted critics.

He created a New England of his own, its ancient towns of Arkham and Dunwich brooding on past glories and present horrors. His "Cthulhu Mythology," complete with its own literature, has influenced a score of writers of weird fiction and caused believing readers to send letters of inquiry to bewildered book dealers. As a ghost writer for Harry Houdini, he produced the most astonishing piece of writing ever linked to the name of the famous magician. But, as Vincent Starrett says, "Lovecraft himself is even more interesting than his stories; he was his own most fantastic creation."

Tall and thin, with spectrally pale skin and bright alert eyes, Lovecraft's appearance was not easily forgotten. "He was the only person I ever met," one intimate friend writes, "who was ashamed of a coat of tan."[41] Suffering from an allergy to cold temperatures, he was sometimes forced to remain indoors for months at a time; and he had a deep-rooted aversion for all sea foods and the sea itself.

A scholarly recluse of antiquarian interests, Lovecraft managed to make a bare living by selling his stories, occasional bits of poetry. and doing ghostwriting or revision work on the material of other writers. Most of his time, however, was spent in writing letters. He had between 200 and 250 regular correspondents, and his letters sometimes ran to fifty or sixty pages. Both his letters and manuscripts were usually written in longhand.

Time, to Lovecraft, was the most grimly terrible thing in the universe. "Conflict with time," he wrote, "seems to me the most potent and fruitful theme in all human expression,"[42] and he longed to merge himself with his beloved eighteenth century. His desire became an obsession, and he often dated his manuscripts 200 years back and used early English expressions in writing and speaking. He dwelled so much in the past that he never considered himself young. During his thirties and early forties he called himself the "old gentleman" and "grandpa," and his small circle of close friends were his "grandsons."

Again, he endeavored to twist time by living at night and sleeping during the day. If forced to work during the day, he drew the window shades and turned on the electric lights. In vanished years he sought his spiritual and mental strength, and he considered our modern culture "a vast mechanical and emotionally immature barbarism."[43]

During the decade that has passed since his death, Lovecraft has become a literary legend. There is little doubt that his fame is destined to grow. His work has been praised by Stephen Vincent Benét, William Bolitho and Vincent Starrett. His stories were selected for O. Henry Memorial collections and yearbooks by the late Edward J. O'Brien; and have been included in anthologies compiled by Dashiell Hammett, T. Everett Harré, Phil Stong,[44] August Derleth, Herbert Wise, Phyllis Fraser and Christine Thomson. Already critics have joined him in august company with Poe, Bierce and Lord Dunsany.

"The older streets of Providence," writes Winfield Townley Scott, the poet, in the *Providence Journal*, "have for generations been distinguished with the haunting memory of the dark and intense and not always firm-footed figure of Edgar Allan Poe, and I think that now we may at last see that a leaner, ascetic, taller gentleman has joined him, walks with him, and is the more especially one of ours."[45]

Born in Providence in 1890, Lovecraft came from old Rhode Island stock of English descent. His father, a traveling salesman, died eight years after his birth, suffering from a mental illness, and he was raised by his mother and an aunt. A frail child, he was excessively coddled by his mother and taught by private tutors. As a result he became extremely introverted and somewhat of a prodigy.

Under the influence of Grimm's *Fairy Tales*, the *Arabian Nights*, and Greek and Roman mythologies, his imagination and sense of the fantastic grew steadily. In solitude he re-enacted story-book roles, and along the wooded shores of the nearby Seekonk River he erected shrines to Pan, Diana and Apollo. Sometimes he actually thought he observed fauns and dryads dancing under the trees.

Shy and lonely, he felt out of place in the modern world. In the books of his deceased grandfather's library and in the midst of the old streets and early houses of Providence around him, he found the glamour of the eighteenth century—the quiet unhurried years that preceded the industrial revolution. This was the period, he decided, when he should have lived. And so he sought escape from the realities of his time by reaching back into vanished yesterdays—attempting to recreate from dreams a world that had ceased to exist.

His first attempt at writing was made when he was seven. During his 'teens, while attending high school, he developed a deep interest in the sciences,[46] and he wrote a series of articles on astronomy for the local newspaper. Illness prevented his attending Brown University, and after leaving high school he became a recluse, living among his books, cultivating a wide range of interests and a phenomenal memory.

In 1914 he joined the United Amateur Press Association, a national organization of literary hobbyists who wrote, produced and exchanged "little magazines." Three years later, when 27, he began writing weird tales. But they failed to sell,[47] and the shadow of economic insecurity that had constantly hovered over the family since his father's death deepened.

Lovecraft's health improved about the year 1920, but in May of the following year his mother died. Suffering from mental and physical exhaustion, she had spent two years in a hospital. And, finally, in 1922, after five years of writing, Lovecraft sold his first story.

For the first thirty years of his life Lovecraft had never spent a night away from home. Now, encouraged by his first few sales, he moved to New York City. There, at the home of a mutual friend, he met Mrs. Sonia Greene. A few months later they were married and established in a Brooklyn apartment.[48]

About this time Lovecraft was the ghostwriter of an article which originally appeared in *Weird Tales* magazine under the byline of the famed Harry Houdini. Entitled "Imprisoned with the Pharoahs," it told of an alleged experience of the magician in Egypt in 1910. Seized by a group of Bedouins while visiting the pyramids one night, he was securely tied with ropes and dropped into a deep burial shaft. After escaping from his bonds, he wandered for hours in a subterranean labyrinth of dark tunnels and observed the phantoms of long-dead gods and kings far below the plateau of Gizeh. At dawn he found himself lying on the sand near the Great Sphinx. As "Houdini" concludes—"I know it was only a dream."

But success and happiness eluded the mystery writer despite his talent for the word-weaving of fantasy. Since his stories had a very limited market, he failed to sell enough of them to meet living expenses. Domestic difficulties arose, and the couple separated. Lovecraft hated the cosmopolitan, hurried life of the great metropolis, the long man-made canyons of Manhattan. New York was no place for an "eighteenth century gentleman." He longed for the old Georgian houses of Providence and the quiet groves along the Seekonk.

During his New York period Lovecraft explored the older sections of the city and Greenwich Village at night. His closest friends were Frank Belknap Long, the writer, and Samuel Loveman, the poet. One evening Long, Loveman and Lovecraft met Hart Crane, the poet, in a cafeteria. Crane, the authority on Poe,[49] and Loveman, who had known Bierce—and, already, to his admirers Lovecraft had inherited the mantles of Poe and Bierce!

"Was Poe symbolically present at that meeting?" wrote Mr. Long years later. "Was Bierce? Was all that lonely high company of dreamers most tragic, the wretched and the great?"[50]

It was Frank Belknap Long who quietly arranged for Lovecraft to return to Providence in 1926 and live with his aged aunt, Mrs. Lillian Clark. And Providence, for him, was home! As he once wrote: "For what is any man but the impress of his home and lineage? What is in us that our pasts have not placed there? Truly, no man is himself save among the scenes that have shaped him and his fathers; nor could I ever hope to find a lasting peace save close to the ancient monument of green-leaved, hill-crowning Providence . . . Providence is I, and I am Providence. One and inseparable!"[51]

Home at last, Lovecraft settled down to become, in the final decade of his life, perhaps the strangest American writer of modern times. He lived as he wished, working at night amid the relics of an earlier era, maintaining his incredible correspondence, and writing enough stories to supply the $15 a week on which he survived. A successful escapist, he found in his nocturnal labor and dreams a curious peace.

"I choose weird stories," he said, "because they suit my inclination best—one of my strongest and most persistent wishes being to achieve, momentarily, the illusion of some strange suspension or violation of the galling limitations of time, space, and natural law which forever imprison us. . . . These stories frequently emphasize the element of horror because fear is our deepest and strongest emotion, and the one which best lends itself to the creation of nature-defying illusions."[52]

Lovecraft was not an imitator of earlier writers of fantasy. Avoiding the stock ghosts, vampires and werewolves of tradition, he created plots of striking uniqueness and originality. He told of a silver key that permitted a man to regain the lost dreams of his youth, of a meteorite from far dark stars that contained a life-destroying intelligence, and of isolated human degeneration into burrowing rodent-like creatures. He wrote of resurrections of forgotten cults and witchcraft, and of alien horrors forever lurking on the dimensional frontier of our world and below the sea.

As a fundamental basis for his tales, he developed a myth-pattern that became known as the "Cthulhu Mythology." It referred to a period in dim antiquity, before the coming of man, when our earth was the home of strange beings with weird powers. As Lovecraft once wrote: "All my stories, unconnected as they may be, are based on the fundamental lore or legend that this world was inhabited at one time by another race who, in practicing black magic, lost their foothold and were expelled, yet live on outside ever ready to take possession of this earth again."

Elements of this mythology were to be found in certain old and rare books—the *Book of Dzyan*, the sinister *Liber Ivonis*, Ludvig Prinn's *De Vermis Mysteriis* and the *Pnakotic Manuscripts*. Most important, however, was the scarce *Necronomicon*, written by the mad Arab Abdul Alhazared, all copies of which were kept under lock and key in certain state and university libraries. So effective was Lovecraft's pseudo-realism, that many readers of his stories believed that these books actually existed.

Lovecraft's work influenced a score of other writers, many of whom drew upon and added to the Cthulhu Mythos. Including such well-known writers of fantasy as August Derleth, Donald Wandrei, E. Hoffmann Price, Robert Bloch, Frank Belknap Long, Clark Ashton Smith, Henry Kuttner, Duane W. Rimel, the late Rev. Henry S. Whitehead, and Bernard Austin Dwyer, the poet, they became known as the "Lovecraft Circle." To Lovecraft, personally, they were his "grandsons."

In 1932 his aunt, Mrs. Clark, died, and Lovecraft moved in with his remaining aunt, Mrs. Annie Gamwell, in the upstairs flat of a small house on the edge of the campus of Brown University. Night after night he carefully and laboriously wrote his letters and manuscripts with a fountain pen, occasionally exercising by tramping the dark, deserted streets. Altogether, he wrote about fifty stories of short novel length,[53] most of them originally appearing in weird and science-fiction magazines.

From time to time he took trips, making antiquarian explorations of Quebec, New England, and the coastal cities of Boston, Charleston, St. Augustine and New Orleans. Searching for hoary buildings and forgotten graveyards, he lived on a few cents a day so he could buy relics and souvenirs. Everywhere he carried a peculiar black case containing his writing materials and a small telescope.

He attacked modernism in literature, art and architecture, terming the latter as "nightmares in chromium, bakelite, glass and concrete." New trends, he said, were due to a mere decadent dissatisfaction with existing things, and he urged a return to our genuine culture stream which originated in ancient Greece and Rome. "Let us therefore accept it as our fathers did," he wrote, "and rejoice in possessing so great a tradition."[54]

Despite his seriousness, he possessed a dry sense of humor. And despite his starvation habits of eating, he was always ready to splurge on ice cream. Donald Wandrei tells of accompanying Lovecraft and his antiquarian friend, the late James F. Morton, curator of the Paterson (N. J.) Museum, to an ice cream parlor at Warren, Rhode Island, advertising 32 flavors. To Lovecraft's disappointment, only 28 varieties were available. Double portions of each flavor were served. Wandrei was forced to drop out of the marathon, but Lovecraft and Dr. Morton continued until every flavor had been enjoyed.

After their repast was over, they wrote a tribute to the excellence of the establishment's product and left it on the table. A year later, on a return visit, they found their testimony framed and hanging on the wall. "Fine," was Lovecraft's comment, "but what a shame that four flavors were missing on that occasion."[55]

Early in 1937 Lovecraft became ill from Bright's disease and intestinal cancer, and he was removed to a hospital. On March 15 he passed away, his death coinciding with that of Montague James, the English writer of fantasy, and he was buried in the family plot at Swan Point Cemetery. Mrs. Gamwell, the last of the family, died in 1941.

Shortly after his death, August Derleth and Donald Wandrei founded Arkham House at Sauk City, Wisconsin, for the purpose of publishing Lovecraft's works in book form. The first volume, *The Outsider and Others*, appeared in 1939 in a limited edition, and is now selling at ten times the original cost among book dealers. Two other volumes, *Beyond the Wall of Sleep* (1943) and *Marginalia* (1944) followed, and a collection of selected letters is now being compiled. R. H. Barlow, Lovecraft's literary executor, has deposited most of Lovecraft's manuscripts and other material in the John Hay Library of Providence, next door to his home.

Lovecraft is gone, but his dreams live on. Only the judgment of time will decide if they are to join the earlier fantasies of Poe and Bierce in the great heritage of American literature to be given to generations unborn. But they served their primary purpose—enabling their creator to escape from the modern world of chaos into a former one of peace, and providing him with the silver key to spaceways and realms distant and strange.

Appendix: Some Vignettes

I can't be very systematic in my suggestions [concerning weird fiction]. I shall have recourse to a funny American thing which was sent me the other day. A periodical, apparently, "The Recluse, issued by W. Paul Cook for His Own Amusement—this being the First Number." In it is a disquisition of nearly 40 pages of double columns on Supernatural Horror in Literature by one H. P. Lovecraft, whose style is of the most offensive. He uses the word cosmic about 24 times. But he has taken pains to search about & treats the subject from its beginnings to MRJ, to whom he devotes several columns. No doubt this is why I am favoured with a copy.
—M. R. James[1]

In this world [of pulp magazines] there are chiefs, evidently. I am inclined to think they must be pretty good. There is Otis Adelbert Kline and H. P. Lovecraft, whom I am sure I would rather read than many fashionable lady novelists they give teas to; and poets too. Meditate on that, you who are tired of the strained prettiness of the verse in the great periodicals, that there are still poets hewre of the pure Poe school who sell and are printed for a vast public.
—William Bolitho[2]

The tales of the supernatural in H. P. Lovecraft's *The Outsider* are all too morbidly fantastic to be convincing. They come nowhere near the high standard of supernatural fiction set by Poe, Fitz James O'Brien and Edith Wharton.
—Don Stanford[3]

I have said elsewhere and before this that my brother [Stephen Vincent Benét] early developed a habit of gritting his teeth and being thrilled by tales of heroic exploits. He will never quite lose that faculty. And he still absorbs pulp-magazines dealing with horror, mystery, and marvel, with as great a relish as he did in his youth. For instance, he was entirely familiar with the work of H. P. Lovecraft long before that little-known master of horror was brought to the attention of the critics.
—William Rose Benét[4]

I . . . have an odd interest in Lovecraft's work because in the few tales of his I have read I found that he was writing in my style, entirely originally

& without in any way borrowing from me, & yet with my style & largely my material.

—Lord Dunsany[5]

I have read three books this year with much more than my eyes alone: *L'Atlantide et les Géants*, by Denis Saurat; *La Coleur Tombée du Ciel*, by H. P. Lovecraft,[6] translated by Jacques Papy; and *Lueurs sur les Soucoupes Volantes*, by Aimé Michel.

. . . Mr. Lovecraft, who is American, invents a terrifying world of space-time; his somewhat loose style has gained by translation into French. . . .

—Jean Cocteau[7]

Notes

I. Recollections of Lovecraft

1. HPL died around 6:45 A.M. on March 15, 1937.

2. HPL was interim president of the National Amateur Press Association in 1922-23, taking over the unfinished term of William J. Dowdell. He contributed occasionally to the "Bureau of Critics" column of the *National Amateur* in 1922-23 and 1931-35.

3. "Idealism and Materialism—A Reflection" (*National Amateur*, July 1919 [distributed summer 1921]); "The Materialist Today" (*Driftwind*, October 1926; also issued as a pamphlet by Driftwind Press, 1926); "Supernatural Horror in Literature" (*Recluse*, 1927; rev. ed. *Fantasy Fan*, October 1933-February 1935).

4. *The Shunned House* was a pamphlet printed by W. Paul Cook in 1928 but not bound or distributed. In 1933 Coates momentarily considered taking over the edition and distributing it, but this plan came to nothing.

5. Samuel Taylor Coleridge, *The Rime of the Ancient Mariner* (1798), ll. 113-14.

6. Edgar A. Guest (1881-1959), British-born American poet whose work was widely derided as a byword for triteness and conventionality.

7. C. Cilnius Maecenas (70 B.C.E.-8 C.E.), celebrated Roman political figure who served as a patron to many leading poets, including Horace and Virgil.

8. Matthew H. Onderdonk, "The Lord of R'lyeh," *Fantasy Commentator* 1, No. 6 (Spring 1945): 103-7, 109-11, a pioneering essay on HPL's philosophy and its ramifications in his fiction.

9. There is no mention of Boland in any of HPL's or Robert E. Howard's extant letters. No letters by HPL to Boland appear to survive.

10. This derivation is wildly inaccurate. HPL's derivation (*nekros*, corpse; *nomos*, law; *ikon*, image = "Image [or picture] of the law of the dead" [*SL* 5.418]) is equally erroneous. The proper derivation is: *nekros*, corpse; *nemo*, to divide (hence to study or classify); -*ikon*, neuter adjectival suffix = A Study [or Classification] of the Dead.

Note: The abbreviation *SL* in the notes refers to Lovecraft's *Selected Letters*, volumes 1-5 (Sauk City, WI: Arkham House, 1965-1977).

11. "The Beast in the Cave" (written April 1905).

12. "The Lurking Fear" (written November 1922), published serially in *Home Brew* (January–April 1923), a professional humour magazine edited by George Julian Houtain, an amateur colleague of HPL.

13. "The Lurking Fear" appearance in *Home Brew* was illustrated by Clark Ashton Smith.

14. When "The Loved Dead" appeared in *Weird Tales* (May-June-July 1924), the issue was apparently banned for a time in the state of Indiana.

15. Chepachet is briefly mentioned in "The Horror at Red Hook" (1925).

16. The First Baptist Church (1775) on Main Street.

17. Nigger-Man disappeared shortly after HPL's move from his birthplace, 454 Angell Street, to 598 Angell Street in 1904.

18. "Under the Pyramids," published as "Imprisoned with the Pharaohs" in *Weird Tales* (May-June-July 1924).

19. Actually, the ms. was typed by HPL as his wife, Sonia, dictated. The typing was done at a stenographer's office in Philadelphia, where the couple had gone for their honeymoon.

20. An adaptation of "The Dunwich Horror" was first broadcast on the CBS radio show "Suspense" on 1 November 1945. It must have been rebroadcast around Hallowe'en of 1947.

II. Criticism in Lovecraft's Lifetime

1. "The Alchemist," *United Amateur* (November 1916).

2. "The Beast in the Cave," *Vagrant* (June 1918).

3. HPL probably had not read the horror tales of Guy de Maupassant (1850–1893) at this time.

4. "Facts concerning the Late Arthur Jermyn and His Family," *Wolverine* (March and June 1921).

5. Long apparently refers to Charles H. Hinton (1853–1907), British mathematician and author of *The Fourth Dimension* (1904) and other speculative works.

6. Benjamin De Casseres (1873–1945), American poet and critic. HPL's friend Clark Ashton Smith was a regular correspondent of De Casseres.

7. The story was in fact rejected by *Weird Tales* in 1925. HPL does not appear to have submitted it to any other magazine before agreeing to let Cook print it as a booklet.

8. In *The Best Short Stories of the Year 1928* (1928), Edward J. O'Brien gave "The Colour out of Space" (*Amazing Stories*, September 1927) a three-star ranking, placing it on the "Roll of Honor." The next year, "The Dunwich Horror" (*Weird Tales*, April 1929) was placed on the Roll of Honor.

9. HPL's stories were, of course, widely published in amateur journals before their appearance in *Weird Tales* and other professional magazines.

10. In the discussion that follows, Orton closely paraphrases several passages from the introduction to "Supernatural Horror in Literature." Orton drew the cover of the issue of the *Recluse* in which HPL's essay appeared.

11. It is not clear what Orton is referring to. HPL's first appearance in book form occurred when "The Horror at Red Hook" appeared in the anthology *You'll Need a Night Light* (London: Selwyn & Blount, 1927). No book of HPL's stories appeared in the UK until after HPL's death.

12. Wilcox's middle name, in "The Call of Cthulhu," is Anthony.

13. HPL, reading this passage, wrote the sonnet "The Messenger" at 3:07 A.M. on the evening of November 30. He sent it to Hart, who published it in his column for December 3; it constitutes the first appearance of the poem.

14. Clark Ashton Smith's "The Gorgon," HPL's "In the Vault," and Edmond Hamilton's "The Earth-Brain," discussed here, all appeared in *Weird Tales*, April 1932.

15. The passage is a crude paraphrase of the opening of Poe's "The Tell-Tale Heart."

III. Comments from Readers

1. H. Warner Munn (1903–1981) later became a friend of HPL; they first met c. mid-1927 (see *SL* 2.157).

2. Farnese (1885–1945) came in touch with HPL years later, in 1932 (see *SL* 4.54). He was a musical composer and set two of HPL's *Fungi from Yuggoth* sonnets to music. He wished to write an opera based on *Fungi from Yuggoth* (with HPL writing the libretto), but the plan came to nothing.

3. Both E. Hoffmann Price's "The Stranger from Kurdistan" and HPL's "The Unnamable" appeared in *Weird Tales*, July 1925.

4. Derleth (1909–1971) came in touch with HPL c. July–August 1926, although Derleth had asked Farnsworth Wright for HPL's address as early as late 1925.

5. Price (1898–1988) became acquainted with HPL only in 1932, when HPL met him in New Orleans.

6. Ray Cummings (1887–1957) was a prolific author of science fiction for the pulps. HPL had little regard for him: "I shall sooner or later get around to the interplanetary field myself—& you may depend upon it that I shall not choose Edmond Hamilton, Ray Cummings, or Edgar Rice Burroughs as my model!" (SL 3.88).

7. *Weird Tales*, April and January 1926, respectively.

8. Actually, HPL had moved back to Providence in April 1926 after two years in New York.

9. Derleth later wrote a story based on this image: "Melodie in E Minor" (*Weird Tales*, February 1929).

10. Shea (1912–1981) began corresponding with HPL in June 1931.

11. Whitehead (1882–1932) met HPL in 1931 when the latter visited him in Florida.

12. John Frederick "Jack" Snow (1907–1956) later wrote several books about L. Frank Baum's "Oz" books and also contributed four stories to *Weird Tales*, the first in September 1927. See further his letter in the January 1946 issue.

13. A four-part serial (Oct.–Dec. 1927 and Jan. 1928).

14. Howard (1906–1936) only began corresponding with HPL in 1930, when he pointed out to HPL an historical inaccuracy in "The Rats in the Walls" when it was reprinted in the June 1930 issue.

15. Published in the February 1928 issue.

16. See such works as *First Principles* (1862).

17. Published in the June 1928 issue.

18. Published in the April 1929 issue.

19. This remark refers to a controversy then raging in "The Eyrie" as to whether *Weird Tales* should publish more weird or science fiction tales; the majority of readers voted for the former.

20. Dwyer (1897–1943) came in touch with HPL through *Weird Tales* in early 1927.

21. Edgar Allan Poe, "Dream-Land," l. 7.

22. First published in the February 1924 issue and reprinted in the September 1929 issue.

23. Reprinted from the July 1925 issue (see n. 3 above).

24. O'Neail published three stories in *Weird Tales* (1929–32).

25. "The Outsider" was in fact reprinted in the June/July 1931 issue.

26. A three-part serial (Oct.-Dec. 1929).

27. According to Howard's own statement, he created the name "Kathulos" on his own and did not derive it from HPL. In a letter to HPL ([9 August 1930]), Howard noted: "I merely manufactured the name at random, not being aware at the time of any legendary character named Cthulhu—if indeed there is." *A Means to Freedom: The Letters of H. P. Lovecraft and Robert E. Howard* (New York: Hippocampus Press, 2009), 1.37.

28. HPL referred to this letter when he wrote to Howard (14 August 1930): "I think it is rather good fun to have this artificial mythology given an air of verisimilitude by wide citation. I ought, though, to write Mr. O'Neil and disabuse him of the idea that there is a large blind spot in his mythological erudition!" (*SL* 3.166).

29. Harlow (1876-1963) wrote a number of articles on superstition (e.g., "The Vampire" in the March 1928 issue, "The Unicorn" in the April 1929 issue) and other oddities throughout 1927, 1928, and 1929.

30. Farnsworth Wright had, beginning in late 1927, given thought to issuing a volume of HPL's tales under the imprint of the Popular Fiction Publishing Co., but the plans came to nothing.

31. Published, respectively, in the issues for October 1928, August-September 1928 (2 parts), and June-July 1930 (2 parts).

32. The reference is to the illustration by Hugh Rankin, on the second page of the story, that anticipates the surprise climax ("[They] . . . were the face and hands of Henry Wentworth Akeley").

33. Ten of HPL's *Fungi from Yuggoth* appeared in *Weird Tales* from September 1930 to April/May 1931 ("Recapture," a separate sonnet later added to the *Fungi*, appeared in May 1930).

34. Published, respectively, in the issues for May 1930, July 1930, and June 1930.

35. Bloch (1917-1994) received his first letter from HPL in April 1933.

36. Smith's story in the July 1933 issue is "Ubbo-Sathla."

37. Ostrow appears to have mistaken HPL for Samuel Loveman, who wrote several "additions" to Shakespeare plays in the amateur journals (but even Loveman did not, so far as is known, write actual "essays" on Shakespeare). HPL refers to the matter in a letter to R. H. Barlow (3 January 1936): "The other day a bird who saw that ancient Eyrie letter (confusing me with Loveman) describing me as a 'Shakespearian authority' wrote to ask me for brief character sketches of Hamlet, Claudius, Ophelia, Mac-

beth, & Lady Macbeth!" (*O Fortunate Floridian: H. P. Lovecraft's Letters to R. H. Barlow* [Tampa: University of Tampa Press, 2007], p. 393).

38. "Bernard J. Kenton" is the pseudonym of Jerome Siegel (1914-1996), co-creator of Superman.

39. Published in the March 1934 issue.

40. A three-part serial by David H. Keller (Jan.-Mar. 1934).

41. "Shambleau" appeared in the November 1933 issue; "Black Thirst" in the April 1934 issue.

42. Kuttner (1915-1958) came in touch with HPL only in February 1936.

43. Nelson corresponded briefly with HPL, exchanging five letters with him in 1934 and 1935, before committing suicide. He published five poems in *Weird Tales* (1934-37).

44. The story was included in Dashiell Hammett's *Creeps by Night* (1931).

45. The two stories were published, respectively, in the issues for January 1935 and June 1934.

46. Published in the April 1935 issue.

47. Wollheim (1914-1990), later a leading science fiction editor, got in touch with HPL in 1935.

48. Frank Belknap Long's "The Space-Eaters" appeared in the July 1928 issue.

49. Reynolds later wrote a letter to "The Eyrie" (November 1935) praising Robert Bloch's "The Shambler from the Stars" (published in the September 1935 issue and featuring a character modelled after HPL) and suggesting that HPL write a story featuring Bloch as a character. HPL responded with "The Haunter of the Dark" (*Weird Tales*, December 1936).

50. Petaja (1915-2000), science fiction fan and writer, began corresponding with HPL in late 1934.

51. Petaja is clearly alluding to *At the Mountains of Madness*, rejected in 1931 by Farnsworth Wright (see *SL* 3.392, 395) and soon to be purchased (through the offices of agent Julius Schwartz) by *Astounding Stories*, which published it in the issues of February, March, and April 1936.

52. Kuttner refers to "The Temple."

53. Bergier (1912-1978) later played a crucial role in introducing HPL to French readers, writing the introduction to the first volume of HPL's work in French, *La Couleur tombée du ciel* (1954). In the article "Lovecraft,

ce grand génie venu d'ailleurs" (*Planète*, October–November 1961), Bergier maintained that he had corresponded with HPL: he had asked him how he had described Paris so accurately in "The Music of Erich Zann" and wondered if HPL had ever visited Paris, to which HPL supposedly responded: "In a dream, with Poe." There is no confirmation that HPL ever corresponded with Bergier, and no letters have come to light.

54. C. L. Moore's "The Dust Gods" appeared in the August 1934 issue; Clark Ashton Smith's "The Gorgon" in the April 1932 issue; H. F. Arnold's "The Night Wire" in the September 1926 issue (reprinted January 1933).

55. "The Dark Demon" appeared in the November 1936 issue. It mentions HPL by name and also features a "reclusive dreamer" named Edgar Gordon, modelled after HPL.

56. Published in the July 1925 issue and purportedly based on a comment in HPL's letter to "The Eyrie" (March 1924): "Take a werewolf story, for instance—who ever wrote a story from the point of view of the wolf, and sympathising strongly with the devil to whom he has sold himself?" But Munn misunderstood the purport of HPL's remark, making his werewolf regret his condition.

57. "The Picture in the House" was reprinted in the March 1937 issue. "The Unnamable" and "The Call of Cthulhu" were never reprinted. "The Horror at Red Hook" was reprinted in the March 1952 issue. "Pickman's Model" was reprinted in the November 1936 issue.

58. Actually, HPL knew only English and Latin fluently, although he had the rudiments of Greek, French, and Spanish.

59. HPL met Quinn during visits to New York in July 1931 and January 1936.

60. Sterling (1920–1995) became acquainted with HPL in March 1935, shortly after his family moved to Providence.

61. Sterling expanded his comments into the memoir "Lovecraft and Science" (in *Marginalia*, 1944).

62. Actually, HPL and Smith began corresponding in August 1922, hence for a total of about 14½ years.

63. Samuel Loveman sent "Beyond the Wall of Sleep" to Smith, probably in 1922 (see *SL* 1.195).

64. Peirce corresponded briefly with HPL in the mid-1930s.

65. William Wordsworth, "London, 1802," ll. 9–11.

66. Lowndes (1916–1998), author and editor, exchanged two letters with HPL in early 1937.

67. "In Memoriam: Robert Ervin Howard" (*Fantasy Magazine*, September 1936).

68. Henry George Weiss (1898–1968), a Canadian-born poet and essayist, wrote science fiction under the pseudonym Francis Flagg. He corresponded with HPL sporadically from 1930 to 1937.

69. C. L. Moore's "Lost Paradise" appeared in the July 1936 issue; Jack Williamson's "The Ruler of Fate" (a three-part serial) in the April, May, and June 1936 issues; Robert E. Howard's "The Hour of the Dragon" (a five-part serial) in the issues of Dec. 1935–April 1936.

70. A story by Manly Wade Wellman (August 1937 issue) about a man who stumbles upon the *Necronomicon* and destroys it with holy water.

71. "Through struggle to the stars"—the motto of the Royal Air Force (RAF).

72. In the omitted section, Pryke discusses the merits of Henry S. Whitehead and Robert E. Howard.

73. Published in the January 1938 issue.

74. Published in the February 1938 issue. The story (published as by William Lumley) was ghostwritten by HPL.

75. Henry Kuttner, "World's End" (*Weird Tales*, February 1938).

76. Sarah Helen (Power) Whitman (1803–1878), whose house is at 88 Benefit Street in Providence.

77. The churchyard of St John's Episcopal Church (1810). The church is on North Main Street, but the churchyard is accessible from Benefit Street, one block to the east.

78. August Derleth, "The Return of Hastur," a pastiche of HPL.

79. Published in the March 1939 issue.

80. Cf. HPL to E. Hoffmann Price, 12 February 1936: "I'm farther away from doing what I want to do than I was twenty years ago" (*SL* 5.224).

81. For Mabbott, see p. 145. He was one of the earliest academic critics to take notice of HPL (see p. 16–17).

82. The first story by Bradbury (b. 1920) in *Weird Tales* was "The Candle" (*Weird Tales*, November 1942).

83. I.e., *The Outsider and Others* (1939).

84. This matter is further elaborated in Conover's *Lovecraft at Last* (1975), pp. 141f.

85. It becomes apparent that the first four paragraphs of the letter were written by Wandrei and the rest by Derleth. Late in life, however, Wandrei mentioned to me that he had had no hand in writing the letter.

86. The ms. is numbered to p. 147, but includes 10 additional pages of inserts.

87. Wandrei's typescript (whether complete or fragmentary) does not survive.

88. Arkham House did not prepare an entirely new typescript: it followed R. H. Barlow's partial typescript (23 pp.) until it ended, then prepared its own. Both the Barlow and the Arkham House typescript contain numerous textual errors.

89. The appearance of *The Case of Charles Dexter Ward* in *Weird Tales* (two-part serial, May and July 1941) was abridged.

90. This paragraph is largely taken from Derleth's article "H. P. Lovecraft, Outsider" (see p. 121), which was itself revised as the introduction to *The Outsider and Others*.

91. There are, of course, dozens of photos of HPL in existence.

92. Published (in abridged form) in the January 1942 issue.

93. The story was published as a book by the Visionary Publishing Co. (Everett, PA), operated by William L. Crawford, in November 1936 (dated April 1936). Only about 200 copies were bound.

94. Published in the September 1941 issue.

95. *At the Mountains of Madness* was written in February–March 1931 and therefore predates "The Shadow over Innsmouth" (November–December 1931).

96. Published, respectively, in the issues for March 1944 and November 1944. The former was retitled "The House on Curwen Street" in *The Trail of Cthulhu* (1962).

97. See *Publishers' Weekly* 148, No. 1 (7 July 1945): 81, in which the Grove Street Bookshop (49 Grove Street, New York) lists "Prinn, Ludvig. Mysteries of the Worm" and "Necronomicon." The hoax was discussed in an article by Jacob Blanck, "News from the Rare Book Sellers," *Publishers' Weekly* 148, No. 25 (22 December 1945): 2726–27.

98. Briney went on to compile the section "Professional Works and Miscellany" in George T. Wetzel's *The Lovecraft Collectors Library, Volume Seven: Bibliographies* (1955).

99. The *R'lyeh Text* was created by August Derleth. The *Book of Dzyan* is a real work (see *SL* 4.155).

100. John Taylor Gatto later wrote a study guide, *The Major Works of H. P. Lovecraft: A Critical Commentary*, for Monarch Press (1977).

101. The book must have been very incomplete, for HPL in "The Dunwich Horror" cites a passage from page 751 of the Latin text.

102. No such edition is recorded in HPL's "History of the *Necronomicon*" (1927).

103. This purports to be the Latin of the "unexplainable couplet," "That is not dead which can eternal lie, / And with strange aeons even death may die." A literal translation of the Latin is as follows: "Believe not that that is dead which lies eternally, / When through astonishing centuries even Death may die." "Quin" in the first line should probably be "quod."

104. Wade went on to write numerous Cthulhu Mythos tales, including "The Deep Ones" (in Derleth's *Tales of the Cthulhu Mythos*, 1969).

105. Howard Brown illustrated *At the Mountains of Madness* in *Astounding*. HPL praised the illustrations in the first instalment: "The illustrator drew the nameless Entities precisely as I had imagined them . . ." HPL to August Derleth, 11 February 1936; *Essential Solitude: The Letters of H. P. Lovecraft and August Derleth* (New York: Hippocampus Press, 2008), 2.725.

106. The reference is to the illustrators Charles Schneeman, Mark Marchioni, and H. Wesso (Hans Waldemar Wessolowski).

107. The reference presumably is to the original novelette version of "The Moon Pool" (*All-Story*, 22 June 1918), not to the subsequent expansion into a novel (1919). HPL himself regarded the novelette as one of the great weird stories in literature.

108. Lloyd Arthur Eshbach (1910–2003), science fiction writer and publisher, began corresponding with HPL in early 1935.

109. Frank Belknap Long, "Cones" (*Astounding Stories*, February 1936).

110. Duane W. Rimel (1915–1996) began corresponding with HPL in 1934.

111. E. E. "Doc" Smith (1890–1965), *The Skylark of Space* (*Amazing Stories*, August–October 1928; book publication 1946), a popular example of "space opera" science fiction.

112. Jack Darrow was a notable science fiction fan of the 1930s. HPL poked fun at him and others in science fiction fandom in "In the Walls of Eryx" (1936).

113. P. Schuyler Miller, "The Chrysalis" (*Astounding Stories*, April 1936).

114. The reference is to Warner Van Lorne (pseudonym of Nelson Tremaine, 1907-1971), a frequent contributor to *Astounding*.

115. Corwin F. Stickney, Jr, was a late correspondent of HPL and editor of *Amateur Correspondent* (1937f.). He was probably in touch with HPL at the time he wrote this letter.

116. James V. Taurasi was later the editor of the celebrated fanzine, *Fantasy-Times*.

IV. Criticism from the Fan World

1. From HPL's letter to J. Vernon Shea, 30 July 1933 (SL 4.232).

2. From HPL's letter to Virgil Finlay, 25 September 1936 (ms.; not published in SL 5.310-11).

3. "The Picture in the House" received a one-star rating in Edward J. O'Brien's *Best Short Stories of the Year 1924* (1924). "Pickman's Model" was cited among "Stories Ranking Third" in the *O. Henry Memorial Prize Stories: 1928*, ed. Blanche Colton Williams (Garden City, NY: Doubleday, Doran, 1928); "The Silver Key" was cited in the 1929 volume among "Stories Ranking Second"; "The Strange High House in the Mist" was cited in the 1932 volume among "Stories Ranking Highest," and "In the Vault" among "Stories Ranking Second." "The Rats in the Walls," "The Music of Erich Zann," and "The Whisperer in Darkness" were never cited in either the O'Brien or the O. *Henry* volumes.

4. From "Some Notes on a Nonentity" (1933).

5. From HPL's letter to J. Vernon Shea, 9 December 1931 (SL 3.441).

6. "The Music of Erich Zann" was reprinted in the *Evening Standard* (London) (24 October 1932).

7. See Section III, n. 93.

8. The reference is to George Santayana's novel *The Last Puritan* (1935), which HPL read and appreciated (see SL 5.312-15).

9. From HPL's letter to Farnsworth Wright, 5 July 1927 (SL 2.150).

10. Actually, an editor at Alfred A. Knopf had asked Farnsworth Wright of *Weird Tales* if he could dispose of 1000 copies of a book of HPL's sto-

ries through the magazine; when Wright said he could not, Knopf turned down the volume.

11. Felix Kowalewski (1913–1989) was an American painter and poet, the son of Polish immigrants. "Death of the Artist" appeared in *Weird Tales* (March 1937).

12. HPL had, in "Literary Review" (*Californian*, Winter 1936), discussed the contributions in the Summer 1936 issue of the *Californian*. In criticising the stories of editor Hyman Bradofsky in the issue, HPL remarks: "His primary need is to draw from life rather than from literature; to delineate the complex emotions and inconclusive acts of the people he sees around him or learns about from non-fictional sources rather than to mirror the dramatically heightened and naively oversimplified feelings and acts commonly encountered in popular fiction. One may add that the stories of Eunice McKee, Jean V. LaForge, and John Blythe Michel indicate a not dissimilar need."

13. W. H. Auden, "A. E. Housman," in Auden's *Another Time: Poems* (1940).

14. John Holmes (1904–1962), American poet, best known for his humorous and light verse. Neil H. Swanson (1896–1983), journalist and historical novelist.

15. Actually, early in his career HPL was an ardent proponent of temperance and did support Prohibition; see the poem "Monody on the Late King Alcohol" (1919). In later years, although still personally believing in temperance, he did not believe that Prohibition was an efficient means to that end.

16. *Charleston* (1936), a mimeographed booklet prepared by H. C. Koenig.

17. The cemetery of St John's Episcopal Church could not be seen from any of HPL's houses in Providence.

18. De Castro's poem, "Edgar Allan Poe," was published in *Weird Tales* (May 1937). HPL's, "In a Sequester'd Providence Churchyard Where Once Poe Walk'd," appeared posthumously (May 1938, as "Where Once Poe Walked"). None of the poems are "sonnets," as they consist of only 13 lines.

19. The house at 135 Benefit Street was never "deserted," although for fictional purposes HPL in the story declares it to have been deserted at various times.

20. "The Very Old Folk," *Scienti-Snaps* (Summer 1940), a transcript of HPL's "Roman" dream as recorded in a letter to Donald Wandrei, 2 No-

vember 1927. A similar letter written to Frank Belknap Long was incorporated into Long's short novel *The Horror from the Hills* (1931).

21. Actually, only one "Dunsanian" story ("Polaris," 1918) was written prior to HPL's reading of Dunsany in the fall of 1919. Later fantasies are consciously modelled after Dunsany's work.

22. Actually five: "The Statement of Randolph Carter" (1919); "The Unnamable" (1923); "The Silver Key" (1926); *The Dream-Quest of Unknown Kadath* (1926-27); and "Through the Gates of the Silver Key" (with E. Hoffmann Price; 1932-33).

23. Actually, HPL declared that Abdul Alhazred lived in the 8th century.

24. The pamphlet was issued posthumously in November 1937.

25. David Cornel De Jong (1901-1967), *Benefit Street* (1942).

26. See p. 000. {185?}

27. Actually, at this period HPL lived at 10 Barnes Street, several blocks north of the Brown University campus. HPL's residence at 66 College Street (1933-37) was directly behind the John Hay Library of Brown.

28. Mabbott refers to HPL's assertion in "Supernatural Horror in Literature" that Roderick Usher, his sister Madeline, and the house itself share a common soul and a common dissolution. See Mabbott's later article, "Lovecraft as a Student of Poe," *Fresco* 8, No. 3 (Spring 1958): 37-39.

29. Mabbott appears to be referring to one or both of two articles by Leiber, "The Works of H. P. Lovecraft: Suggestions for a Critical Appraisal" (*Acolyte*, Fall 1944), and "Some Random Thoughts about Lovecraft's Writings" (*Acolyte*, Winter 1945), both of which were incorporated into Leiber's "A Literary Copernicus" (1949).

30. This appears to be a paraphrase of Alexander Pope's *An Essay On Man*: "All Chance, Direction, which thou canst not see; / All Discord, Harmony, not understood" (1.290-91).

31. Little is known of HPL's late correspondent Jack H. Birss (1908-1994). He appears to have been a resident of Providence, so possibly Mabbott is mistaken in believing that he and HPL toured the Metropolitan Museum in New York together.

32. Cook appears to mean not *Creeps by Night* (1931), the anthology by Dashiell Hammett that included HPL's "The Music of Erich Zann," but August Derleth's *Sleep No More* (1944), which included "The Rats in the Walls." The review in the *Herald Tribune* has not been located; it may have

been by Will Cuppy, who was a longtime reviewer of mystery and adventure books for that paper (1926–49).

33. Derleth's "The Weird Tale in English Since 1890" (cited erroneously by Cook), published in the *Ghost* (May 1945), was his honors thesis at the University of Wisconsin, 1930. It lavished praise on HPL's stories, especially "The Outsider."

34. Wilson's celebrated attack on HPL was "Tales of the Marvellous and the Ridiculous" (*New Yorker*, 24 November 1945). He had dismissed detective stories in "Why Do People Read Detective Stories?" (*New Yorker*, 14 October 1944) and "Who Cares Who Killed Roger Ackroyd?" (*New Yorker*, 20 January 1945). He had previously discussed the horror tale in "A Treatise on Tales of Horror" (*New Yorker*, 27 May 1944).

35. In the following passage, Harrison appears to paraphrase sections of the introduction (by Derleth and Wandrei) to *The Outsider and Others* (1939), itself an adaptation of Derleth's "H. P. Lovecraft, Outsider" (see p. 121).

36. "Though I speak with the tongues of men and angels . . ." 1 Cor. 13:1.

37. Possibly a reference to one of Harrison's early novels, perhaps *Weep for Lycidas* (1934) or *Spring in Tartarus* (1935).

38. Hillman refers to *The Dunwich Horror* (New York: Bartholomew House, 1945), containing the title story, "The Thing on the Doorstep," and "The Shadow out of Time." It was assembled by F. Orlin Tremaine, who had accepted *At the Mountains of Madness* and "The Shadow out of Time" when he was editor of *Astounding Stories*.

39. *The Weird Shadow over Innsmouth and Other Stories of the Supernatural* (New York: Bartholomew House, 1944), also assembled by Tremaine.

40. "The Dunwich Horror," in *Avon Ghost Reader*, [ed. Herbert Williams] (1946); "The Haunter of the Dark," in *Terror by Night*, ed. Herbert Williams (1947); "The Shunned House," in *Who Knocks?*, ed. August Derleth (1946); "The Colour out of Space," in *The Night Side*, ed. August Derleth (1947).

41. Hillman refers to the *Avon Fantasy Reader* (1947–52), edited by Donald A. Wollheim, a series of 18 paperback anthologies that regularly reprinted HPL's stories.

42. The quotation is from "Notes on Writing Weird Fiction" (1933).

43. "An Appreciation of H. P. Lovecraft," an abridgment of *In Memoriam: Howard Phillips Lovecraft* (1941).

44. David H. Keller, "Shadows over Lovecraft" (*Fantasy Commentator*, Summer 1948), whose central contention—that HPL had congenital syphilis, acquired from his parents—has been proven false.

45. *Startling Stories* (1939-55), American science fiction magazine.

46. Brunner refers to "A Martian Odyssey" (*Wonder Stories*, July 1934) by Stanley G. Weinbaum (1902-1935); the science fiction stories of Henry Kuttner (1915-1958), Leigh Brackett (1915-1978), and John W. Campbell, Jr (1910-1971); "The City of the Singing Flame" (*Wonder Stories*, January 1931) by Clark Ashton Smith (1893-1961); and *Assignment in Eternity* (1953), a short story collection by Robert A. Heinlein (1907-1988).

47. At the *Mountains of Madness* was reprinted in August Derleth's anthology *Strange Ports of Call* (1949).

48. Brunner refers to Sherwood Anderson (1876-1941), American novelist and short story writer; Nigel Balchin (1908-1970), British novelist and screenwriter; Stuart Cloete (1897-1976), South African novelist and essayist; Colette (pseudonym of Sidonie-Gabrielle Colette, 1873-1954), French actress and novelist; William Faulkner (1897-1962), American novelist; James Elroy Flecker (1884-1915), British poet and playwright; George Bernard Shaw (1856-1950), Anglo-Irish playwright and essayist; and James Thurber (1894-1961), American humorist.

49. J. Michael Rosenblum was a leading British science fiction fan and editor of the period. He founded and edited the most celebrated British science fiction fanzine, the *Futurian* (1938-58), which underwent various title changes during its long run; it ran as the *New Futurian* in 1954-58. The article on HPL cited by Brunner has not been located.

50. Graham Stone (b. 1926), a leading Australian science fiction fan and critic.

51. Cyril Pearl, *The Girl with the Swansdown Seat* (1955), a study of prostitution in the Victorian era.

52. H. G. Wells (1866-1946), "The Red Room," in *The Plattner Story and Others* (1897) and *Thirty Strange Stories* (1897). HPL himself enjoyed this story when he read it (under the title "The Ghost of Fear") in Joseph Lewis French's anthology *Ghosts, Grim and Gentle* (1926).

53. Brunner refers to William McGonagall (1825?-1902), a notoriously bad Scottish poet.

54. Aldous Huxley (1894-1963), "The Subject-Matter of Poetry," in *On the Margin: Notes and Essays* (1923).

55. Jethro Bithell (1878–1962) was a British scholar on German literature and culture. Brunner is probably referring to Bithell's *Modern German Literature, 1880–1938* (1939).

56. L. Ron Hubbard (1911–1986), "Fear" (*Unknown*, July 1940); Henry Kuttner, "The Devil We Know" (*Unknown*, August 1941).

57. Moskowitz seriously misquotes Brunner. Brunner would have been two years old when HPL's stories appeared in *Astounding*.

58. See Section I, n. 20.

59. Keller obtained HPL's astronomical notebook (1909–15). See his article, "Lovecraft's Astronomical Notebook" (*Lovecraft Collector*, October 1949).

60. Leiber refers to *Last and First Men* (1930) by W. Olaf Stapledon (1886–1950), *Brave New World* (1932) by Aldous Huxley, *Nineteen Eighty-four* (1949) by George Orwell (1903–1950), and *Men Like Gods* (1923) by H. G. Wells.

61. *The Worm Ouroboros* (1922) by E. R. Eddison (1882–1945); *The Lord of the Rings* (*The Fellowship of the Rings*, *The Two Towers*, and *The Return of the King*) (1954–55), by J. R. R. Tolkien (1892–1973).

62. *The Duchess of Malfi* (1623), a tragedy by John Webster (1578?–1632?).

63. Stanley G. Weinbaum, "The Black Flame" (*Startling Stories*, January 1939; book publication 1948).

64. David Lindsay (1876–1945), a Scottish novelist best known for the philosophical science fantasy *A Voyage to Arcturus* (1920).

65. George R. Stewart (1895–1980), American writer and scholar who was professor of English at the University of California at Berkeley and a founder of the American Name Society. He wrote the post-apocalytic novel *Earth Abides* (1949).

66. Alan Paton (1903–1988), South African author best known for the novel *Cry, the Beloved Country* (1948).

67. Frank Edward Arnold (1914–1987), "Wings across Time" (*Science Fiction Quarterly*, 1942); reprinted in the collection *Wings across Time* (1946).

V. Notices from the Literary Community

1. See Section IV, n. 5.

2. William M. Sloane (1906-1974), author of two weird novels, *To Walk the Night* (1937) and *The Edge of Running Water* (1939). Sloane held editorial positions at several leading New York publishers during his career, including Henry Holt & Co. His novels were likely influenced by HPL; see Matthew H. Onderdonk, "Apostle of the Outside: William Sloane and Howard Phillips Lovecraft: A Curious Affinity," *Fantasy Commentator* 1, No. 7 (Summer 1945): 150-55.

3. August Derleth, *Restless Is the River* (1939), a volume in Derleth's Sac Prairie saga; *The Narracong Riddle* (1940), a Judge Peck detective novel.

4. The number is only six: Popular Fiction Publishing Co. (1927); Simon & Schuster (1930); G. P. Putnam's Sons (1931); Vanguard Press (1932); Alfred A. Knopf (1933); and Loring & Mussey (1935). In 1936-37 Wilfred B. Talman attempted to interest William Morrow & Co. in a novel by HPL.

5. Actually, the longest known HPL letter covers 70 pages, or 35 sheets written on both sides.

6. Probably no more than 5% to 10% of HPL's letters now survive.

7. The so-called Arkham House transcripts run to 41 volumes. The volumes average 100 single-spaced typed pages, although a few are a bit longer and several much shorter.

8. The second volume, *Beyond the Wall of Sleep* (1943), did not contain any letters.

9. Shakespeare, *Hamlet* 1.2.135-37.

10. Thomas Traherne (d. 1674), "Insatiableness," ll. 37-40.

11. "I believe because [it is] absurd." A paraphrase of the axiom by the early Christian thinker Tertullian (160?-240 C.E.): *Certum est, quia impossibile est* ("It is certain because it is impossible": *De Carne Christi* 5), oftentimes rendered *Credo quia impossibile* [or *incredibile*] *est* ("I believe because it is impossible [or incredible]").

12. From Thomas De Quincey (1785-1859), *Confessions of an English Opium-Eater* (1821).

13. The quotation is from Machen's "The Red Hand" (1895), which HPL used as the epigraph to "The Horror at Red Hook" (1925).

14. The quotation is from Blackwood's *The Centaur* (1911), which HPL used as the epigraph to "The Call of Cthulhu" (1926).

15. Parker refers to Smith's *Out of Space and Time* (1942).

16. *Weird Tales* (May 1930).

17. *Weird Tales* (November 1930).

18. Henri Rousseau (1844–1910), referred to as "Le Douanier" (the customs officer), based on his place of employment.

19. *Wonder Stories* (January 1931).

20. From Yeats's preface to Lady Gregory's *Gods and Fighting Men* (1904).

21. Hannes Bok (pseudonym of Wayne Woodard, 1914–1964), celebrated fantasy artist for the pulp magazines. Bok was born in Kansas City, MO, and moved to Seattle only after completing high school. He later spent time in Los Angeles and New York City.

22. The quotation is from HPL's "The Hound" (1922). De Vries, surprisingly, does not seem aware that the story was probably a self-parody.

23. "The Curse of Yig" (1928), ghostwritten by HPL for Zealia Bishop.

24. Machen is paraphrasing a passage in Tennyson's *Maud* (1855), 18.3.1–7.

25. *Great Tales of Terror and the Supernatural*, ed. Herbert A. Wise and Phyllis Fraser (New York: Random House/Modern Library, 1944).

26. Collins refers to *Who's Who in America* (1900f.); *Twentieth-Century Authors*, ed. Stanley J. Kunitz and Howard Haycraft (1942); and W. J. Burke and Will D. Howe, *American Authors and Books: 1640–1940* (1943).

27. *The Dunwich Horror and Other Weird Tales* was published by the Editions for the Armed Services, c. 1945.

28. *The Best Supernatural Stories of H. P. Lovecraft* (Cleveland: World Publishing Co./Tower Books, 1945) went through 4 printings through 1950 and sold more than 67,000 copies.

29. C. S. Lewis, *Out of the Silent Planet* (1938) and *Perelandra* (1943), the first two volumes of Lewis's space trilogy. Frank Baker (1908–1988), British musician, actor, and novelist, and author of *Sweet Chariot* (1942), a novel of the supernatural.

30. The musical composition is by Alfred Galpin.

31. The quotation is from Winfield Townley Scott's article "His Own Most Fantastic Creation" (*Marginalia*, p. 330).

32. Winfield Townley Scott, *To Marry Strangers: A Book of Poems* (1945).

33. HPL's treatise was first published in the *Recluse* (1927); a revised version was serialised in the *Fantasy Fan* (1933–35).

34. Harrison Smith, "The Rise of Fantasy in Literature" (*American Scholar*, Summer 1948).

35. The articles were gathered as *The Immortal Storm: A History of Science Fiction Fandom* (1951; rev. ed. 1974).

36. E. F. Bleiler, *The Checklist of Fantastic Literature* (1948).

37. A. E. Van Vogt (1912–2000), *The World of Null-A* (1948) and *The Pawns of Null-A* (*Astounding Science Fiction*, October 1948–January 1949; book publication 1956).

38. William Tenn (pseudonym of Philip Klass, 1920–2005), "Child's Play" (*Astounding Science Fiction*, March 1947).

39. *The Haunter of the Dark and Other Tales of Horror* (London: Gollancz, 1951), the first British edition of HPL's work.

40. *The Case of Charles Dexter Ward* (London: Gollancz, 1951), the first separate publication of the novel.

41. The comment is from W. Paul Cook's *In Memoriam: Howard Phillips Lovecraft* (1941), but it is false. See HPL to Helm C. Spink, [26 May 1934]: "I go hatless & coatless [in Florida], & am accumulating an excellent coat of tan" (ms., John Hay Library).

42. From "Notes on Writing Weird Fiction" (1933).

43. From HPL's letter to August Derleth, 6 October [1929]; cited in Derleth's "Lovecraft as a Formative Influence" (*Marginalia*, p. 357).

44. "In the Vault" was included in *The Other Worlds*, ed. Phil Stong (1941).

45. From Scott's "The Case of Howard Phillips Lovecraft of Providence, R.I.," *Providence Sunday Journal* (26 December 1943): Sec. III, p. 6.

46. HPL's interest in chemistry dated to the age of eight; his interest in astronomy was awakened in early 1902, when he was eleven.

47. HPL made no attempt to market his fiction professionally at this time.

48. HPL had met Sonia Greene in 1921, long before he moved to New York City in 1924; in fact, it was his marriage to Sonia that impelled his move.

49. Crane was not an "authority" on Poe, although he included a celebrated passage on Poe in *The Bridge* (1930).

50. From Long's "Some Random Memories of H.P.L." (*Marginalia*, p. 336).

51. From "Observations on Several Parts of [North] America" (1928) (*Marginalia*, pp. 266–67).

52. From "Notes on Writing Weird Fiction."

53. Of HPL's fifty-odd stories, only three are of "short novel length."

54. The two quotations are from "Heritage or Modernism: Common Sense in Art Forms" (*Marginalia*, p. 164). This essay has now been ascertained to be the first section of "A Living Heritage: Roman Architecture in Today's America" (1934).

55. Actually, what HPL said (according to Donald Wandrei) was: "What a disappointment that the other four varieties were not available!" See Wandrei's memoir, "The Dweller in Darkness: Lovecraft, 1927" (*Marginalia*, p. 369).

Appendix

1. From a letter by M. R. James to Nicholas Llewelyn Davies (12 January 1928); first published in *Ghosts & Scholars* No. 8 (1986): 28–33.

2. From Bolitho's "Pulp Magazines," *New York World* (4 January 1930): 11. The article was reprinted in the editorial column of *Weird Tales* (April 1930). Bolitho (1890–1930) was a noted American journalist, critic, and historian. HPL took note of Bolitho's remarks, writing: "Another recent thing which rather tickled me was a favourable mention of my tales in William Bolitho's column in the N.Y. World—although it was spoiled by the coupling of my name with that of the amiable hack Otis Adelbert Kline!" (HPL to August Derleth, [mid-January 1930]; *Essential Solitude* 1.244).

3. From Stanford's "*The Beloved Returns* and Other Recent Fiction," *Southern Review* 6, No. 3 (Winter 1940–41): 628.

4. From Benét's "My Brother Steve," *Saturday Review of Literature* 24, No. 30 (15 November 1941): 25. For William Rose Benét, see p. 205. Stephen Vincent Benét (1898–1943) was a distinguished American poet, novelist, and short story writer, some of whose work—such as the story "The Devil and Daniel Webster" (1937)—is laced with the weird.

5. From a letter by Lord Dunsany to August Derleth (28 March 1952); first published in *Lovecraft Studies* No. 14 (Spring 1987): 38.

6. *La Couleur tombée du ciel* (Paris: Editions Denoël, 1954), the first foreign-language edition of HPL. The translations were by Jacques Papy.

7. From "Books of 1954: A Symposium," *Observer* (London) (26 December 1954): 7. Cocteau (1889–1963) was a celebrated French poet, novelist, and playwright.

Index

Ackerman, Forrest J 12
Acolyte 28, 145, 161, 163, 171
Across the River and into the Trees (Hemingway) 172
Adams, Abigail 140
Addams, Charles 168
Addison, Joseph 165
Aerostatic Spy 215
Ah! Sweet Idiocy! (Laney) 14, 161
Aisenstein, Alan J. 113
"Alchemist, The" 48, 137
Alhazred, Abdul 71, 82, 84, 100, 103, 138, 195, 209, 228
Allgeier, Donald 110
Amateur Correspondent 127
Amato, Anthony 74
Amazing Stories 10, 139, 152, 157, 210n, 217
American Author 56
American Authors and Books (Burke-Howe) 199
American Literature 16-17, 183, 207
American Scholar 214
Anderson, Howard 65
Anderson, Sherwood 165
Andreyev, Leonid 55
Aprea, Andy 12, 115-16
Arabian Nights 122, 191, 225
Argosy 217
Aristotle 217
Arjen, Leif 104
Arkham House 16, 17, 51, 102, 139, 148-49, 163, 164, 180-82, 186, 197, 199, 200, 201, 203, 204, 206, 210n, 218, 221, 229
Arnold, Frank Edward 176
Arnold, H. F. 80
Ashley, Mike 201
Asquith, Cynthia 218
Assignment in Eternity (Heinlein) 165
Astounding Science Fiction 213
Astounding Stories 10, 11-12, 14, 15, 25, 110-18, 139, 157-58, 171, 180, 187, 195, 210n, 221
At the Mountains of Madness 11-12, 15, 102, 110-16, 117, 118, 139, 165, 171, 172, 174, 183, 187, 188-89, 209-10, 238n51
Atherton, Gertrude 123, 180
Auden, W. H. 132
Autolycus 131-35
Avon Fantasy Reader (Wollheim) 158
Avon Ghost Reader (Williams) 158

Bailey, J. O. 17, 209-13, 215
Bailey, Margaret Emerson 141
Baird, Edwin 125
Baker, Frank 201
Balchin, Nigel 165
Baltadonis, John V. 117
Barlow, R. H. 99-100, 130, 131, 137, 229, 341n88
"Bat's Belfry" (Derleth) 102
Baudelaire, Charles 122, 167
"Beast in the Cave, The" 48, 137
"Bells, The" (Poe) 41
"Beloved Dead, The" (Lovecraft-Eddy). *See* "Loved Dead, The"
Benefit Street (De Jong) 140-41
Benét, Stephen Vincent 205, 225, 231
Benét, William Rose 205-7, 231
Bennett, Carl 11, 110
Bennett, John W. 75-76
Bensom, Harold F. 111
Benson, E. F. 55
Bergier, Jacques 80, 91
Bert, Charles H. 79, 94
Best in Science Fiction, The (Conklin) 219
Best Short Stories of 1929, The (O'Brien) 56
Best Supernatural Stories of H. P. Lovecraft 16, 157, 200, 218
Beware After Dark! (Harré) 54, 55, 123, 124, 139, 180
"Beyond the Threshold" (Derleth) 101

"Beyond the Wall of Sleep" 137
Beyond the Wall of Sleep 16, 139, 149, 157, 161, 162, 193-97, 199, 200, 204, 205, 206, 210n, 222, 229
Bierce, Ambrose 29, 37, 50, 70, 103, 123, 125, 155, 162, 183, 196, 202, 205, 220, 227, 229
Binder, Eando 112
Binder, Otto 93
Birss, Jack 147
Bithell, Jethro 169
Bizarre 135
Black, Robert 96-97
Black Cat 189
"Black Flame, The" (Weinbaum) 175
"Black Swamp" 36-37
"Black Thirst" (Moore) 77
Blackwood, Algernon 51, 70, 76, 80, 91, 96, 124, 139, 160, 187, 191, 197, 198, 201-2, 218
Bleiler, E. F. 215
Bloch, Robert 13, 14, 25-27, 76, 80, 81, 84, 88, 102, 153, 165, 218, 238n49
"Boiling Point, The" (*Fantasy Fan*) 12
Bok, Hannes 192
Boland, Stuart M. 13, 28-32
Bolitho, William 10, 225, 231
Book of a Thousand Nights and a Night 191
Book of Dzyan 94, 104, 228
Book of Enoch 207
Book of the Dead 28
Books and Bipeds (Starrett) 196, 204
Bradbury, Ray 97-98, 108, 215, 218
Bradofsky, Hyman 13, 22-24
Brackett, Leigh 165
Brattleboro Daily Reformer 10, 52
Brave New World (Huxley) 172
Brown, Howard 113, 242n105
Brown, Paul 78
Brunner, John 15, 164-76
Bryan, Bruce 87
Budge, E. Wallis 147
Burleson, Donald R. 18
Burroughs, Edgar Rice 214
Butler, Samuel 48, 191

Californian 22, 128
"Call of Cthulhu, The" 54-56, 67-68, 71, 74, 77, 81, 85, 100, 102, 123, 155, 157, 171, 179, 187-88
Campbell, John W., Jr. 131, 152, 165, 172
Cannon, Peter 13
Capone, Al 77
Cardozo, Nathan 109
Carnacki the Ghost-Finder (Hodgson) 206
Carr, Robert S. 67
Carroll, Lewis 175
Case of Charles Dexter Ward, The 99-100, 139, 194, 196, 223
Casserley, Jeffrey St. John 95-96
Castle of Otranto, The (Walpole) 218
"Cats of Ulthar, The" 104
"Celephaïs" 137, 139
Cepheid 150
Cervantes, Miguel de 133
Chambers, Robert W. 91, 103, 123, 125, 155, 162
Charleston 244n16
Chatterton, Thomas 146
Chaucer, Geoffrey 169
Checklist of Fantastic Literature, The (Bleiler) 215
Chesterton, G. K. 206
Chicago Sun Book Week 193
Chicago Tribune 18, 196, 198, 204, 220
"Chrysalis, The" (Miller) 115
"City of the Singing Flame, The" (Smith) 165, 190-91
Clark, Lillian D. 33, 227, 228
Claviculae of Solomon, The 207
Cloete, Stuart 165, 176
Coates, Walter J. 21-22, 233n4
Cobb, Irvin S. 123, 180
Cocteau, Jean 232
Cole, Edward H. 23, 144
Coleman, Ronald 171
Coleridge, Samuel Taylor 233n5
Colette 165
Collier, John 173, 175, 219
Collins, Charles 198-201
"Colossus of Ylourgne, The" (Smith) 78
"Colour out of Space, The" 15, 85, 102, 110, 112, 122, 125, 139, 142,

149, 151, 157, 183
Colter, Eli 67
"Cones" (Long) 112
Conklin, Groff 219
Conover, Willis, Jr. 98-99
Conrad, Joseph 108
Conservative 9, 47
"Conversation of Eiros and Charmion, The" (Poe) 216
Cook, W. Paul 9, 10, 15-16, 21, 48-49, 51, 137, 140, 144, 146, 148-50, 162, 194, 233n4
"Cool Air" 97-98
Couleur tombée du ciel, La 232, 238n53
Crane, Charles 52
Crane, Hart 203, 227
"Crashing Suns" (Hamilton) 73
Creeps by Night (Hammett) 123, 124, 139, 148, 180
Croutch, Leslie A. 118
Crypt of Cthulhu 201
"Cthulhu Mythology: A Glossary, The" (Laney) 161
Cthulhu Mythos 14, 71, 83, 93, 100, 101-2, 103-5, 107, 108, 123, 125, 138, 146-47, 152-53, 159, 173, 174, 218, 224, 228
Cummings, Ray 66, 75
Cuppy, Will 16, 150, 179-80, 194, 202
"Curse of Yig, The" (Lovecraft-Bishop) 196

da Vinci, Leonardo 145
"Dagon" 9, 48, 49, 50, 80, 86, 137, 179
Dahlbrun, Lyle 111
"Dark Demon, The" (Bloch) 81
"Dark Eidolon, The" (Smith) 78
Darrow, Jack 115
Davidson, O. M. 116
Davis, Sonia H. 221, 222. *See also* Greene, Sonia H.
De Casseres, Benjamin 51
de Castro, Adolphe 71, 137, 220
De Jong, David Cornel 140-41
de la Mare, Walter 124, 139
De Quincey, Thomas 186

De Vermis Mysteriis (Prinn) 228
De Vries, Peter 17, 193
"Deaf, Dumb and Blind" (Lovecraft-Eddy) 39
"Death of the Artist" (Kowalewski) 128
Derleth, August 16, 17, 22, 30, 54, 65, 66, 74, 97, 98, 99-100, 101-2, 108, 111, 121-7, 131, 135, 144, 148, 149, 150, 153, 155, 157, 158, 159, 163, 165, 169, 175, 179, 180-82, 183, 186, 189, 195, 197, 199, 200, 201, 202, 204, 206, 207, 210n, 218, 220, 221, 222, 225, 228, 229
"Devil We Know, The" (Kuttner) 169
"Diary of Alonzo Typer, The" (Lovecraft-Lumley) 94-95, 96
Dickens, Charles 62, 108
Donne, John 173, 175
"Doom That Came to Sarnath, The" 50, 96, 137
Dowdell, William J. 233n2
Doyle, Sir Arthur Conan 196
Dracula (Stoker) 199
Dream-Quest of Unknown Kadath, The 104, 139, 147, 172
"Dreams in the Witch House, The" 75-76, 85, 102
Driftwind 21
Duchess of Malfi, The (Webster) 173, 175
Duerr, Howard J. 74-75
Dunsany, Lord 9, 50, 51, 96, 97, 103, 104, 122, 124, 138, 151, 152, 160, 183, 187, 191, 197, 217, 218, 231-32
"Dunwich Horror, The" 15, 42, 56, 69-70, 71, 72, 73, 74, 76, 77, 78, 80, 83, 85, 89, 92, 100, 102, 104, 122, 125, 139, 157, 158, 171, 172, 200
Duschnes, Philip C. 104
"Dust of Gods" (Moore) 80
"Dweller in Darkness, The" (Derleth) 102
"Dweller in the Gulf, The" (Smith) 12
Dwyer, Bernard Austin 69-70, 72, 94, 228
Dyalhis, Nictzin 171

Dyer, Jim 13
Eadie, Arlton 92
"Earth-Brain, The" (Hamilton) 57, 61
Eddison, E. R. 173
Eddy, C. M., Jr. 13, 32, 34, 35, 36-37, 39, 41
Eddy, Muriel E. 13, 14, 32-40, 41
Eddy, Ruth 13, 41-43
Edkins, Ernest A. 23
Emerson, Ralph Waldo 51
"End of the Story, The" (Smith) 75, 189
Enemy of the People, An (Ibsen) 75
Epictetus 146
Eshbach, Lloyd Arthur 111

"Facts concerning the Late Arthur Jermyn and His Family" 9, 50
Fairy Tales (Grimm) 225
"Fall of the House of Usher, The" (Poe) 62, 145, 168, 183, 197, 204
Famous Fantastic Mysteries 206
Fantasy Commentator 25, 41, 162, 215
Fantasy Fan 12, 207
Fantasy Review 157
Farber, Marjorie 17, 203-4
Farnese, Harold S. 16, 65, 73, 87
Faulkner, William 108, 165
Faust (Goethe) 65
"Fear" (Hubbard) 169
"Festival, The" 88
Fine, Calvin 113, 117
Finlay, Virgil 139, 206
First Steps in Egyptian (Budge) 147
Fischer, Marjorie 219
Fisher, Genevieve W. 70
Fitz, E. W. 200
Flagg, Francis 90-91
Flecker, James Elroy 165
Forrestal, John 213
Frankenstein (Shelley) 216
Fraser, Phyllis 199, 219, 225
Freud, Sigmund 173
Frost, Robert 134
Fungi from Yuggoth 21, 22, 75, 235n2, 237n33

Gaddis, Vincent J. 18, 223-29
Galpin, Alfred 49-50, 250n30

Gamwell, Annie E. Phillips 14, 33, 40, 129-30, 228, 229
Gatto, John 104
Gauer, Harold 101
Gehman, Richard B. 17, 213-20
Gentleman from Angell Street, The (Eddy) 13, 32
Gernsback, Hugo 217
Ghost 140, 148
"Ghost of Fear, The" (Wells) 247n52
Girl with the Swansdown Seat, The (Pearl) 168
Goethe, Johann Wolfgang von 65
Goodenough, Arthur 10, 52
Gordon, Samuel 90
"Gorgon, The" (Smith) 57, 60, 61-62, 80
Grant, Donald M. 32
Great Tales of Terorr and the Supernatural (Wise-Fraser) 199, 200, 219
"Green Thoughts" (Collier) 219
Greene, Sonia H. 38-39, 226. *See also* Davis, Sonia H.
Griffes, Charles 203
Grimm, brothers 225
Guest, Edgar A. 23
Gulliver's Travels (Swift) 191

H.P.L.: A Memoir (Derleth) 158, 210n
Hadley, Thomas P. 32
Haggard, H. Rider 217
Hamilton, Edmond 10, 57, 61, 67, 73, 75, 76, 86
Hamlet (Shakespeare) 185
Hammett, Dashiell 123, 124, 225
Harper's Weekly 217
Harré, T. Everett 54, 55, 123, 124, 225
Harrison, Michael 153-57
Hart, B. K. 10, 54-56
"Haunter of the Dark, The" 26, 91, 102, 157, 158, 238n49
Haunter of the Dark and Other Tales of Horror, The 222-23
Hauser, Kaspar 79
Hawthorne, Nathaniel 84, 183, 208
"He" 137
Heald, Hazel 11, 76, 77, 78-79, 83, 87, 88, 96

Heinlein, Robert A. 165, 172
Hemingway, Ernest 172
Hendrickson, Paul 68
"Herbert West—Reanimator" 137, 139, 196
"Heritage or Modernism: Common Sense in Art Forms" 251n54
Heyward, Dubose 123, 180
Hillman, Arthur F. 157-60
Hinton, Charles H. 51
"History [and Chronology] of the Necronomicon" 138, 196, 242n102
Hitler, Adolf 143, 185
Hockley, G. W. 75, 76
Hodgson, William Hope 173, 175, 206-7
Holmes, John 134
Holmes, Sherlock 150-51, 153, 196
Home Brew 137-38
"Horror at Red Hook, The" 39, 77, 80, 81, 86, 137, 234n15, 235n11
"Horror in the Museum, The" (Lovecraft-Heald) 11, 76, 77, 96
Hoskins, W. B. 12, 117-18
Houdini, Harry 38, 202, 204, 206, 224, 226
"Hound, The" 70-71, 77, 83, 89, 250n22
"Hour of the Dragon, The" (Howard) 91
Housman, A. E. 132
Houtain, George Julian 234n12
Howard, Robert E. 10, 28, 29, 31, 32, 67-68, 71, 73, 75, 76, 83, 86, 89, 91, 92, 95, 97, 139
Hubbard, L. Ron 169
Humphries, Rolfe 219
Huxley, Aldous 169
"Hypnos" 78

"Ibid" 123
Ibsen, Henrik 75
"Idealism and Materialism—A Reflection" 22
"Imprisoned with the Pharaohs" (Lovecraft-Houdini). See "Under the Pyramids"
In Memoriam: Howard Phillips Lovecraft (Cook) 144

"In the Vault" 57, 60-61, 109, 243n3
"Inhabitant of Carcosa, The" (Bierce) 123, 125, 155
Inside and Science Fiction Advertiser 164

Jackson, Joseph Henry 17, 221-22
James I (King of England) 166-67
James, M. R. 124, 139, 160, 202, 223, 229, 231
Jeffers, Robinson 134
Jensen, L. M. 110
Jolson, Al 61
Journey to the Center of the Earth (Verne) 216
Joyce, James 203

Kafka, Franz 219
Kant, Immanuel 51
Keil, Paul Livingston 13, 40-41
Keller, David H. 162, 171, 238n40
Kelvin, Lord 167
Kenton, Bernard J. 11, 77
Keown, Eric O. D. 17, 222-23
King in Yellow, The (Chambers) 91, 123, 125, 155
Kleiner, Rheinhart 9, 23, 47-48, 221, 222
Kline, Otis Adelbert 10, 56, 231
Knopf, Alfred A. 243n10
Koenig, H. C. 206
Kowalewski, Felix 128
Kreisler, Fritz 92
"Kubla Khan" (Coleridge) 175
Kuttner, Henry 11, 13, 77, 80, 81, 86, 88, 95, 102, 159, 165, 169, 218, 228

Ladd, James 116
"Lament for H. P. L." (Galpin) 203
Laney, Francis T. 14, 28, 161-64
Last and First Men (Stapledon) 172, 175
"Last Incantation, The" (Smith) 75
Last Man, The (Shelley) 216
Last Puritan, The (Santayana) 243n8
"Last Test, The" (Lovecraft-de Castro) 71
Lawrence, D. H. 203
Lawson, Horace L. 49
"Lazarus" (Andreyev) 55

Leiber, Fritz 15, 146, 171, 172-73, 175, 221, 222
Lewis, C. S. 167, 175, 201
Lewis, Cameron D. 12, 114, 115
Liber Ivonis 228
Lindsay, David 175
London Evening Standard 123
Long, Frank Belknap 10, 13, 40-41, 50-51, 54, 76, 131, 139, 159, 218, 227, 228
"Lord of R'lyeh, The" (Onderdonk) 25
Lord of the Rings, The (Tolkien) 173
"Lost Dream" (Petaja) 94
"Lost Paradise" (Moore) 91
Lost Worlds (Smith) 206
Lovecraft, H. P.: and amateur journalism, 9-10, 22; as critic, 207-9, 231; criticism of, 9-18, 148, 150-51, 154, 158-59, 163-64, 171, 199, 225; death of, 21-24, 81-91, 229; and fantasy fandom, 14-16, 121-76; as letter writer, 23-24, 28-29, 37, 41, 182; and mainstream press, 16-18, 179-229; memoirs of, 13, 26-43, 128-31; philosophy of, 29-30, 131; as poet, 24, 47-48, 145, 166, 172, 174, 196; and pulp magazines, 10-13, 34-35, 65-118, 231; and science fiction, 15, 110-18, 164-65, 209-13, 217-18; and weird fiction, 31-32, 34-35, 48-49, 50, 51, 53-54, 55-56, 57, 60-61, 65-109, 122-23, 124-27, 137-40, 142-44, 146-47, 149-50, 151-53, 155-58, 159-60, 161-62, 165-71, 172, 173, 179-81, 183, 186-88, 193-96, 197-202, 203-7, 222-23, 227-28, 231-32
Lovecraft Remembered (Cannon) 13
"Loved Dead, The" (Lovecraft-Eddy) 34, 35
Loveman, Samuel 131, 221, 227, 237n37
Lowndes, Robert A. W. 13, 89-90, 128
Lumley, William 94-95, 96
"Lurking Fear, The" 34, 68, 70, 78, 88, 89, 138
Lurking Fear and Other Stories, The 158

Luten, J. Randle 10, 56-62
Mabbott, Thomas Ollive 16, 97, 145-47, 183, 206
McElfresh, Allen 201
McGonagall, William 169
Machen, Arthur 51, 55, 80, 91, 96, 103, 108, 124, 139, 151, 160, 173, 187, 196, 197, 198, 202, 209
McIntire, Elaine 92
Maecenas, C. Cilnius 24
Malone, John 78
Man into Beast (Spectorsky) 219
Man Who Was Thursday, The (Chesterton) 206
Marchioni, Mark 110
Marginalia 135, 159, 162, 200, 202-6, 229
Markham, David 93
"Martian Odyssey, A" (Weinbaum) 165, 171-72, 174-75
Marx, Karl 134
Materialist Today, The 21, 22
Mather, Cotton 37
Maupassant, Guy de 49
"Melodie in E Minor" (Derleth) 236n9
Men Like Gods (Wells) 172
Mengshoel, E. L. 70, 75
Merritt, A. 91, 110, 113, 139, 217
"Messenger, The" 235n13
Metamorphosis, The (Kafka) 219
Michael, Bob 104
Michel, J. B. 14, 128-32
Micromegas (Voltaire) 191
Miller, P. Schuyler 14, 150-53
Milton, John 88, 166
Miske, J. Chapman 135-40
Moe, Maurice W. 23
Monk and the Hangman's Daughter, The (Voss-Bierce-de Castro) 220
Montgolfier brothers 215
"Moon-Bog, The" 78, 80
"Moon of Skulls, The" (Howard) 73
"Moon Pool, The" (Merritt) 91, 110, 113
Moore, C. L. 31, 77, 80, 91, 110, 139, 171
Morton, James F. 9, 13, 23, 40-41,

229
Mosig, Dirk W. 18
Moskowitz, Sam 11, 15, 170-72, 174, 215
Motz, Ward 65
Munn, H. Warner 65, 81
Munsey's 217
"Music of Erich Zann, The" 78, 88, 122, 125, 139, 183, 238n53
Mussolini, Benito 122
Myers, Max F. 67
Mysteries of the Worm (Prinn) 102, 241n97

Narracong Riddle, The (Derleth) 180
Narrative of Arthur Gordon Pym of Nantucket, The (Poe) 123, 125, 155, 209, 210
National Amateur Press Association 22, 33, 76, 122
Necronomicon (Alhazred) 28-29, 66, 70, 71, 75, 81, 82, 83, 92, 93, 100, 102-3, 104-6, 107, 110, 138, 195, 209, 210, 228, 241n97
"Negotium Perambulans" (Benson) 55
Nelson, Robert 78
New Futurian 166
New Republic 172, 213
New York Herald Tribune 16, 148, 150, 179, 194, 202
New York Times Book Review 195-96, 203
New Yorker 150-51, 193
Nickman, Steven 103-4
Night Land, The (Hodgson) 206-7
Night Side, The (Derleth) 158, 218
"Night Wire, The" (Arnold) 80
Nineteen Eighty-four (Orwell) 172
Noguere, Gene 113
Not at Night anthologies (Thomson) 123, 124, 139, 180, 235n11
"Notes on Writing Weird Fiction" 14, 159, 246n42, 251n42
"Nyarlathotep" 50

O. Henry Memorial Prize Stories 122, 125-26, 139, 225
O'Brien, Edward J. 51, 56, 122, 125, 139, 225

O'Brien, Fitz-James 90, 216, 231
"Observations on Several Parts of America" 251n51
O'Donnell, Elliott 21
Old Man and the Sea, The (Hemingway) 172
"Old Roses" (Perry) 74
Olympian 144
"Omnipresent Philistine, The" 40
On the Margin (Huxley) 169
Onderdonk, Matthew H. 233n8, 249n2
O'Neail, N. J. 71, 88
Orton, Vrest 10, 51-54
Ostrow, Alexander 76
"Other Gods, The" 194
Other Side of the Moon, The (Derleth) 165, 218
Out of Space and Time (Smith) 189n, 206
"Out of the Aeons" (Lovecraft-Heald) 78-79
Out of the Silent Planet (Lewis) 201
"Outsider, The" 16, 66, 67, 69, 70, 71, 73-74, 79, 85, 88, 122, 125, 149-50, 158, 183, 223
Outsider and Others, The 16, 98-99, 100, 101, 121, 126, 139, 149, 157, 159, 179-83, 186, 194, 197, 199, 200, 201, 204, 205, 206, 207, 210n, 213, 218, 222, 229, 231

Parker, Robert Allerton 17, 184-92
Paton, Alan 176
Pattee, Fred Lewis 17, 207-9
Pauke's Quill 40
Paul, St. 156
Paulive, Robert 103, 104, 105, 106
Pause to Wonder (Fischer-Humphries) 219
Pearl, Cyril 168
Peirce, Earl, Jr. 86-87
"Pendrifter, The" 52
Perelandra (Lewis) 201
Perils of Pauline, The (film) 193
Perry, Stella G. S. 74
Pershing, A. V. 69, 70-71
Petaja, Emil 79, 94

Petrarch (Francesco Petrarca) 169
Phazaton, Cecile 112
Phoenix 40, 153
"Pickman's Model" 67, 74, 80, 81, 85, 88, 243n3
"Picture in the House, The" 69, 81, 243n3
Pigg, Gene 111
Pilgrims through Space and Time (Bailey) 17, 215
Pizzano, Charles 117
Pnakotic Manuscripts 210, 228
Poe, Edgar Allan 9, 10, 35, 40-41, 49, 50, 52, 54, 58, 60, 62, 65, 66, 67, 68, 69, 70, 76, 77, 79, 80, 84, 90, 91, 96, 97, 98, 103, 108, 112, 122, 123, 125, 133, 136, 137, 140, 145-46, 153, 154, 155, 166, 167, 173, 183, 187, 197-98, 199, 203, 206, 208-9, 210n, 216, 217, 218, 222, 224, 225, 227, 229, 231, 236n21
"Polaris" 50, 94, 137, 244n21
Pope, Alexander 48, 147
Poster, William 17, 195-96
Powell, Anthony 17, 223
Power, Lorne W. 82
Prediction 153
Price, E. Hoffmann 10, 66, 75, 76, 80, 82, 89, 94-95, 96-97, 139, 221, 228
"Prince Borgia's Mass" (Derleth) 74
Prinn, Ludvig 102, 228, 241n97
Proust, Marcel 122
Providence Journal 10, 38, 54, 140, 225
Pryke, Reginald A. 92
Publishers' Weekly 16, 102-3, 180
Punch 222

Queen, Ellery 206
"Quest of Iranon, The" 97, 139, 172, 194
Quinn, Seabury 67, 73, 76, 84

Rachmaninoff, Sergei 66
Rankin, Hugh 78, 92, 237n32
"Rats in the Walls, The" 15-16, 35, 42, 43, 69, 73, 74, 77, 80, 85, 89, 122, 125, 139, 148, 200, 202
"Raven, The" (Poe) 41
Reader and Collector 206

Reading and Collecting 124
Recluse 159, 231, 235n10
"Red Room, The" (Wells) 168
Restless Is the River (Derleth) 180
"Restless Souls" (Quinn) 73
"Return of Hastur, The" (Derleth) 101
Reynolds, B. M. 79, 80
Rhein, Richard 117
Rhode Island on Lovecraft (Grant-Hadley) 14, 32
Rimel, Duane W. 112, 228
River 121
R'lyeh Text 104
Roosevelt, Franklin D. 14
Rousseau, Henri 189
Rosen, Robert 101
Rosenblum, Mike 165
"Ruler of Fate, The" (Williamson) 91
Rush, Charles, Jr. 73
Russell, James L. 112
Russell, Robert Leonard 12, 74, 83
Ruzella, Peter, Jr. 115
Ryan, Joseph Allen 93

Saati, Oliver E. 112
"Sadastor" (Smith) 75
San Francisco Chronicle 17, 221
Santayana, George 134, 243n8
Saturday Evening Post 214
Saturday Review of Literature 205
Schneeman, Charles 110
Schwartz, Julius 93
Science Fiction Fan 128, 132
Scienti-Snaps 135, 137, 139
Scott, Winfield Townley 205, 206, 225, 250n31
"Seed" (Snow) 102
Selected Letters 127, 149, 200, 221
Senf, C. C. 92
"Shadow out of Time, The" 11-12, 102, 104, 115-17, 151, 158, 171, 210-12
"Shadow over Innsmouth, The" 101-2, 158, 172
Shadow over Innsmouth, The 123, 124, 126-27, 201
Shakespeare, William 69, 76, 144, 165, 175, 214

"Shambleau" (Moore) 77
"Shambler from the Stars, The" (Bloch) 81
Shaw, George Bernard 165
Shea, J. Vernon 66-67, 73-74, 93-94, 95
Shelley, Mary 216
Shelley, Percy Bysshe 146
Sherman, R. W. 127-28
Shiel, M. P. 124, 167, 218
"Shunned House, The" 22, 93-94, 137, 144
Shunned House, The 10, 50-51, 137
"Shut Room, The" (Whitehead) 73
"Silver Key, The" 11, 73, 83, 243n3
Simpson, Dale V. 71-72
Sivia, H. 95
"Skull-Face" (Howard) 71
Sky Hook 161
Skylark of Space, The (Smith) 113
Sleep No More (Derleth) 200, 218
Sleeping and the Dead, The (Derleth) 218
Sloane, William 180
Smith, C. W. 33
Smith, Clark Ashton 12, 31, 56, 57, 60, 62, 69, 74, 75, 76, 78, 80, 85-86, 123, 131, 138, 139, 153, 159, 165, 171, 180, 184, 186, 188-91, 192, 206, 218, 228, 234n13
Smith, E. E. "Doc" 113
Smith, Harrison 214, 219
Smith, Paul S. 89, 96
Snow, Jack 67, 68, 102-3
"Solitary Hunters, The" (Keller) 77
"Some Current Motives and Practices" 22
"Some Notes on a Nonentity" 243n4
"Some Notes on Interplanetary Fiction" 159
Something about Cats and Other Pieces 220-22
Soper, Cleveland C., Jr. 12, 114, 115, 117
Southey, Robert 146
"Space-Eaters, The" (Long) 78
"Spawn of Eternal Thought" (Binder) 112

Spectorsky, A. C. 219
Spencer, Herbert 68
Spinoza, Benedict de 90
Stanford, Don 231
Stapledon, Olaf 172
Starrett, Vincent 18, 196-98, 204-5, 206, 220-21, 222, 224, 225
Startling Stories 164
"Statement of Randolph Carter, The" 50, 65, 81, 137
Sterling, George 29, 206
Sterling, Kenneth 13, 84-85
Stern, Philip Van Doren 200, 219
Stevenson, Robert Louis 183
Stewart, George R. 175-76
Stewart, J. H. 106
Stickney, Corwin, Jr. 116
Stiller, H. P. 73
Stoker, Bram 21
Stone, Graham 166, 169
Stong, Phil 225
"Strange High House in the Mist, The" 79, 89, 139, 172, 179
Strange Ports of Call (Derleth) 171, 218
"Stranger from Kurdistan, The" (Price) 65, 71
Superman 11
"Supernatural Horror in Literature" 17, 21, 126, 139, 159, 179, 181, 183, 186, 206, 207-9, 215, 231, 235n10
Swanson, Neil 134
Sweet Chariot (Baker) 201
Swift, Jonathan 48, 191

Tales of Magic and Mystery 10
Taurasi, James 117
Taylor, Harold Z. 11, 114
Tchaikovsky, Peter Ilyich 118
Tead, H. P. 65
"Tell-Tale Heart, The" (Poe) 235n15
"Temple, The" 80, 171, 172, 238n52
Tenn, William 217
Tennyson, Alfred, Lord 198
"Terrible Old Man, The" 109
"Terrible Parchment, The" (Wellman) 92, 93
Terror by Night (Williams) 158
Tertullian 249n11

"Thing in the Moonlight" (spurious) 135
"Thing on the Doorstep, The" 81, 83, 89, 102, 157, 179, 223
Thompson, Robert 113, 115
Thomson, Christine Campbell 123, 124, 225
"Through the Gates of the Silver Key" (Lovecraft-Price) 11, 77, 80
Thurber, James 165
Tierney, Richard L. 18
Time 214
Time Machine, The (Wells) 219
"Time-Raider, The" (Hamilton) 67
Times Literary Supplement 223
Tolkien, J. R. R. 173
"Tomb, The" 65, 66, 137, 145, 183
Torrance, Lewis F. 78, 113
Traherne, Thomas 185
"Trail of Cthulhu, The" (Derleth) 30, 102
Travelers in Time (Stern) 219
Treasury of Science Fiction, A (Conklin) 219
"Tree, The" 139
Tryout 33
Turn of the Screw, The (James) 202
Twentieth-Century Authors (Kunitz-Haycraft) 199
Twenty Thousand Leagues Under the Sea (Verne) 216

"Ulalume" (Poe) 183, 209
"Uncharted Isle, The" (Smith) 189-90
"Under the Pyramids" (Lovecraft-Houdini) 226, 234n18
Underground City, The (Verne) 216
United Amateur 47, 137
United Amateur Press Association 9, 50, 122, 137, 226
"Unnamable, The" 81
Utpatel, Frank 124

VVV 184
Vagrant 48, 137
Van Lorne, Warner 116
Van Vogt, A. E. 217, 218
Variety 149

"Vermont: A First Impression" 22
Verne, Jules 191, 216, 217
"Very Old Folk, The" 137
Villon, François 133
"Vivisector, The" 49
Voltaire (François Marie Arouet) 130, 191
Voss, Richard 220
Voyage to Arcturus, A (Lindsay) 175
"A Voyage to Sfanomoë" (Smith) 75

Wade, James 108, 109
Walpole, Horace 218
Walter, Dorothy 140-45
Wandrei, Donald 69, 76, 98, 99-100, 111, 135, 144, 153, 155, 157, 159, 179, 180-82, 183, 186, 189, 195, 197, 199, 202, 204, 218, 228, 229
War and Peace (Tolstoy) 172
War of the Worlds, The (Wells) 216
Washington, George 140
Wasso, J. 71
We (Zamiatin) 191
Weinbaum, Stanley G. 165, 171-72, 174-75
Weird Shadow over Innsmouth and Other Stories of the Supernatural, The 200, 246n39
"Weird Tale in English Since 1890, The" (Derleth) 149
Weird Tales 10-11, 12-13, 21, 25, 26, 34, 35, 38, 39, 52, 57, 65-109, 125, 132, 137, 138, 139, 157, 159, 166, 171, 180, 187, 189, 195, 197, 210n, 217, 218, 221, 226, 252n2
Weisinger, Mort 93
Wellman, Manly Wade 83, 92, 93, 106, 240n70
Wells, H. G. 91, 168, 191, 216, 217, 219
"Werewolf of Ponkert, The" (Munn) 81
Wesso, H. 110
Wharton, Edith 123, 180, 231
"What Was It?" (O'Brien) 216
Wheatley, Dennis 167
"Whisperer in Darkness, The" 74, 83, 89, 100, 101-2, 122, 157, 158, 171

"White Ship, The" 50, 67, 69, 137
Whitehead, Henry S. 67, 73, 92, 95, 123, 180, 228
Whitfield, Jack T. 69
Whitman, Sarah Helen 140
Whitman, Walt 146
Who Knocks? (Derleth) 158, 218
Who's Who in America 199
Wilcox, Joseph V. 107-8, 109
Wilde, Oscar 167
Wilkin, John 215
Williams, Charles 173, 175
Williamson, Duke 75
Williamson, Jack 91
Wilson, Edmund 17, 150-51
Wilstach, John 149
"Winged Death" (Lovecraft-Heald) 77
"Wings across Time" (Arnold) 176

Wise, Herbert A. 199, 219, 225
Wollheim, Donald A. 78, 92, 128-29, 131
Wolverine 49
Wonder Stories 12, 25
Wood, Edward 15, 174, 175
Wordsworth, William 88
World Set Free, The (Wells) 216
Worm Ouroboros, The (Eddison) 173
Wright, Farnsworth 11, 125, 171
Writers Forum 224
Wylie, Elinor 206

Yeats, W. B. 191

Zamiatin, Eugene 191
Zoilus. *See* Galpin, Alfred

www.ingramcontent.com/pod-product-compliance
Lightning Source LLC
Chambersburg PA
CBHW060115170426
43198CB00010B/906